Virtual Reality – Real Visuality

Visual Learning

Edited by András Benedek and Ágnes Veszelszki

Volume 7

PETER LANG
EDITION

András Benedek / Ágnes Veszelszki (eds.)

Virtual Reality – Real Visuality

Virtual, Visual, Veridical

PETER LANG EDITION

Bibliographic Information published by the Deutsche Nationalbibliothek
The Deutsche Nationalbibliothek lists this publication in the Deutsche Nationalbibliografie; detailed bibliographic data is available in the internet at http://dnb.d-nb.de.

The publication of this volume was sponsored
by the Gergely László Foundation, Hungary.

ISSN 1435-845X
ISBN 978-3-631-73104-8 (Print)
E-ISBN 978-3-631-73105-5 (E-PDF)
E-ISBN 978-3-631-73106-2 (EPUB)
E-ISBN 978-3-631-73107-9 (MOBI)
DOI 10.3726/b11592

Peter Lang Edition is an Imprint of Peter Lang GmbH.

Peter Lang – Frankfurt am Main · Bern · Bruxelles · New York · Oxford · Warszawa · Wien

This publication has been peer reviewed.

www.peterlang.com

Contents

András Benedek
Preface ... 7

Figurative, Virtual, Rhetorical

Zoltán Kövecses
A Radical View of the Literal-figurative Distinction ... 17

Petra Aczél
Beyond Persuasion – Rhetoric in a Virtual World ... 29

Eszter Deli
Can Images be Arguments? The Possibility of Visual Argumentation in the WWF Nature Conservancy Campaigns ... 41

Pictorial, Veridical, Cross-Cultural

Kristóf Nyíri
Pictorial Truth ... 51

István Danka
The Pictorial, the Virtual and the Trivial. On Pictorial Realism and Relativism ... 59

Orsolya Endrődy-Nagy
Images and Iconography in Cross-Cultural Context ... 67

Diagrammatic, Visual, Practical

Amirouche Moktefi
Diagrams as Scientific Instruments ... 81

András Benedek
Visual Learning and Open Content Development (OCD) ... 91

György Molnár
How Digital and Virtual Life Trapped in Visuality and New Media Systems Affect Teaching and the Learning Process 101

SOCIAL, VISUAL, DIGITAL

James E. Katz, Daniel Halpern
Image Self-Involvement and Romantic Relationships: The Case of Selfies 121

Rachel A. Katz
All About Image: Development of Visual Literacy through American Dating Apps 131

Ágnes Veszelszki
Verbal and Visual Aggression in Trolling 141

APOCALYPTIC, REAL, MEDIAL

László Attila Hubbes
Revolution of the Eye. The Spectacular Rhetoric of the Apocalyptic 159

Philipp Stoellger
"In Images We Trust". On Belief in Images as the Real Reality 175

Notes on Contributors 189

Index 195

András Benedek

Preface

We began examining the topic of visuality from an interdisciplinary perspective nearly a decade ago. At that time, my philosophy-based discussions with Kristóf Nyíri about the role of images in human activities inspired us to build on our ongoing research into the more and more complex effects of mobile communication tools on learning, and to establish the Visual Learning Lab (www.vll.bme.hu) at the Budapest University of Technology and Economics in the autumn of 2009 as an opportunity for a new scientific dialogue.

We held workshops for those interested in the topic, arriving from various fields of scholarship. Today our series of regular meetings, which has introduced new research results, has an eight-year history. The widest possible interpretation of *visuality* has attracted the interest of the representatives of several disciplines. The special program of the professional platform initiated by the philosopher and the education researcher received contributions from linguists, sociologists, and engineers from the very beginning. Also, we had the privilege of receiving support and outstanding lectures from international participants (James Elkins, Kurt Röttgers, and Theo Hug) who enriched our agenda with the issues of distance education and m-learning. International scientific interest and the recognition of the opportunity of dialogue prompted us to organize an international Visual Learning Conference each year since 2010. Despite its modest dimensions including 30 to 40 papers and talks by European and even overseas researchers, these conferences can contribute to the modern interpretation of *visuality*, an increasingly diverse topic, as well as to the analysis of the complex developments in various areas of our life.

The Visual Learning Conferences have reached beyond creating a platform and a scientific dialogue. In addition to the possibilities offered by the electronic publication of abstracts and presentations, we produced a peer-reviewed book each year, which included invited papers by approximately one third of the conference speakers. It is worth mentioning how we came up with topics for the Visual Learning volumes, now published as a series. The first book, co-edited by Kristóf Nyíri and myself, published in 2011 with the title *Image in Language: Metaphors and Metamorphoses*, recalls the atmosphere of our first meeting with the topic of *visuality*. The titles of the later volumes, *The Iconic Turn in Education* (2012), *How to Do Things with Pictures: Skill, Practice, Performance* (2013), *The Power of the Image – Emotion, Expression, Explanation* (2014), *Beyond Words: Pictures, Parables,*

Paradoxes (2015), and *In the Beginning was the Image: The Omnipresence of Pictures: Time, Truth, Tradition* (2016), the latest one co-edited with Ágnes Veszelszki, clearly show that an increasingly complex interpretation has added up-to-date explanations to the analysis of the interconnections between various disciplines.

The present volume is an edited selection of the studies finalized by the speakers of the 2016 VLL Conference. As usual, the title is important: *Virtual Reality – Real Visuality: Virtual, Visual, Veridical.* Virtual reality is connected to our current environment with multiple ties. Today it is no longer just a way of giving colours to the world of toys. It affects the everyday operation of the media and hence all of our lives. The application of virtuality is a means and method of research at various levels and in specific fields. This raises the question of what visuality really is and how it is possible to explain it. And the answers are not at all evident, especially when they are given by different disciplines, all from their respective perspectives.

The opening part of this volume is titled *Figurative, Virtual, Rhetorical* and presents three papers applying aspects and interpretations of rhetoric that has received a special attention from cognitive linguistics, communication theory, and the perspective of visuality from the very beginning of our work. Zoltán Kövecses's study titled *A Radical View of the Literal-figurative Distinction* argues at the level of deep interconnections and from the perspective of cognitive linguistics that even our most concrete experiences can be conceptualized figuratively and not literally. The core element of his paper is Conceptual Metaphor Theory (CMT), by which it is an essential recognition that abstractions are routinely conceptualized as basic concrete experiences. Its approach sets out from the analysis of the nature of metaphors perceivable in our present, historically demonstrating the basic difference between literal meaning and figurative meaning through the examples Anger is Insanity and Knowledge is Vision, pointing out that "… in the case of literal meaning (or concrete concepts) the ontological content predominates over the cognitive-construal part".

Petra Aczél's study titled *Beyond Persuasion – Rhetoric in a Virtual World* connects to this, just like the first step taken towards virtuality at the level of language and rhetoric. The author is a key figure of VLL, who also represents the development of our common thinking with her permanent presence. She has written a paper in each of the volumes published so far. Her latest work built on an up-to-date examination of the literature aims to find out more about the connection between the rhetorical and the virtual. In fact, it endeavours to frame the concept of *virtual rhetoric* with the investigation into how virtual is rhetorical and how rhetorical is virtual. No doubt, the concept of the naturally virtual has become the object of high-profile scientific analyses only during the latest two decades, and the introduction and application of the notion of virtual rhetoric in the interconnections of visual communication definitely amounts to an original approach. According to Professor Petra Aczél's latest comments, "visuality for virtuality functions the same way as sounded words functioned for primarily oral cultures where practices of rhetoric can find their origins". The rhetorical approach allows the author to place this recent phenomenon into a wider cultural-historical and philosophical framework: "Rhetoric can be seen as an ancient head mounted display through which we can enter into spectacular shared worlds, experience visual persuasion, emotional states, abbreviated decisive processes – that is, a kind of virtuality that preceded digital technology with thousands of years."

Eszter Deli connects to this study presenting concrete examples of the explanation framework of visuality in her writing titled *Can Images be Arguments? The Possibility of Visual Argumentation in the WWF Nature Conservancy Campaigns.* The paper can be seen as a case study in line with the comprehensive title of the present volume as well as with the linguistic-rhetoric part. It surveys the changes in the role of image-based argumentation in communication as a constructive critical analysis of the almost half-a-century old idea of *New Rhetoric* (Perelman and Tyteca). This subtle analysis connects to the latest rhetoric interpretations that "attempted to prove that argumentation is as much a visual as a verbal art" (Aczél) and responds to a number of counter-arguments, recalling that "after centuries of the reign of the written word, we are witnessing the revival of visual rhetoric in a new world of imagery and sight" (Nyíri).

This last quotation is also important because it leads to the next part of the book, which includes, under the title *Pictorial, Veridical, Cross-cultural*, another three studies, including Kristóf Nyíri's keynote paper *Pictorial Truth.* In his study, entering the domain of modern philosophical thinking, the author builds the subject of his investigation on the classical pillars of the literature, related to the essential statements of Arnheim, Gombrich, J. M. Kennedy, and Wittgenstein. A central element of the study is the claim that metaphors that are "used in everyday thinking and in science express essential aspects of reality – they are literally true." Given the interconnections between words and images, it is an essential idea that "Metaphoric language cannot be reduced to non-metaphoric language because the visual foundations of thinking actually cannot be eliminated. Sacrificing images would amount sacrificing truth".

The next work is *The Pictorial, the Virtual and the Trivial. On Pictorial Realism and Relativism* by István Danka. The author argues that an examination of pictoriality and virtuality as philosophical themes can provide ammunition for commonsense realism in its fight against extreme forms of relativism. Setting out from the conceptual system of Common-sense realism (CSR), the author highlights the Triviality Thesis, which has been accepted by several thinkers during the latest decades and "...helps the realist avoid problems with perspectivism". The author's conclusions are especially noteworthy: "Connectivity as having access from one perspective to another, along with an overlap of routes, seems to be sufficient for warranting the sort of unity required by CSR".

Orsolya Endrődy-Nagy's study, *Images and Iconography in Cross-Cultural Context*, presents a new analytical dimension of the pictoriality problem. The author's educational philosophy approach converges with the philosophical systems appearing in the previous conceptional-theoretical writings. It is the comparative visual analysis of Cross-Cultural Context and European and Japanese children's drawings and woodcuts that gives a special thematic framework to the author's investigation. This paper offers excellent evidence of the possibilities of interdisciplinary approaches to the subject. In her conceptual framework, the author includes the notions of Childhood History and Childhood Studies and Education, and presents the changes in these notions with recourse to practical considerations. Relying on the rich literature of childhood research, the study introduces plenty of illustrating material to document that "Using micro historical perspectives, we can explore and understand several situations and aspects of everyday life and mentality". Examining the possibilities of iconographic analyses, the author consciously expands the scope of visual research to conclude that "Pictures could be coded texts; their conservative function helps us to break the silence regarding the attitude towards children both in Japan and in Europe."

The next part includes three studies under the title *Diagrammatic, Visual, Practical*. Amirouche Moktefi's paper, *Diagrams as Scientific Instruments*, deals with the role of diagrams as one of the most frequent demonstration tools applied in scientific thinking and reasoning and in science and technical education. Referring to the latest literature, the study states that "We rather use imagination, not rules, to manipulate diagrams in order to solve problems. The formalist mode would be the realm of symbolic demonstrations alone. When it comes to diagrams, the strategy is different: we work *with* diagrams (as tools), rather than *on* diagrams (as objects)." Remarkably, it declares that if diagrams are scientific instruments, the reliability of a diagram can simply be restated as the reliability of a scientific instrument. From the perspective of visuality, the author summarizes his paper in a noteworthy way, underlining that he "explored the idea that diagrams are *literally* scientific instruments ... [and] considered the applicability of epistemological strategies that are widely used in the natural sciences, where visual elements contribute to the robustness of results."

The next two studies, written by researchers at the Department of Technical Education of the Budapest University of Technology and Economics, which hosts the Visual Learning Lab, have the most direct relation to the world of education. As is natural, the education science approach in the given technical educational environment pays special attention to technological aspects, and adds specific components to the interdisciplinary character of this volume. András Benedek's study titled *Visual Learning and Open Content Development (OCD)* introduces the conceptual elements of a pedagogical methodological project launched lately. Open content development, which moves from the rigid system of central content development towards the more dynamic content innovation, where both teachers and students can participate through cooperative techniques, has a strong visual character. In the up-to-date info-communication technological (ICT) environment, a new pedagogical opportunity appears: the Open Access principle and its adoption in a wider context of practice have stirred up pedagogical thinking, which means the trend of opening up education. As the author puts it, "According to these inputs and outputs, our network concept, which is characterized by active student contribution, encouraged the development of new educational content. The result of these activities integrated the original OCD model to formulate a real open environment where information exchange is organized into an informal network."

György Molnár's study, *How Digital and Virtual Life Trapped in Visuality and New Media Systems Affect Teaching and the Learning Process*, connects to this work through an analysis of the educational opportunities offered by ICT. The author attributes outstanding importance to the new functions of ICT devices. "Besides the importance of visuality, virtual reality and cyberspace society can provide their citizens with a fruitful and desirable way of life both in social and in learning aspects since students of these environments attend these courses only when they want to or have the time for it." The study contains several figures and statistical data to present the new perspectives of applying ICT tools with the following key conclusion: "The appreciation of visuality is assisted by virtual and augmented reality spaces. Cyberspace, which houses both, offers a promising and beneficial way of life to digital citizens in both public life and learning as they attend courses only when they wish or have the time."

The next part, titled *Social, Visual, Digital*, directs the reader to a wider social context to discuss the sociological issues of using the new media. The first paper, titled *Image Self-involvement and Romantic Relationships: The Case of Selfies*, is written by professor James E. Katz, honorary doctor of the Budapest University of Technology and Economics, and Daniel Halpern, professor at the Catholic

University of Santiago, Chile. Demonstrating the special connections between visuality and reality, the study provides theoretical suggestions and is basically of an empirical nature. Its starting point is the term *perpetual contact* to underscore how individuals strain toward connectedness with each other. "Selfies, as with other types of social media, may be negatively affecting the quality of personal relationships" is an especially remarkable comment as an earlier work on Facebook found a link between the rise of divorces and the spread of that technology. This makes the author's question so relevant today, "Could the same be true of selfies? In this study, a longitudinal panel of Chileans in a romantic relationship was surveyed at a one-year interval to see if their involvement with selfies was associated with a directional change in paired evaluations of the quality of their relationships."

Rachel A. Katz offers a direct follow-up on the subject. In her study titled *All About Image: Development of Visual Literacy through American Dating Apps*, she analyses the peculiar visuality of the community media usage of young people. The examination of the role of images in this context leads us to the world of Digital Dating and selfies that are now researched by more and more theoretical experts, and the young author presents the interconnections with convincing genuineness and through a critical eye at the same time. In addition to providing a look at the widening conceptual background, the author writes about the experiences of empirical surveys made amongst the youth: "…'image reading' differs from historical notions of codes in images and of representational conventions in art studies, where there was a decisive understanding of image based on a written scholarly code. Rather, this form of communication has developed socially and organically among users without a driving 'correct' dictionary of codes developed by gatekeepers. Digital natives are constructing their own visual language through technology." All these reflect the presence of visuality at all the times and everywhere; as the author puts it: "Dating app technologies have given new significance to the power of visual communication. Their contribution to everyday practices of interpreting visual images will be affecting not only any given person's life course, but additively, the larger picture of how society will operate in the future."

The fourth part concludes with a study by Ágnes Veszelszki, co-editor of the present volume. Her paper titled *Verbal and Visual Aggression in Trolling* is really topical in our days. Visual aggression is a form of presence that is existent in everyday life, also in the more closed world of the private sphere, beyond the mass publicity of politics and the media. Its examination exploits several approaches, and researchers are more and more engaged in this topic. Verbal aggression, which is well-known and thoroughly elaborated in terms of its historical aspects, is capable, owing to the demolition of space and time limits and up-to-date ICT devices, of taking on several online forms in our days. Direct verbal aggression is usually taken to include mocking, taunting, teasing, cursing, making personal remarks to or verbally abusing the partner, and using profanities and foul language. At the same time, "As opposed to verbal language with its conventionalized symbols permitting only linear decoding, visual language can be decoded quickly and simply. The perception of visual information differs from that of verbal information, which enhances its role in conveying offensive attitudes, further differentiating it from texts." Owing to the public nature of the Internet, trolls play a new and especially interesting role from the perspective of researchers. The author analyses the visual effects of trolls and the complexity of their denotative meaning through several examples and illustrations. As she undertakes to give a comprehensive view of the types related to this phenomenon as well as to systematize the main characteristics. Her final comment also gives food for thought: "Probably the most useful suggestion is that users should stay alert and have a critical view of online information (more generally: media awareness)."

In case the reader has now become slightly exhausted by the elaborate descriptions of all these chapters, their interest will surely be grasped by the title of the last part of the book. The title *Apocalyptic, Real, Medial* refers to two studies. László Attila Hubbes' study is pictorial even in its title, and its content gives a strong focus to our enterprise. The title is impulsive: *Revolution of the Eye. The Spectacular Rhetoric of the Apocalyptic*. Despite the rhetorical outset and the communication theory terminology, the author's intention is clear: "…the apocalyptic produces and reproduces spectacular representations which gain their strong expressiveness from combining images of the real and the uncanny, the monstrous and the desirable." Starting from the modern interpretation of the terms *apocalyptic, imagery* and *rhetoric*, his study discusses the pictorial and rhetoric representation of the apocalypse within modern philosophy, although with some references to the history of religions. The author makes an original contribution to scholarly thinking: "…that apocalyptic rhetoric is a distinct form of pervasive discourse that uses metaphoric language and mythical narratives, built upon specific eschatological *topoi*, not only to explain the present state of affairs and answer the ultimate question of evil, but also to convince its audience to revert their perspective through a *cathartic metanoia*".

Finally, Philipp Stoellger's *In Images We Trust. On Belief in Images as the Real Reality* is a truly appropriate closing chapter because of its profound arguments and the way in which it opens up new perspectives. It is an important study which represents well what we hope is an important volume. The author is Professor of

Systematic Theology: Dogmatics and Philosophy of Religion at Heidelberg University and was a keynote speaker at several of our Visual Learning Conferences. His study is a comprehensive theoretical work in which the issues of belief, trust and verification are subjects of deep philosophical analysis. Perhaps it is not by chance that the author, who gives a thorough elaboration of some quite basic questions, does not make a definite statement after a detailed explanation of the key notions. Instead he concludes by formulating a further question: "Does a critical belief in images mean to believe in a truth beyond all images as well? Yes, but only if this external truth is accessible in and by verbal and visual communication."

This volume contains 14 studies. The different theoretical foundations necessarily reflect the researchers' intentions, and the agenda, which relies on probably multiple reader interests, gives rise to high-quality and fresh scientific orientation in newer and newer directions. Structuring the diversity of topics posed a real challenge for the editors. On the other hand, the authors certainly felt restricted by strict limits and the editors' demand for a modest use of graphical demonstration. We are thankful to each contributor for keeping to the strict deadlines of only a few months and to Peter Lang Publishing for its professionalism and for taking care of our volume for the seventh time. Special thanks go to Kristóf Nyíri, who provided us with considerable help both in setting the agenda and selection criteria for our volumes and preparing the annual VL conferences, as well as to co-editor Ágnes Veszelszki for a really valuable job for the second time and making the authors keep the timeframes of our joint work in an empathic but uncompromising manner. Looking into any of our VL volumes, the reader can see how far our loose professional-scientific community has come in exploring visuality from various interdisciplinary perspectives, welcoming the specialities in each other's disciplines and their enriching role, and how we position ourselves in a scientific environment that is reflected by the impressive reference and literature lists. At the same time, the existence of this series demonstrates the dynamics in scholarly life, which is so important but quite difficult to document. The thematically changing focuses in this series, the emergence of novel core elements and the authors' choice of topics form a continuous development in which visuality, image and metaphor, as well as ontological, historical and political questions of reality and virtuality are given a central role.

Budapest, May 2017

Figurative, Virtual, Rhetorical

Zoltán Kövecses

A Radical View of the Literal-figurative Distinction

1. Introduction

In this paper I argue that our most concrete experiences can be conceptualized figuratively, and not literally. This does not, however, prevent them from being used as source domains for figurative conceptualization. We seem to have a huge body of figuratively conceptualized concrete experiences that we take over from previous generations, use them as if they were literally-construed experiences, and turn them into vehicles for the further comprehension of more abstract things. Much of what we take to be literal is only ontologically literal (i.e., constitutes basic concrete experience), but as regards its cognitive status it is figuratively constructed experience. We re-use this apparently literal conceptual material in a figurative way to comprehend and construct abstractions without being aware of their original metaphorical or metonymic cognitive status.

I argue below that even basic concrete experience is commonly construed figuratively, that is, by means of metaphor and metonymy. This is not a new and original observation – Nietzsche suggested that "language is a graveyard of dead metaphors." The notion that even our basic concrete experiences are figuratively construed raises an important question for conceptual metaphor theory (CMT). CMT postulates (and empirically finds) that abstractions are routinely conceptualized as basic concrete experiences. But if this is the case and it is also true that language, including concepts that denote basic concrete experiences, is figuratively construed, why is it that we conceptualize the abstract in terms of the concrete? In other words, our fundamental distinction between the concrete and the abstract loses its significance, if both of them turn out to be figuratively understood. Thus, we gain nothing by conceptualizing the abstract in terms of the concrete, so the CMT explanation for the unidirectionality of metaphorical mappings from concrete to abstract (and not the other way around) loses its validity (since the concrete is also figuratively conceived).

In classical accounts of literal meaning (such as Searle's), literal meaning is identified with meaning that denotes concrete things and that is conventionally used, including dead metaphors. This is a large and foundational set to which figurative meaning can always be "translated." The highest level generalization that supporters of both the classical theory of metaphor and conceptual metaphor theory make is that there is such a thing as literal meaning. Where they differ is in the role they attribute to it. Supporters of the classical view claim that literal meaning is the foundation of meaning in general and that figurative (metaphoric and metonymic) meaning depends on it. Adherents of conceptual metaphor theory suggest, by contrast, that literal meaning is not foundational in that sense and that figurative meaning does not depend on it.

But researchers in the conceptual metaphor tradition greatly limit the extent of literal meaning, that is, the kinds of linguistic expressions that can be considered to have a literal meaning. They tend to delimit the extent of literal meaning in a variety of ways. In this paper, I offer a radical view of the extent of the figurative, which greatly reduces or even eliminates the literal—at least in a certain sense.

2. Delimiting the Literal

Let us begin with dead metaphors. Despite their name, dead metaphors are not really metaphors according to the classical theory. They are expressions that acquired a new literal meaning. As we saw above, however, conceptual metaphor theory treats dead metaphors as metaphors, the justification being that dead metaphors are conceptually very much "live" as examples of fully active *conceptual metaphors*. The conventionalized status of dead metaphors does not prevent them from being active in the conceptual system via the conceptual metaphors they belong to.

As we just saw, the decision concerning what is literal is made in conceptual metaphor theory on the basis of how an expression is processed. If it activates two conceptually linked domains, it is metaphorical; if it does not, it is literal. Lakoff (1993: 205) handles the distinction between literal and metaphorical in the following way: "those concepts that are not comprehended via conceptual metaphor might be called "literal"." But this still leaves us with cases that are hard to classify. For example, it is clear that "Time passed quickly" and "The time will come" are metaphorical due to the TIME IS MOTION conceptual metaphor. But what about *early* in sentences like "March comes earlier than April," a sentence used in one of Boroditsky's (2001) experiments? Is *early* literal or metaphorical? It is usually taken to be literal. But in the experiment Boroditsky (2001) found that speakers of English responded faster (saying TRUE/FALSE) when they received a horizontal prime, and speakers of Chinese were faster when they received a vertical prime. The results of this priming study indicate that a word we would take to be literal (since it is unrelated to motion) is comprehended metaphorically (since speakers are affected by a conceptual metaphor—horizontal vs. vertical motion—in processing it). Thus, if the "comprehension via conceptual metaphor" criterion is correct, the word would have to be taken as metaphorical, not literal.

The criterion of "comprehension via conceptual metaphor" would give us a similar dilemma in a large number of cases, including that of the domain of time. As a matter of fact, the word *time* is open to the same question: is it literal or metaphorical? If the word *early* is understood metaphorically, and thus counts as metaphorical, then surely the word *time* is also understood metaphorically and has thus a metaphorical meaning. Or should we distinguish the name (the word) of a domain from the domain itself (the concept of TIME)? But can we separate word meaning from conceptualization in a cognitive linguistic framework? Isn't word meaning dependent of conceptualization?

We encounter the same problem in all the cases where there is an abstract target domain (ANGER, THEORY, TIME, DESIRE, etc.) involving many linguistic expressions that we would not hesitate to take to be literal (such as *anger, rage, ire, irritation, fury* for anger; *theory, idea, scheme, belief* for theory; *time, period, moment, minute, hour* for time; *desire, urge, longing, want, yearn* for desire; etc.). Can abstract concepts such as these be literal? That's how we feel about them intuitively. But this should not be the case if we apply the criterion of "comprehension via conceptual metaphor." Clearly, the concepts corresponding to them are all comprehended metaphorically via a number of different conceptual metaphors, such as ANGER IS FIRE, KNOWLEDGE IS VISION, TIME IS MOTION, DESIRE IS HUNGER, etc. My claim here would be that abstractions can only be conceptualized metaphorically, and consequently the linguistic items expressing these metaphorical conceptualizations can only be metaphorical.

However, we do not view them as such. The question is why. It seems to me that in such cases we apply a criterion different from "comprehension via conceptual metaphor" to establish what is literal. This seems to be the following: They do not involve any overt morphological markers of more concrete source domains that would suggest their metaphorical nature. The words above do not morphologically reflect any of the well-known conceptual metaphors (source domains) associated with the target domains in question (ANGER, KNOWLEDGE, TIME, DESIRE mentioned above). In this regard, they are very different from lexical expressions such as *burn* (with anger), *clear* (idea), *passage* (of time), and *hungry for* (love), which explicitly show the concrete source domains to which they belong.

At the same time, the assumed literal expressions belonging to abstract target domains such as the ones above can be regarded as complying with the Lakoffian criterion for metaphorical meaning: "comprehension via conceptual metaphor," as a result of which they would cease to be literal expressions. They would comply with it etymologically, that is to say, in a historical perspective. Etymologically, all of these words derive from figurative (metaphoric or metonymic) conceptualizations. For instance, the words *rage* and *fury* for anger go back to Latin, where they had to do with madness, and the words *theory* and *idea* in the knowledge domain have to do with vision and seeing in Ancient Greek (cf., e.g., Sweetser 1990). Both of these cases show that the words that we take to be literal today are actually motivated by some of the same conceptual metaphors that motivate many of today's metaphorical expressions; namely, ANGER IS INSANITY and KNOWLEDGE IS VISION. In some other examples, the metaphor or the metonymy is not clear in the etymology, but the metaphoric or metonymic origin appears to be certain. According to etymological dictionaries (such as the Online Etymology Dictionary), *anger* originates from the Indo-European root meaning "tight, narrow, painfully constricted." This could probably be considered a case of metonymic conceptualization: THE CAUSE OF ANGER FOR ANGER, a generic-level metonymy for anger.

In other words, it seems that a large number of expressions (that belong to abstract domains) are taken to be literal, but in synchrony their corresponding concepts are metaphorically comprehended and from a historical perspective they have metaphorical or metonymic origins. Their perception as literal seems to be based on the fact that their morphology does not reveal to contemporary speakers any metaphoric origins.

The same argument can be taken further. In a historical perspective, many non-abstract concepts (i.e., concrete ones) also emerged as a result of figurative processes. For example, in English the word *book* derives from the Proto-Germanic word **bokiz* meaning "beech" according to the Online Etymology Dictionary. The explanation offered by the dictionary is that runic writing was inscribed on beechwood tablets. We may have a series of metonymies at work here. As another example, consider the word *storm*. The same dictionary suggests that it ultimately derives from the PIE root **(s)wer-* meaning "to turn, whirl." Again, this seems to be metonymic: THE EFFECT OF AN EVENT FOR THE EVENT. The concepts that arose by means of certain figurative processes, such as BOOK and STORM, later became source domains for more abstract concepts (e.g., ANGER IS A STORM). We are of course no longer aware that these concepts were produced by figurative means; we take them to be literal. But it is clear that the same kind of figurative conceptual processes were responsible for their emergence as the ones we use today.

3. So What Exactly is Literal Meaning?

Most of this information is of course well-known. The reason I am discussing the issue here is to provide an answer to the question raised in the subtitle above.

The answer seems to depend on (1) whether we allow a fuller application of the "comprehension via conceptual metaphor" criterion in synchrony (to cases like *anger* and *rage*) and (2) whether we allow a fuller application of the criterion from synchrony to diachrony. It is a further issue whether it would be legitimate and how legitimate it would be to apply the principle more extensively. My view is that if we want to approach the issue from a coherent cognitive perspective, we can and should embrace the more extensive versions of the principle, that is, to extend it both to all the words and expressions that belong to a particular abstract target in synchrony and to concrete concepts in diachrony.

In my view, the extended application of the principle would be legitimate because, on the one hand, the linguistic expressions belonging to a particular abstract target are *all* comprehended metaphorically or metonymically (like *rage* and *fury* in ANGER), not just the prototypical item in the domain (i.e., *anger* for ANGER). And, on the other hand, the move would be legitimate because many of our categories for concrete objects and events had been comprehended figuratively in previous times. This latter step would also be justified because, by taking it, we would recognize our cognitive unity with others who lived before us. The fact that we comprehended figuratively many concrete objects and events that we take to be literal today is a very thin line that separates us from previous generations. Their figurative conceptualizations have become unmotivated to us since we do not know many things about the past, and thus we do not see the morphological cues that would reveal the figurative devices they have employed. But etymologies often tell us these stories.

What these stories indicate very clearly is that humans have always engaged in figurative ways of understanding the world—not only in the case of abstractions but also in comprehending its concrete, physical aspects. The main difference between the two simply is that in the case of abstractions we have conceptually constructed previously nonexistent realms of reality, whereas in the case of concrete things already existing entities and events have been figuratively comprehended (such as rain as "God's tears"). The emphasis of conceptual metaphor theory on the former case is understandable: It is the realm where conceptual metaphors work most fully, and they teach us important lessons about the way we function in our world. As for the latter case, we cannot even be certain that the same systematic mapping patterns we find in conceptual metaphors are applicable to the realm of the concrete. We do not know, but paying attention to this realm may turn out to be just as informative regarding the way we function cognitively.

4. The Radical Claim

Overall, then, taking the stand I sketched out here would lead to a considerable reduction of the extent of the literal. There would remain very little that would be understood in a literal way. If we accept this position, we would actually reverse the assumption of the classical view of metaphor according to which it is the literal that is foundational for language and thought. Indeed, we would go even beyond the accepted view in conceptual metaphor theory according to which the literal is needed in order to be able to comprehend the world and to be able to create conceptual metaphors. In the radical alternative I suggest, the figurative would be foundational, and, in many cases, the literal would be regarded as figuratively comprehended aspects of the concrete realm, where we lost track of the figurative comprehension of the concrete. At the same time, it may be that this figurative comprehension of the concrete is not a passive one but a *conceptual construction* of existing things and events. The challenge would be to see whether this "conceptual construction" is or is not the same type of conceptual construction that we find in creating abstractions—the well-studied area of conceptual metaphor theory.

But all this is not to say that literal meaning does not exist. It does, and it plays an important role in conceptual metaphor theory as well. Without literal meaning, conceptual metaphor theory would become incoherent. In the theory, abstract experiences are comprehended and created via concrete ones that are expressed by apparently literal language. If there is no literal language of some kind (corresponding to concrete experience), no metaphorical comprehension and creation can take place.

What I have really argued for above is that the extent of the literal may be considerably smaller than we commonly assume. If we do not count as literal (i) dead metaphors, (ii) abstract entities or events without explicit morphological markers for particular source domains, and (iii) the large class of cases where a concrete entity or event is figuratively conceptualized historically, we are left with a rather limited set of cases. Actually, it is very difficult to assess the exact size of this remaining set. Based on research in a variety of disciplines, we can probably include in that set basic-level objects and events, a variety of spatial relations, basic emotions, body parts, and probably some others (cf. Lakoff 1993).

But *can* we? Even here, we run into problems. In all of these groups, we find items that are comprehended / constructed figuratively. For example, the basic-level category of wolf in Hungarian is *farkas*, literally meaning "the one with a tail," or "that which has a tail." This is the result of comprehending wolves metonymically due to some taboos on naming this animal in the ancient belief system. The English preposition *in* corresponds to the suffix *-ban/-ben* in Hungarian, and the

Hungarian preposition goes back to the word *bél* ("bowels") in its etymology. In this case, the body serves as the source domain for spatial relations. The English basic emotion term *anger*, as we saw above, has a metonymic origin. *Surprise* (deriving from old French, and ultimately Latin, *surprendre*), another basic emotion term, is the product of a metaphorical process that can be characterized by the metaphor SURPRISING (SOMEONE) IS UNEXPECTED SEIZURE/ATTACK (cf. Kövecses 2015). Finally, the French word for the face, *visage*, derives from the Latin *visus* "sight." This is probably also metonymic. What the examples show is that even concepts that we can take to be based on our most basic and direct experiences, such as the animals that surround us in nature, fundamental spatial relations, basic emotions, and the parts of the human body can all be conceptualized figuratively.

In other words, under a broad definition of what is figurative, very little of the literal remains. This could seriously undermine a major claim of conceptual metaphor theory; namely, that a sufficiently large part of language and thought is about concrete things and is thus literal and that we use this language and thought to conceptualize abstractions. What we saw above was that our most concrete experiences can be conceptualized figuratively, and not literally. But this does not mean that they cannot be used as source domains for figurative conceptualization. Rather, we seem to have a huge body of figuratively conceptualized concrete experiences that we take over from previous generations, use them as if they were literal experiences, and turn them into vehicles for the further comprehension of more abstract things. Ultimately, much of what we take to be literal is only ontologically literal (i.e., constitutes basic concrete experience), but as regards its cognitive status it is figuratively constructed experience. We re-use this apparently literal conceptual material in a figurative way to comprehend and construct abstractions without being aware of their original metaphorical or metonymic cognitive status.

5. Smell as a Target Domain

We can see the same situation in the case of the concept of smell. Probably there is general consensus that the sense of smell is one of the most basic ways in which humans (and animals) gather information about reality. For this reason it serves as a perfect source domain, very much in line with what we would expect. For instance, the concept of suspicion is conventionally conceived of as smell, hence the conceptual metaphor SUSPICION IS SMELL (as in, "I can smell trouble"). Immorality and, more generally, badness is conceptualized as (bad) smell (as in, "I can smell a rat"), yielding BAD IS SMELLY. And the vague and loose concept of "general atmosphere of something" is understood in terms of smell (as in, "What he did smells of fraud"), giving us the conceptual metaphor THE GENERAL ATMOSPHERE (OF SOMETHING) IS SMELL.

Thus we assume that smell is an ideal source domain. Given this, we would *not* expect it to be understood metaphorically, that is, as a target domain. But it is conceptualized as such. How is this possible? The reason, I suggest, is that smell like any other concept is characterized by a number of conceptual dimensions, or to put it in the framework of Langacker (1987), it is part of a domain matrix. Thus the concept of smell is connected to the idea that it is something that exists, that it is something that can have various degrees of intensity, that it is something that the perceiver, or experiencer, cannot help perceiving, that is, that he or she has no control over whether or not s/he perceives it. In other words, we can identify at least the following three dimensions for the concept of smell: existence, intensity, and lack of control.

In a "domain matrix" view of the conceptual system, the three dimensions are high-level, generic concepts that characterize many concepts, concrete and abstract alike. They function as shared dimensions of concepts. Existence, intensity, and (lack of) control are concepts that form an integral part of many domains, such as smell. An important property of these dimensional concepts is that they are all generic-level ones and abstract. The question is what kinds of conceptual metaphors are formed by making use of them in relation to smell.

5.1 Existence

Let us begin with existence. Consider some examples for how the existence of smell is presented by a dictionary:

> VERB + SMELL **be filled with, have** *The air was filled with a pervasive smell of chemicals. The cottage had a musty smell after being shut up over the winter.* | **give off** *The skunk gives off an unpleasant smell when attacked.* | **catch, detect** *As she walked into the house she detected the smell of gas.* (boldface in the original)

The examples indicate a variety of ways in which the existence of smell can be conceptualized. In the case of *fill*, the smell is viewed as a substance and the object or location with the smell is viewed as a container, and the existence of the smell as the substance being in the container. In the case of *have*, existence of the smell corresponds to the possession of an object that is smell itself. In the case of *give off*, causing smell to come into existence is the transfer of an object and the source of the smell is a surface. Finally, *catch* and *detect* are not dedicated to denoting the existence of smell, they simply assume its existence.

The examples and their construals of the existence of smell they reveal point to the following conceptual metaphors:

filled with:

SMELL IS A SUBSTANCE
THE OBJECT / LOCATION THAT HAS THE SMELL IS A CONTAINER
THE EXISTENCE OF SMELL IS FOR THE SUBSTANCE TO BE IN THE CONTAINER

have:

SMELL IS AN OBJECT
THE EXISTENCE OF SMELL IS THE POSSESSION OF AN OBJECT

give off:

SMELL IS AN OBJECT
CAUSING SMELL IS TRANSFERRING THE OBJECT
SOURCE OF SMELL IS A SURFACE

The three cases conceptualize the experience of smell as the existence of a state. The state is either a substance or an object. Existence is viewed as a substance being in a container, as possessing an object, and as transferring an object. The three specific cases of existence metaphors for smell are thus instances of three generic-level metaphors for existence:

- EXISTENCE IS BEING IN A CONTAINER
- EXISTENCE IS POSSESSION
- (CAUSING) EXISTENCE IS TRANSFER

These conceptual metaphors apply to a large number of specific-level instances of existence, not just to the existence of smell.

5.2 Intensity

Another generic-level concept that is linked to smell is intensity. In the case of smell, intensity involves a scale of values from weak to strong. Collocation dictionaries give us a good idea of this notion in relation to smell:

- ADJ. **overpowering, pervasive, pungent, rich, sharp, strong** *There was an overpowering smell of burning tyres.* | **faint** | **distinct** | **distinctive, particular, unmistakable** | **funny, peculiar, strange, unusual** *What's that funny smell?* | **familiar** | **lingering** | **aromatic, delectable, delicious, fragrant, fresh, lovely, nice, savoury, sweet, wonderful** *the aromatic smells of a spring garden full of herbs* | **warm** | **appalling, awful, bad, evil, horrible, nasty, offensive, terrible, unpleasant, vile** | **acrid, nauseating, putrid, rank, sickly** *An acrid smell filled the air.* | **damp, dank, musty, rancid, sour, stale** *the sour smell of unwashed linen* | **earthy, fishy, masculine, metallic, musky, oily, smoky, spicy** | **cooking** *Cooking smells drifted up from the kitchen.* (boldface in the original)

Many of these adjectives deal with the different kinds of smell, but some of them denote the intensity aspect of smell. These latter adjectives (and the verb *fill*) appear to be based on several different conceptual metaphors—in some cases, on etymological grounds:

- *overpowering, strong, faint*: INTENSITY OF SMELL IS STRENGTH OF EFFECT
- *sharp, pungent*: INTENSITY OF SMELL IS SHARPNESS OF AN OBJECT
- *vaguely*: INTENSITY OF SMELL IS DEGREE OF BRIGHTNESS OF LIGHT
- *pervasive, fill*: INTENSITY OF SMELL IS QUANTITY OF A SUBSTANCE

These conceptual metaphors that relate to the intensity aspect of smell also have their generic-level variants:

- *overpowering, strong, faint*: INTENSITY IS STRENGTH
- *sharp, pungent*: INTENSITY IS SHARPNESS
- *vaguely*: INTENSITY IS BRIGHTNESS
- *pervasive, fill*: INTENSITY IS QUANTITY

5.3 Lack of Control

The issue of control is also relevant to smell and perception in general. A curious property of perceptual experience is that we do not have control over what we perceive. If our sense organs are normal and no external circumstance blocks the perception, we undergo the perception of any existing perceptual stimulus. This is also often rendered in metaphorical ways—one of the chief ways among them (according to dictionary information) is by means of the verb *hit* in the case of smell. Consider the example taken from a dictionary: *Then the pungent smell hit us—rotting fish and seaweed.* We can analyze the metaphorical use of *hit* as follows:

- SMELL IS A PHYSICAL FORCE
- INTENSE SMELL IS A STRONG PHYSICAL FORCE
- SENSING AN INTENSE SMELL IS COMING INTO CONTACT WITH A STRONG PHYSICAL FORCE

The three basic conceptual metaphors above can be combined into a complex one that describes the metaphorical conceptualization of the perceptual experience of strong smell:

- THE EXPERIENCER OF AN INTENSE SMELL IS A PERSON COMING INTO ABRUPT PHYSICAL CONTACT WITH A STRONG PHYSICAL FORCE

But most importantly, the main point is, as before, that the specific-level conceptual metaphors are licensed by corresponding generic-level ones:

- CAUSES ARE FORCES
- INTENSITY IS STRENGTH
- SENSING IS CONTACT

Again, these generic-level metaphors pervade the conceptual system and allow us to conceptualize various kinds of causes, intensity, and sensation, not just smell as a cause, not just the intensity of smell, and not just sensing smell. In other words, smell as an extremely basic and direct experience has aspects to it that lend themselves to metaphorical conceptualization.

6. Conclusions

On the basis of the evidence we saw in this paper, it seems that figurativity (that is, understanding concepts by means of metaphor or metonymy) does not really distinguish literal from figurative meaning, or concrete concepts from abstract ones. Both types of meaning (literal and figurative) and both types of concepts (concrete and abstract) are characterized by being understood metaphorically and metonymically. As a result, we cannot account for the unidirectionality of metaphorical mappings in conceptual metaphors. We cannot claim that the concrete is understood in a literal way and we make use of this in comprehending and creating abstractions.

Does this situation mean we have to discard CMT? In my view, it should not mean that. We can propose, given the evidence we saw, that concepts consist of two parts: an ontological part that specifies what kind of ontological materials make up a concept and a cognitive part that specifies the ways in which concepts are cognitively construed or constructed. I assume that this distinction is similar, but at least related, to a distinction made by Langacker (1987, 2008) between the content part and the construal part of concepts.

Now, given the distinction, we can suggest that in the case of literal meaning (or concrete concepts) the ontological content predominates over the cognitive-construal part. The construal part is limited to certain generic-level dimensions of concepts, as we saw in the case of smell. These dimensions shared across many concepts in the conceptual system are figuratively (metaphorically, metonymically) understood. In the case of abstractions, however, the construal part predominates over the ontological part. The cognitive-construal part of abstract concepts is essentially figurative (metaphoric, metonymic). The actual ontological part, the ontological content is small. We call this small ontological essence or core "embodiment." Embodiment retains the tangible content ontology of abstract concepts. This is what cognitive linguists and scientists mean when they talk about abstract concepts as not being "transcendental."

Thus, both concrete and abstract concepts have both embodied content ontology and figuratively constructed comprehension—but in different proportions. In conceptual metaphors, we have predominantly content-ontology-based concepts as source domains and predominantly figuratively-construed concepts as target domains. There are probably no pure ontology-content-based concepts and no pure figuratively-construed concepts. This view explains, in addition, why an "ideal" source domain, such as smell, can also function as a target domain. The reason is that we can profile the ontology part in some cases (and we get a concept as a source domain, such as smell as source), but in others we can profile the figuratively construed part (and we get target domains, such as smell as target).

References

Boroditsky, Lera (2001): Does Language Shape Thought? Mandarin and English Speakers' Conception of Time. *Cognitive Psychology* 43: 1–22.

Kövecses, Zoltán (2015): Surprise as a Conceptual Category. *Review of Cognitive Linguistics* 13/2: 270–290.

Lakoff, George (1993): The Contemporary Theory of Metaphor. In: Ortony, Andrew (ed.): *Metaphor and Thought*. Cambridge – New York: Cambridge University Press. 202–251.

Langacker, Ronald (1987): *Foundations of Cognitive Grammar*. Stanford: Stanford University Press.

Langacker, Ronald (2008): *Cognitive Grammar. A Basic Introduction*. New York: Oxford University Press.

Searle, John (1979): Metaphor. In: Ortony, Andrew (ed.): *Metaphor and Thought*. Cambridge – New York: Cambridge University Press. 92–123.

Sweetser, Eve (1990): *From Etymology to Pragmatics*. Cambridge – New York: Cambridge University Press.

Petra Aczél

Beyond Persuasion – Rhetoric in a Virtual World

0. Prologue

"At the end of 20th century the phenomenon of 'virtual reality' achieved an unexpected success, among others because of its unclear and fuzzy definition", claim Taube and Leenders (1998: 345) at the beginning of their single-page subchapter on virtual reality. It was 20 years ago and, apparently, only the century changed. Virtual reality has become our everyday vision and our best instrument "for dealing with a radically uncertain future" (Nyíri 2012: 192). Virtuality is the magic word that evolves from its predecessor: 'innovation'. Technology moguls strive to pave the path for this brave new space to make it everybody's. Virtual is meant to enrich what is 'mass' and 'smart' in communication. Alongside with games, serious contents are being published for the virtual consumer. In November 2015, the New York Times in cooperation with Google shipped to its subscribers a million units of the Google Cardboard VR headset together with the new NYT VR app, which improves online reading with immersive 360-degree visual experience. The massive giveaway was repeated in May 2016, when the newspaper's eighth virtual-reality story about the planet Pluto was 'published'. A great effort was made but not only by the content provider. Even though virtual technology is as near as a Pokémon these days, it is not always as hassle-free to use as a touchscreen. It needs exclusive focus and total immersion in an era of multitasking, with eyes captured and cognition fully engaged. Virtual reality thus has to be a persuasive and attractive concept in itself to facilitate participative consumption. This is when it first meets rhetoric.

This chapter, however, aims to find out more about the connection between the rhetorical and the virtual. In fact, it endeavors to frame the concept of *virtual rhetoric* with the investigation into how virtual is rhetorical and how rhetorical is virtual. This inquiry highlights three elements: visuality, persuasion, and immersion, in rhetorical and virtual terms.

1. Introduction

Contemporary scholarship supports the claim that there are three approaches to the concept of *virtual rhetoric*. The first offers a functionally adaptive view of the two-millennia-old faculty, suggesting that rhetoric as a *praxis* and *paideia* are capable of virtual conversion. By this, academic practitioners mean that rhetoric can be taught and learnt exclusively or mainly online, and that web-based rhetorical training courses are interchangeable with and not less effective than their brick-and-mortar alternatives. Summarizing her research in this topic, Katie Böhme (2009: 4–5) assumes that web-based rhetorical training courses, though doubted earlier, are virtually possible and if the basic requirements are met they can exceed the success of face-to-face classroom courses. Moreover, virtual rhetoric as an educational program and logic has proven to be more effective in deepening theoretical insights and improving analytical skills. The conclusions of web-based rhetorical education provide the perspective of *rhetoric in the virtual*, which is further exploited in empirical studies of computer-mediated communication (Sundar 2015). The second interpretation of virtual rhetoric focuses on *virtual as rhetorical*, examining the ways virtual spaces are created to persuade and immerse users. The third meaning offers a view of rhetoric as a mode of creating a virtual space of imaginative communication. *Rhetoric*, constructing shared, imaginary and social spaces can be seen *as inherently virtual (and visual)*. Being a *techné* (τέχνη), a systematic, disciplined, skillful art, rhetoric originally shares characteristics with (media) technology, the study and body of procedures and processes of (message) production/circulation. Still, there remains a need to show how immediate, immersive, visual and sensible the rhetorical experience is meant to be (Aczél 2016). In what follows I aim to theorize about the concept of virtual rhetoric by dwelling upon persuasion, immersion and visuality.

2. Naturally Virtual

Virtual is something latent, something that is visible but does not exist, like our body's reflection in the mirror. It is something very close to being something without being it, offering other spaces, "heterotopias" (Foucault 2002) that share attributes of real ones without sharing their material existence and/or mirroring everyday activities in a festive way. Virtual is not the opposite of the real but a sort of reality itself (Lister et al. 2003: 124). It is the alternative reality or hyperreality that is either a creation or a simulation or a representation serving as an opportunity to parallel (or overcome) reality and its interactions (Aczél 2016). With the advent of new media technologies, the virtual refers to a spatial experience that promises "to transform interpersonal communication to the very extent of our imaginations. [...] VR will eventually provide the means by which interactants will transcend the real and create communication environments that are hyperreal" (Palmer 1995: 290).

Computerized virtual reality is a visually and spatially designed, photorealistic space each frame of which requires 80 million 'polygons' (three dimensional objects which are created out of many two dimensional figures amidst straight lines). For the illusion of motion at least ten frames per second should be created with the above visual potential. This way, the visual complex of altogether 800 million polygons per second 'equals' reality and creates a full-fledged virtual space (Taube-Leenders 1998: 345). This is massive, indeed, but definitely not enough. As game designers put it, to stimulate a subtle visual-virtual experience, and an immersive display, developers work with particle systems in which the behavior and appearance of simple shapes can be programmed and thus modified in response to the user (Therrein 2012: 273). Behind the virtual experience there is an intention of visual creation and recreation of worlds in an interactive and thus persuasive way.

The term *virtual* is readily and frequently used as a synonym of digital/cyber/simulated, that is, of the numerically based, networked capacity of ephemeral, infinite and intense communicative processes, codes, platforms and activities. In this prospect, virtual stands for the technological imagery that formulates spaces for individual and collective actors; online virtual realities. *Virtual reality* (VR) is one of those terms that are used widely without much consensus about its meaning. First written about by Ivan Sutherland as "computer generated illusion" and later coined by Jaron Lanier (1989), it is generally accepted that virtual reality is a digitally constructed simulation without the qualities of the 'actual'. Virtual reality comprises of spaces, each of which "is a hybrid of technical, social and economic practices" (Kuksa–Child 2014: 4). In terms of mediation, virtual spaces perform the highest form of immediacy, that is, the absence of the perception that there is a technology (interface) that mediates. In VR there feels to be no interface with which mental absorption of the human agent may be technologically reflected or the physical body objected. VR offers the experience of a physical and psychological involvement in a simulated and dynamic (because of feedback loops) world. It is based on new media's potential for real-time communication and on the holistic sensations that digital simulations are able to formulate. Presence, vividness and immersion are the main conditions of such intensification of the sensual, cognitive and emotional functions. In fact, these are at the heart of the rhetorical persuasion and practice as well.

Virtual is not the antithesis of the real. It is better imagined in a continuum which contains the real, the augmented and the virtual. The extremes of this continuum, the real and the virtual, embrace mixed reality, that is, when the real is enhanced with computer generated information and graphics (augmented reality) or when the virtual is augmented by real images and objects (augmented virtuality) (Milgram–Drascic 1997).

Virtual reality is constantly (re)produced by an apparatus to serve as a symbolic dimension for the individuals' telepresence, whereas the apparatus is operated by its human wearer who (re)produces herself within the boundaries of the digital sphere. Virtual reality is where physical bodies and spatial illusions are intertwined via technological imagery. These are online environments, digitally shaped spaces for embodiment and immersion in which the visual has a dominant, creative force.

Visuality for virtuality functions the same way as sounded words functioned for primarily oral cultures where practices of rhetoric can find their origins (Aczél 2016). Sounded language for oral peoples, for whom writing was non-existent, was a mode of action, a way of (re)creating the world. Words in these cultures were sounds that could not be made notes. Therefore, the thoughts and actions they expressed and provoked had to be imaginable, memorable, rhythmic and sensory. In primary orality, speech was aggregative rather than analytic, additive rather that subordinative, empathetic and participatory rather than objectively distanced and homeostatic, the latter referring to the embeddedness of speech into the very present situation (Ong 2002: 35–46). These psychodynamics are analogically observable in the primarily visual digital-virtual space where images bolster the sense of the present and presence. In virtual spaces visual elements are likewise memorable, additive, aggregative, empathetic and immersive. Rhetoric has its roots in oral cultures, in the world of powerful words that created rather than denoted reality. Thus, the dynamics of online visual-virtual spaces and original persuasive speeches bear a notable resemblance (Aczél 2016).

3. Persuasion and Immersion – Virtual as Rhetorical

"Virtual reality is a new, complex form of communication, and as in any other medium of communication, we can use rhetoric in virtual reality to convey arguments and change how individuals view the real world. [...] Visual rhetoric refers to the ability of images to convey arguments, primarily through invoking an emotional response [...]" (Ulrich 2011: 6). In this view, rhetoric means the apparatus of persuasion in virtual environments, theoretically framing persuasive technologies; interfaces, spaces and procedures designed to influence their users. Design can be persuasive intentionally, that is when the designer applies rhetorical principles to the interface to capture and move users (audiences). However, persuasive technologies operate unintentionally, too, where there is a critical-rhetorical literacy needed to make influential gestures overt. Virtual as rhetorical thus comprises two approaches: the practical ("utens") and the critical ("docens"). The first deals with the creation of persuasive virtual realities (planning, structuring and designing effects) while the other concerns the reception and interpretation of the persuasive intention and display.

Technologies and the virtual spaces created by them can definitely persuade: they keep us engaged, make us attentive, feel real and personal. Persuasive displays are designed to be influential. Design here manifests the persuasive intent of its creator by which attitudes and behaviors of recipients can be modified. This perspective of virtual persuasion is by nature rhetorical, the virtual 'artifact' – reality – being its speech. Fogg (2003) terms these rhetorically formulated complex technological operations, their applications and research *captology*, a neologism specifying the critical approach to study designed persuasive effects of human-computer (internet) interactions and to investigate "how people are motivated or persuaded when interacting *with* computing products rather than *through* them" (2003: 16). As Fogg asserted, in coming years computing products and software applications would be more persuasive and motivational by being designed more supportive and empathetic with the human psyche. He was definitely right: computers as technologies are gradually disappearing into transparency, getting to be less and less 'machines' and more and more information and simulation appliances (Norman 1998 cited by Bolter–Gromala 2003).

In Fogg's taxonomy, computers can be persuasive in three different functional roles: as tools, as mediums and as social actors. A medium, Fogg explains, "can be persuasive by allowing people to explore cause-and-effect relationships, providing people with vicarious experiences that motivates, helping people to rehearse a behavior" (Fogg 2003: 62). Computers can become sensory media that provide users with simulated spaces and roles where the intense intensity of the hyperreal cyberspace carries users into a flow of influtainment. That flow motivates users to adopt new attitudes and behaviors in a safe place, involving them in cause-and-effect chains that unfold in a compressed time span without immediate real-life consequences. Being integrated into the virtual, the user is often biased by the intensity of sensory media and forgets to reflect on the designers' biases built into the programming and display.

Persuasion is a function of digitally constructed spaces that clearly connects virtual design with rhetorical thinking. However, it is not the only one. There is a crucial concept when it comes to understanding the human experience in virtual realities: immersion. Immersion denotes a complex relationship that forms between a human, a medium and its message. The human agent's understanding of, and interaction and engagement with, the media results in what we call immersion, which acts on the emotions, body and mind. (Cashman 2010) Concluding from the persuasiveness of computerization we claim that there is indeed a rhetorical element in designing and exploiting immersive virtual environments.

In parallel, immersion presents itself as the original function of rhetorical speech as well. It is thus the concept through which the connectedness of virtual to the rhetorical can further be explicated.

A rhetorical speech is immersive in terms of its force to stimulate the mind's eye and excite imagination, of its vividness to engage people in a world designed by symbols (language, context, environment, etc.). Vivid, imagistic explanation of places, actions, conflicts and emotions help interactants incorporate into an aesthetically and logically constructed, shared psychological-social reality. It is the intensity of the language, the 'visibility' and presence created by the speech that allure recipients to be a part rather than a listener of what they are told. When a rhetorical speech unfolds, audiences are invited into a space where temporal immediacy and spatial logic frame the possibility for recipients to immerse.

Virtual reality can be immersive in terms of its capacity to manipulate human perception, emotion, cognition and imagination (Cashman 2010; Kuksa–Child 2014). The more these experiences are enhanced, the more immersive that particular virtual media-message is considered. Nevertheless, these experiences can occur separately and cause immersion exclusively, so even though immersion feels to be an overwhelming involvement in a virtual or augmented sphere, the manipulation of cognition alone can trigger it. This recognition points to the need of finding an integrative model which is capable of overcoming the narrowness of definitions that concentrate on only one dimension of immersive design. Of the three distinguishable approaches, one describes immersion as the result of altering human perception (seeing, hearing, smelling, being) (Slater 2003). Here immersion stands for a kind of physical-sensual submerging into a virtual-digital world the displays of which are designed in all sensory modalities with fidelity to their real-world equivalents. Technology embraces the body and the senses, and induces them to react to artificially formulated, simulated stimuli. The virtual space integrates its user by the excitement of her senses. It is the feeling of "as if I was there" without a clear reflection on what is simulated and what is real (or augmented). Visual, haptic and audial fidelity, concreteness and subjectivity can effectively serve this sensation. The other approach highlights the significance of emotional arousal through the manipulation of desires (Murray 1997). This is what stories apply in order to motivate and facilitate the psychological engagement of their recipients. Immersion in this sense means the imaginative integration of the human agent into a simulated social situation. This is where interactions, role-playing and, most importantly, identifications are facilitated in order to incorporate the person into an emotionally important and shared narrative. The third explanation takes attention as central to define immersion as a cognitive act of focusing (Lanham 2006). Mental absorption (Grau 2003) into the virtual redirects attention that is driven by the flow of acts, goals, rewards, punishments and the very presence of conclusions.

All three definitions implicitly point to the very rhetorical nature of immersive design and experience. However, in order to bridge these three and add a new facet to the understanding of immersion, rhetoric offers a more explicit method. Within it we can consider immersion a complex communicative and persuasive act in which the communicative exigence, the thesis/topic (narrative), the spatial-temporal arrangements, style and identification, emerging personal and cultural memories/associations are to be examined (Cashman 2010: 90). The narrative means of immersion refers to the plot scheme, the spatial and temporal regard the arrangement of the virtual space and timing of its actions. The social means of immersive design entails style that motivates identification with characters and roles. Memory means unveils intertexts in a virtual display, while exigence serves as the dynamic force of participation (Cashman 2010: 109–110).These are the elements that clearly correlate with what classical and modern rhetoric categorized under stasis (the case/narrative itself), circumstantiae (the circumstances), situation (the participants and dynamics) and identification (consubstantiality between parties; persuasion). Moreover, these are the means the inquiry into which can lead to a multifaceted understanding of why/how immersion may occur.

The immersive function of digitally formulated virtual spaces and activities is rhetorical in nature, while rhetoric is aimed to immerse audiences in a psychological reality created by the speech: immersion thus marks a significant intersection of the rhetorical and the virtual.

4. Rhetoric – Visual and Virtual

Rhetoric, according to Aristotle (1355b), is "the faculty of observing in any given case the available means of persuasion". It is broadly referred to as the theory and practice of suasory communication enabling men to participate actively in public an in front of publics. Although traditionally viewed as strongly tied with exclusively verbal persuasion, rhetoric has always tended to outgrow this limitation. Platitudinous, semi-forgotten elements of the ancient faculty prove that rhetoric requires creative visual imagination from both parties (orator-audience) and that it emanates from and embeds in visuospatial, sensual experiences. Among these are the ars memorativa (the semi-conventional, picture and space-based system of memory), phantasia (the inner sense of the speaker and the receiver, that connects imagination, cogitation and memory), ingenium (the creative force in meeting, cognizing and expressing the world), enargeia (the energizing force that guides speakers to create vivid descriptions and to make their audiences to picture what is said in order to persuade), ekphrasis (the rhetorical description that unfolds before the audience's eyes) or thaumazein (the initial shock of seeing and sensing the world uniquely, the wonder that comes from experience and recognition).

As the extensive analysis of these terms cannot be aimed here, I limit myself to flash up some characteristics of memory, presence and enargeia to cast light upon rhetoric as something virtual in its origins, operations and effects. I assert that rhetorical communication is based upon immediate and intense impressions and thus can it create visuospatially, emotionally and sensibly cognizable psychological-virtual spaces for its perceivers.

Classical rhetorical theory held memory in high regard. Even with its most skeptical writers it was considered the centre of the orator's arsenal, the cornerstone of the rhetorical discipline. It was defined either a mental art (a revival or recollection of perfect, ideal images), a part of the virtue of prudence, or a prescribed, trainable strategy. Often called the treasure-house of ideas, memory was originally related to invention that is built on the use of 'loci' and 'imagines', backgrounds and images. The locus has to be thought of as a real place that the speaker is familiar with. The background should be mentally divided into separate scenes and thus it forms a continuous series in the mind providing linkage in the 'material' and keeping it in the right sequence. This background, once learned, can be used repeatedly as a board that is there to be erased or reused when needed. Further on in memorization, the subject matter is divided up into scenes and each marked point is represented by a physical object, an incredibly intense impression (Yates 1974). Loci mnemonic was thus imagistic and synthetic, and orchestration of the senses, impressions and meanings offering a virtual space for the speaker where rational, emotional and associational processes can go on. Creativity, selectivity, situatedness and spatiality of seeing are recognized by the operations of the ancient system, which may serve as a mirror model of the programming of today's virtual spaces (Aczél 2011).

Presence is what grounds the rhetorical situation and experience. As such, it founds the immersive experience of the digital virtual participant. Perelman and Olbrechts-Tyteca (2008) address the concept of rhetorical presence assuming that the effectiveness of argumentation is greatly affected by how successfully the speaker can make the elements of her proposal stand out for the audience, "to make these elements more salient and memorable. This can be done partly by the simple act of selecting and pointing out those elements. [...] Indeed, such a choice endows these elements with a presence" (Perelman–Olbrechts-Tyteca 2008: 116).

Rhetorical presence is more for the 'viewer' than for the listener. Fahnestock insists that the "intense realization of an actual or hypothetical event, as though occurring before the eyes, have crucial purpose: rhetoricians believe that such mental images could induce and emotional state in the audience" (Fahnestock 2011: 336). The "psychological assumption here [...] is that the emotions are reached through the senses, so the best way to create an emotion is to recreate the situation with a deictic immediacy stimulating the senses that would then evoke the emotion", as underlined by Fahnestock (2011: 337). The deictic immediacy directly operates on the 'passions' and creates the feeling of here and now, a kind of immersion. Presence and immediacy are likewise foundational in VR, where a whole world is made up around the virtually re/embodied agent. Presence entails the usage of vivid illustrations in order to create vivid impressions in the receiver both in rhetoric and in VR. Vividness – a phenomenon that contemporary psychology invests considerable interest into without referring much to the ancient roots and rhetorical knowledge – comes from the rhetorical virtue of enargeia. Enargeia, as the word itself suggests, energizes rhetorical descriptions with the visualization of things in activity (Aczél 2014). It brings words in front of the eyes by creating lively images of active persons and things, thus giving the impression of presence, of the here and now. It involves the audience into the happening of things as if they were unfolding right then, right there. The virtue of enargeia enacts the idea of actualization and the formulation of a common, shared reality; a reality that is virtual and rhetorical. Vivid information has its source in the communicator's enargeia and is identified as concrete, emotionally interesting, imagery-provoking information and proximate in a sensory, temporal, or spatial way (Nisbett–Ross 1980: 45). Concrete, intense language, imagistic, figurative expressions (metaphors), personal narratives and first-had experiences serve vividness well, actual experience being the most vivid on the scale. Some psychological experiments in the field have demonstrated that vivid information prompts more emotional responses and thus turns out to be more persuasive (Hill 2004: 32).

Memory, presence and enargeia exemplify the spatial, visual, emotional volume of rhetorical practice (and theory). Even though the logical-verbal paradigm has long been domineering over the inquiry into rhetorical processes and products, there is a rich body of evidence that visuospatial-emotional elements are equally relevant and applicable in its tradition. However neglected this line of thinking may be, this is what makes rhetoric so lucrative in the analysis of virtual spaces and this is what calls for further quests into rhetoric as virtual (visual) itself (Aczél 2016).

5. Epilogue

In our supernow, technologically revolutionized era it is an intriguing challenge to apply one of the oldest faculties of the social human being to the understanding of the ambitiously bred digital virtuality. Having been hyper-connected, augmented and nested into the internet of things, acquiring a new fluency of hybrid codes in global interactions, what we head for now is the virtual. Virtual is becoming the new real and so will its interpretations further proliferate. The efficiency of employing rhetorical operations in the design and analysis of virtual realities and displays is indisputable when it comes to the phenomena of persuasion and immersion. In reverse, analysis of virtual communications can augment and intensify the urge for the rediscovery of rhetorical communication's hidden visual and immersive capacities.

Rhetoric can be seen as an ancient head mounted display through which we can enter into spectacular shared worlds, experience visual persuasion, emotional states, abbreviated decisive processes – that is, a kind of virtuality that preceded digital technology with thousands of years. This chapter is meant to be a humble contribution to this provocative metaphor by conceptualizing rhetoric in a virtual world.

References

Aczél, Petra (2011): Enchanting Bewilderment: Concerns for Visual Rhetoric. In: Benedek, András – Nyíri, Kristóf (eds.): *Images in Language*. Series Visual Learning vol. 1. Frankfurt: Peter Lang. 85–98.

Aczél, Petra (2014): Expressivity and Emotion in Visionary Rhetoric. In: Benedek, András – Nyíri, Kristóf (eds.): *The Power of the Image: Emotion, Expression, Explanation*. Series Visual Learning vol. 4. Frankfurt: Peter Lang. 61–72.

Aczél, Petra (2016): Virtual Rhetoric. A Theoretical Approach. *Res Rhetorica* 2016/4. 2–15. Online: http://resrhetorica.com/index.php/RR/issue/view/9.

Aristotle (1991): *On Rhetoric: A Theory of Civic Discourse*. Transl. by G. A. Kennedy. New York, NY: Oxford University Press.

Böhme, Katie (2009): Web-based rhetorical training – a virtual impossibility? Problems and perspectives of improving public speaking skills in virtual learning environments. *Journal of Education, Informatics, and Cybernetics* 1/1: 1–6.

Bolter, David J. – Gromale, Diane (2003): *Windows and Mirrors. Interaction Design, Digital Art, and the Myth of Transparency*. Cambridge, MA: MIT Press.

Cashman, Shaun Lee (2010): *The Rhetoric of Immersion in Video Game Technologies*. Dissertation. Raleigh: North Carolina State University. Online: https://repository.lib.ncsu.edu/bitstream/handle/1840.16/6105/etd.pdf?sequence=1.

Fahnestock, Jeanne (2011): *Rhetorical Style: The Uses of Language in Persuasion*. New York: Oxford University Press.

Fogg, B. J. (2003): *Persuasive Technology. Using Computers to Change What We Think and Do*. New York, NJ: Morgan Kaufmann – Elsevier.

Foucault, Michel (2002): Of Other Spaces. In: Mirzoeff, N. (ed.): *The Visual Culture Reader*. London – New York: Routledge. 229–237.

Grau, Oliver (2003): *Virtual Art: from Illusion to Immersion*. Cambridge, MA: MIT Press.

Hill, Charles A. (2004): The Psychology of Rhetorical Images. In: Hill, Ch. A. – Helmers, M. (eds.): *Defining Visual Rhetorics*. Mahwah, NJ: Lawrence Erlbaum Associates. 25–40.

Kuksa, Iryna – Childs, Mark (2014): *Making Sense of Space. The Design and Experience of Virtual Spaces as a Tool for Communication*. Oxford: Chandos – Elsevier.

Lanham, Richard A. (2006): *The Economics of Attention: Style and Substance in the Age of Information*. Chicago: University of Chicago Press.

Lanier, Jaron (1992): Virtual Reality: The Promise of the Future. *Interactive Learning International* 8: 275–279.

Lister, Martin – Dovey, Jon – Giddings, Seth – Grant, Iain – Kelly, Kieran (2009): *New Media. A Critical Introduction*. New York, NY: Routledge.

Milgram, Paul – Drascic, David (1997): *Perceptual Effects in Aligning Virtual and Real Objects in Augmented Reality Displays*. Paper presented at the 41st Annual Meeting of Human Factors and Ergonomics Society, Albuquerque, New Mexico. Sept. 1997. Online: https://pdfs.semanticscholar.org/22c6/5fbadc83cd752302c71e2d358039e8204f12.pdf.

Murray, Janet (1997): *Hamlet on the Holodeck: The Future of Narrative in Cyberspace*. New York: Free Press.

Nisbett, Richard – Ross, Lee (1980): *Human Inference: Strategies and Shortcomings of Social Judgement*. Englewood Cliffs, NJ: Prentice Hall.

Norman, Donald (1998): *The Invisible Computer: Why Good Products Can Fail, the Personal Computer is So Complex, and Information Appliances Are the Solution*. Cambridge, MA: MIT Press.

Nyíri, Kristóf (2012): Images in Conservative Education. In: Benedek, András – Nyíri, Kristóf (eds.): *How to Do Things with Pictures: Skill, Practice, Performance*. Series Visual Learning vol. 3. 191–207.

Ong, Walter J. (1982/2002): *Orality and Literacy. The Technologizing of the Word. 30th Anniversary Edition*. New York, NY: Routledge.

Palmer, Mark T. (1995): Interpersonal Communication and Virtual Reality: Mediating Interpersonal Relationships. In: Biocca, Frank – Levy, Mark R. (eds.) *Communication in the Age of Virtual Reality*. Hillsdale, NJ: Lawrence Erlbaum Associates. 277–302.

Perelman, Chäim – Olbrechts-Tyteca, Lucie (1969/2008): *The New Rhetoric: A Treatise on Argumentation*. Trans. John Wilkinson and Purcell Weaver. Notre Dame, IN: University of Notre Dame Press.

Slater, Mel (2003). *A Note on Presence Terminology.* Online: https://pdfs.semanticscholar.org/ed27/7f9067a0b6aadd90c055d31aecc8ab92aa2f.pdf

Sundar, Shyam S. (ed.) (2015): *The Handbook of the Psychology of Communication Technology*. Malden, MA: Wiley – Blackwell.

Taube, Mieczyslaw – Leenders, Klaus (1998): *The Search for Terrestrial Intelligence*. Singapore: World Scientific Publishing Co.

Therrien, Carl (2012): The Language of Illusion. In: Wolf, Mark J. P. (ed.): *Encyclopedia of Video Games. The Culture, Technology and Art of Gaming.* Vol. 1. Santa Barbara, CA: Greenwood. 272–273.

Ulrich, Mark (2011): Seeing is Believing: Using the Rhetoric of Virtual Reality to Persuade. *Young Scholars in Writing*, 5–15. Online: http://cas.umkc.edu/english/publications/youngscholarsinwriting/documents/9/3SeeingIsBelieving.pdf.

Yates, Frances A. (1974): *The Art of Memory*. Chicago: The University of Chicago Press.

Eszter Deli

Can Images be Arguments? The Possibility of Visual Argumentation in the WWF Nature Conservancy Campaigns

1. Visual Argumentation

The role of images within argumentation has always been a hotly debated and scientifically controversial issue, therefore the present paper focuses on the opportunities and challenges of argumentation within the realm of visuality. I will argue that images play an essential role in the communication of propositions as the necessary components of argumentation itself. Furthermore, I will assert that images communicate propositions directly, without verbalising them, through the mental representation of the given information.

The primary motivation for this topic is that little attention is paid to the visual components of argumentation and persuasion, even though the present period is mostly called the *"modern era of pictures"* or the *"pictorial turn"*, to quote Mitchell, with pictures towering over words as never before (1995: 12–13). However, a thorough look at the literature on the subject reveals that many researchers, for more than one reason, refute the very existence of non-verbal reasoning. In their book *The New Rhetoric*, Perelman and Tyteca exclusively focus on the discursive means of obtaining the adherence of minds, which means that the only thing worth exploring is the technique which uses language to persuade and convince (1971: 8). Eemeren, Grootendorst and Kruiger also consider argumentation to be necessarily verbal, as this process involves a person who makes an assertion or statement, assumes or doubts something, denies something, etc. by uttering words (Fleming 2005: 2), while Balthrop claims that an argument is inherently discursive and linguistic (Fleming 2005: 2). Toulmin et al. also suggest that reasoning could not exist in the absence of language (1984: 201). In fact, Toulmin believes that one of the primary functions of arguments is to be justificatory, brought forward in support of verbal assertions, in the structures they may be expected to have, the merits they can claim and the ways in which we set about classifying, assessing and criticising them (2003: 12). On the other hand, others, such as Aspeitia, assert that images contribute directly to the communication of premises or conclusions (2011: 123), while Groarke believes that visual arguments can contain a premise-conclusion structure which is amenable to standard forms of argumentative analysis (1996: 107). Agreeing with the latter theoreticians, the present paper confirms that visual argumentation is not only possible but it is also one of the most significant fields of our age.

In this modern era of pictures, Gombrich assumes that the image takes over the written word, therefore it is essential to examine whatever an image knows compared to a word and what kind of possibility it is for communication. To this end, I first present the functions of language then I apply them to images, too (Horányi 2003: 92–107). According to Karl Bühler, language as one of the most important means of human communication has three functions: expression, appeal, and description. A speech act is expressive if it informs the listener about the speaker's state of mind, while the function of appeal is to induce a state of mind in the addressee. These two communication functions also occur in non-human species but the last one, description, shows that human language is capable of something more. The descriptive function has evolved in human language and it is used to inform others about past, present or future facts, and remote, real or possible events. Thus we can say "it is raining", "it was raining" and "it is going to rain", but description can also include small particles such as "if," "when," "because," "some", etc., which enable speakers to draw logical conclusions (Horányi 2003: 92–107). By contrast, Gombrich believes that not all functions can be used for images. In his view, pictures are brilliant at appealing, quite problematic at expressing and, without additional cues, totally incapable of fulfilling the descriptive function of language. Based on Gombrich's train of thoughts, there are three common counter-arguments against the possibility of visual argumentation. The present paper attempts to refute each.

1. One of the most widespread prejudices about visual argumentation is that it is generally vague and arbitrary, thus reinforcing the view that images are less precise than words, especially written words (Birdsell – Groarke 1996: 2).
2. Another essential, and maybe the most relevant, objection to visual argumentation is that it contains no truth value, therefore it cannot convey propositions, although argumentation does require the presence of certain propositions in order to fulfil its task (Hill – Helmers 2008: 47).
3. The final criticism against visual argumentation is that even though non-verbal tools can be applied, they do not function as an argument in the reasoning process as long as they are not linguistically translated (Fleming 2005: 2).

In order to present the first counter-argument about the vague and ambiguous nature of pictures, Gombrich gives the following example: "*The cat is on the mat.*" According to him, the problem does not merely stem from the fact that the visual medium is never as abstract as language. While his elementary school-level example is obviously not an abstract sentence, we cannot picture it exactly.

In his view, we cannot know if *the* cat or *a* cat is concerned, we cannot know whether it *was* or still *is* seated on there, etc. However, I agree with numerous researchers (e.g. Birdsell – Groarke 1996: 2, Blair [Hill – Helmers 2008: 46] or Noth) in that it is worth taking into account the possibilities of the visual, and the limitations of verbal meaning. Pictures can definitely be ambiguous and unclear but these properties alone do not distinguish them from words and sentences, which may be ambiguous and imprecise, too. On the other hand, fuzziness and ambiguity may not always be considered a defect within the communication processes. To use Blair's example, if we are asked about our age, we do not have to give the minutes, hours, days or weeks exactly. It is enough to reveal the year which is also quite obscure, but in most social situations perfectly acceptable (Hill – Helmers 2008: 46–47). In addition, visual signals can often help us reduce the uncertainties caused by verbal language, e.g. by accompanying our story with a smile or a wink (Birdsell – Groarke 1996: 2). This makes it much easier to identify the speaker's intentions and thoughts together with such figures of classical rhetoric as irony and the closely related caustic, bitter sarcasm (Szathmári 2003: 145).

The second objection to visual argumentation is that images are not able to make allegations and hence convey propositions, even though the argumentation process does require the presence of certain propositions in order to perform its task (Hill – Helmers 2008: 47), therefore visual argumentation itself is nothing but a paradox (Horányi 2003: 92–107). In response to this criticism, I will first attempt to define the concept of propositions. King et al. believe that propositions are equal to the information content of declarative phrases, which can be true or false based on the truth value of the encoded information. Thus, these authors believe that propositions are the primary carriers of truth and falsity as the truth value of statements necessarily depend on the truth of the propositions they express (2014: 5).

2. Analysis of World Wildlife Fund Posters

The present study addresses the problem of propositions by presenting visual elements, specifically, the posters of WWF (World Wildlife Fund), an international non-governmental organisation founded in 1961 (W1). The first example demonstrates the 2009 campaign poster, in which argumentation is performed by a mixture of the verbal and the visual. In Roque's view, words and images are strongly intertwined, so that it is absolutely impossible to conceive of a universe of images without words. However, the opposite is also true as the universe of words depends on images, too (2009: 4). The first two illustrations are meant to prove the falsehood of the common prejudice that the visual and the verbal are irreconcilably distinct (Groarke 1996: 107) and that the visual is not only capable of embellishing the verbal but also completing it. The picture below (*Figure 1*) imitates a tic-tac-toe game where the 3 × 3 grid is incomplete as one space is left empty, while the rest contain either a bag or a crocodile. According to the rules of the game, the blank field could be completed both with the icon of the bag and with the crocodile. The caption is a simple sentence: *"It's your turn"*.

Figure 1: WWF Noughts and Crosses Campaign

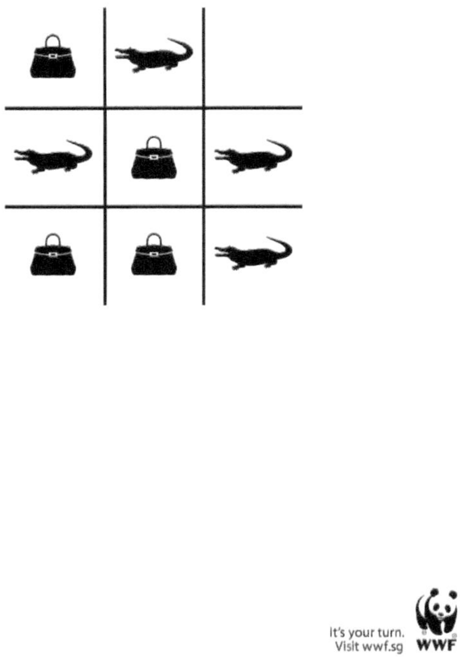

(source: W2)

The configuration involves the viewer both intellectually and kinetically, by inviting them first to find the relation between the crocodile and the bag, and then to complete the empty space by selecting either symbol. The image becomes argumentation as no matter which symbol the viewer chooses, they will support one of the two options and by this the image will gain its propositional value (Tseronis 2013: 13).

Figure 2: WWF Biodiversity Protection Campaign

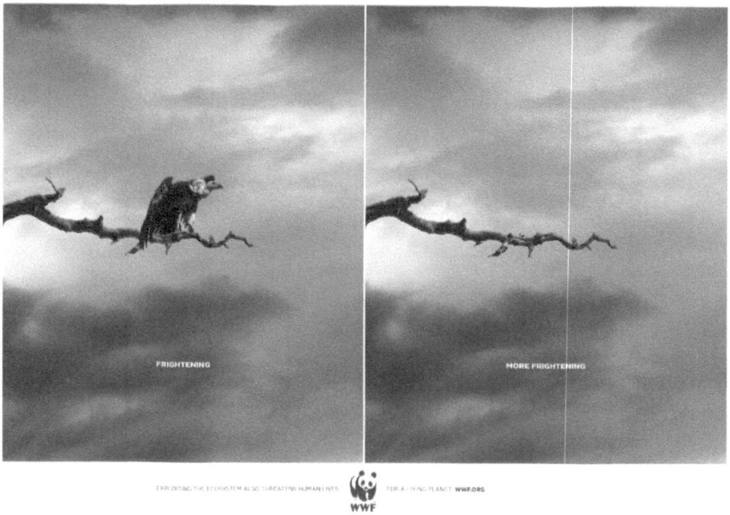

(source: W3)

The next image is an advertisement from the WWF Biodiversity Protection Campaign. The picture on the left shows a vulture sitting on a branch with the caption *"Frightening"* while the picture on the right shows an empty branch and says *"More frightening"*. Here again, the proposition is clear: the extinction of vultures is an existing and frightening problem. As with the previous example, argumentation is achieved through a blend of the verbal and visual. At the same time, the poster's message would be obviously unintelligible without the image as the words do not explicitly refer to vultures and could easily be misunderstood. Therefore, the image is not playing merely a decorative role by completing or illustrating the picture. Instead, it is carrying the main meaning. The image, then, directly contributes to transmitting the proposition as the key component of argumentation (Aspeitia 2011: 123).

The last example comes from the WWF Global Warming Campaign. In the picture a scoop of ice cream is fused with the globe, melting its greens and blues and whites all over the cone. This image does not contain any verbal messages but the proposition is crystal clear: The Earth is melting due to global warming and this will have serious consequences for humanity. This example is meant to demonstrate that an image is perfectly capable of conveying its propositions in a comprehensible and perspicuous way without any verbal support.

Figure 3: WWF Global Warming Campaign

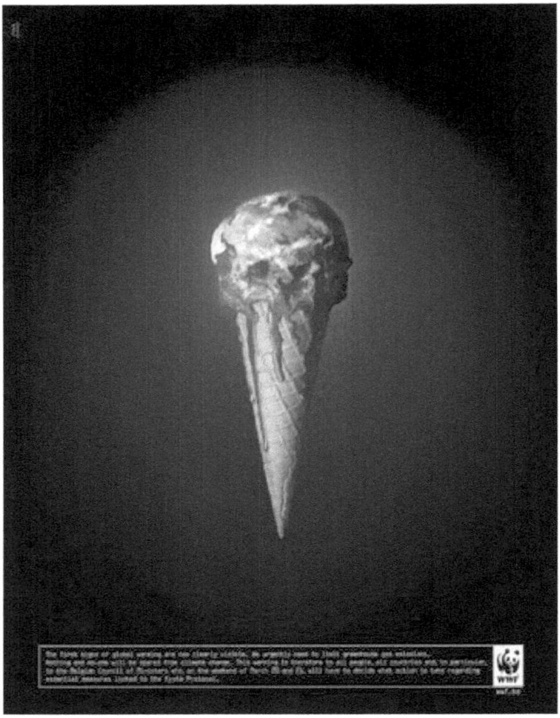

(source: W4)

The last criticism about the possibility of visual argumentation is that visual elements cannot function as an argument in the reasoning process until they are linguistically translated (Fleming 2005: 2). In Roque's opinion, this statement stems from the arrogance of linguistic imperialism, since by saying that an image needs language to become an argument, it loses its visual nature and falls into the realm of language (2009: 4). In order to prove that visuality is often enough to convey a message, suffice it to cite Lewis E. Walkup's example which examines the visualisation of a combination of cubes (1965: 38). He asked a number of people to envision a large cube made up of 27 smaller ones, just like the famous Hungarian Rubik's Cube. Then he asked them to imagine painting the entire outer surface of the large cube. His question was how many of the smaller cubes would be painted on one, two, three, or no sides at all. Walkup observed that even those who were professionally engaged in science and art were simply unable to solve this problem mentally because they could not visualise the task in any way. According to Arnheim, the easiest way to find the solution is to imagine the central one of the twenty-seven cubes surrounded by all the others, covering it like a shell (2013: 491). Shielded from the outside, the one central cube evidently remains unpainted, while all the others touch the surface. Now, we look at the two-dimensional version of the three-dimensional image, and notice that each side has a central element that will only be painted on one side, which leaves us with six cubes with one surface painted. Then we inspect the twelve edges of the large cube and find that each edge has two sides painted, and lastly only the eight corners are left for us to observe, which cover three surfaces each. Did we need language to perform this action? Not in the least. Even though language could help us codify our results, all we needed was visualisation, intelligence, inventiveness and creative discovery (Arnheim 2013: 491).

3. Conclusion

The present paper attempted to prove that argumentation is as much a visual as a verbal art (Aczél 2015: 176). Although Gombrich admits that we have entered a visual age, he does not accept that visuals may prove to have the same expressive function as verbal language. He asserts that visual meaning is so vulnerable that the verbal always needs to give it a helping hand. Similarly to many other scholars, he believes that the visual is not able to convey propositions but even when it is, it needs verbal translation to do so. With the attempt to respond to all of these counter-arguments, this treatise endeavoured to prove that "after centuries of the reign of the written word, we are witnessing the revival of visual rhetoric in a new world of imagery and sight" (Nyíri 2016: 44).

References

Aczél, Petra (2015): Ingenious Rhetoric: The Visual Secret of Rhetoricality. In: Benedek, András – Nyíri, Kristóf (eds.): *Beyond Words – Pictures, Parables, Paradoxes.* Series Visual Learning vol. 5. Frankfurt: Peter Lang Edition. 165–176.

Arnheim, Rudolf (1980): A Plea for Visual Thinking. *Chicago Journals* (The University of Chicago Press) 6/3: 489–497.

Aspeitia, Axel A. (2011): *Words and Images in Argumentation*. Springer Science + Business Media B.V. 355–368.

Birdsell, David S. – Groarke, Leo (1996): Toward a Theory of Visual Argument. *Argumentation and Advocacy. The Journal of the American Forensic Association*: 1–10.

Blair, J. Anthony (2004): The Rhetoric of Visual Arguments. In: Hill, Charles A. – Helmers, Marguerite (eds.): *Defining Visual Rhetorics*. Mahwah, NJ: Lawrence Erlbaum Associates. 41–61.

Fleming, David (1996): Can pictures be arguments? *Argumentation & Advocacy* 33/1: 1–12.

Gombrich, Ernst H. (2003): A látható kép. In: Horányi, Özséb (ed.): *Kommunikáció I–II*. Budapest: General. 92–107.

Groarke, Leo (1996): Logic, Art and Argument. *Informal Logic* (Philosophy Publications) 18: 105–129.

King, Jeffrey C. – Soames, Scott – Speaks, Jeff (2014): *New Thinking about Propositions*. UK: Oxford University Press.

Mitchell, William J. (1995): *Picture Theory: Essays on Verbal and Visual Representation*. Chicago: University of Chicago Press.

Noth, Winfred: Can Pictures Lie? *The Semiotic Review of Books* 6/2. http://projects.chass.utoronto.ca/semiotics/srb/pictures.html [19. 02. 2017]

Nyíri, Kristóf (2016): Elfelejtett képelméletek. In: Benedek, András – Nyíri, Kristóf (eds.): *Képi Tanulás Műhelye Füzetek*. Budapest: BME GTK Műszaki Pedagógia Tanszék. 3–55.

Perelman, Chaim – Olbrechts-Tyteca, L. (1971): *The New Rhetoric – A Treatise on Argumentation*. London: Notre Dame University Press.

Roque, Georges (2009): What is Visual in Visual Argumentation? In: Ritola, J. (ed.): *Argument Cultures*. Windsor, ON: OSSA. 1–9.

Szathmári, István (ed.) (2003): *A retorikai-stilisztikai alakzatok világa*. Budapest: Tinta Könyvkiadó.

Toulmin, Stephen – Rieke, Richard – Janik, Allan (1984): *An Introduction to Reasoning*. Second edition. USA: Macmillan Publishing Company.

Toulmin, Stephen (2003): *The Uses of Argument*. New York: Cambridge University Press.

Tseronis, Assimakis (2013): *Argumentative Functions of Visuals: Beyond Claiming and Justifying*. University of Windsor. Scholarship at UWindsor. 1–17.

Walkup, Lewis E. (1965): *Creativity in Science through Visualisation*. Battelle Memorial Institute, Columbus Laboratories. Columbia, Ohio: Southern Universities Press.

W1 = http: //www.worldwildlife.org/about/history [19. 02. 2017].

W2 = http: //theinspirationroom.com/daily/2009/wwf-its-your-turn/ [19. 02. 2017].

W3 = http: //www.adforum.com/creative-work/ad/player/34457675/vulture/wwf [19. 02. 2017].

W4 = https: //jh7304a.wordpress.com/analysis/ad/ [19. 02. 2017].

Supported by the ÚNKP-16-3 New National Excellence Program of the Ministry of Human Capacities.

Pictorial, Veridical, Cross-Cultural

Kristóf Nyíri

Pictorial Truth

1. Introduction

The concept of pictorial truth refers, first of all, to truth in the sense of seeing the world as it really is. We speak of pictures – sights, views – opening up before us. In the spirit of common-sense realism I will argue in the first section of the paper that those pictures very much tend to be veridical. In the second section, I will assume that we can also speak of pictorial truth in the sense of correct depiction, that is, resemblance. Of course pictures – drawings, paintings, photographs – resemble the objects they depict in a limited manner only; however, as in particular Arnheim and Gombrich have shown, resemblance in the sense of structural equivalence, and equivalence in the form of possible response, can certainly obtain: Goodman's extreme conventionalism and relativism are misguided. Bringing up the problem of correct depiction I will touch on children's drawings on the one hand, and the issue of linear perspective on the other. – Now while I take the notion of pictorial truth to be covering veracity also in the sense that images can correctly state *facts*, in the third section I will argue that *static* images – *single* static images – can only achieve this if they are complemented by captions. Statements can be made with a sequence of images (in this case captions need not be necessarily relied on), or indeed with moving images. One should, however, note that the term "statement" is used here in a transposed mode of speech, as it were metaphorically. Metaphor is the topic of the fourth section of the paper: I side with the view that the metaphors used in everyday thinking and in science express essential aspects of reality – they are literally true. However, I stress that understanding a metaphor essentially involves experiencing mental images. In the fifth section I conclude by emphasizing that not only is it possible to convey truths via images, but also that in a fundamental sense it is *only* via images that truths can be conveyed at all.

2. The World Viewed

The above section title is borrowed from Cavell (1979). In his epilogue to the enlarged edition, Cavell writes of "a more or less vague and pervasive intellectual fashion, apparently sanctioned by the history of epistemology and the rise of modern science, according to which we never really, and never really can, see reality as it is", of "a general dismissal of reality" that "depends upon theories (of knowledge, of science, of art, of reality, of realism) whose power to convince is hardly greater than reality's own", and mentions Heidegger and Wittgenstein as philosophers influencing his resistance to anti-realist scepticism (Cavell 1979: 165). When referring to the former, Cavell has the work *Being and Time* (Heidegger 1927/1962) in mind. I myself would add here a reference to Heidegger ([1929] 1997), a book that provides, in the span of a few pages, some brilliant answers to the fundamental questions of pictorial representation (cf. Nyíri 2014: 18–19). Heidegger discusses the image in the sense of likeness ("copy", in particular the photograph), but above all he wants to take the expression "image" in its "most original sense", "according to which we say that the landscape presents a beautiful 'image' (look)" (Heidegger [1929] 1997: 64). As to Wittgenstein, a focused text by him on the issue of realism and visual perception is *Philosophical Investigations* (1958 [1953]: Part II; for details cf. Nyíri 2017). And very unequivocal is a remark he jotted down in 1950: "Being and seeming may, of course, be independent of one another in exceptional cases, but that doesn't make them logically independent; the language-game does not reside in the exception" (Wittgenstein 1977: 29).

Mainstream philosophical-psychological theory on visual perception today does not lean towards realism. We are being told that what is mirrored on the retina at any given moment is very different from what one, as it were, sees; what one actually sees, today's mainstream theory concludes, is a mental construct rather than an aspect of some unique objective reality. I believe this conclusion is wrong. I side with, say, Rudolf Arnheim and the realist Gestalt tradition he represents; and with Ernst Gombrich and his relentless opposition to relativism. As Arnheim puts it in a memorable passage: human cognition reflects "the objective structure of physical reality as conveyed to the mind through the senses. To this objective structure art, science, and the common sense of practical life strive to do justice. In emphasizing the objective conditions of reality, I try to counteract the destructive effects of philosophical relativism" (Arnheim 1986: xi). Or as Gombrich wrote in a seldom-quoted paper: "there is a limit to perceptual relativism. What looks like a leaf to modern European must also have looked like a leaf in fairly distant geological epochs" (Gombrich 1973: 200).

3. Correct Depiction

Modern common-sense thinking is fundamentally realist. However, contemporary common sense faces a major problem when it comes to the specific issue of children's drawings. In drawings, common sense today expects the rules of naturalism and linear perspective to obtain. Children's drawings of course do not conform to those rules. Hence common sense, as also most of the earlier literature on children's drawings, regards these attempts at representation as deficient. By contrast, more recent literature, mainly under the influence of Rudolf Arnheim, emphasizes the creativity of children's drawings (cf. esp. Golomb 2004), claiming, too, that realism has many varieties, and that children's drawings, just like modern art and non-Western art, can display a degree of realism which drawings observing the rules of linear perspective often cannot. Still, it is possible to maintain that naturalism and linear perspective should be regarded as essential cognitive and cultural achievements. Here Arnheim and Gombrich, though both epistemological realists, have diverging views.

Gombrich coins a formula called the "eye-witness principle". According to this principle, "perspective enables us to eliminate from our representation anything which could not be seen from one particular vantage point" (Gombrich 1980: 193). So "if you want to follow the programme of the eye-witness principle of not including in your picture anything that is not visible from a given point, you can and indeed you must stick to the method of central perspective which the camera has taken over from the painter" (Gombrich 1980: 197). Perspectival drawings/paintings enhance visual credibility, they are experienced as visual truths, creating a "feeling of participation" (Gombrich 1980: 202). Gombrich acknowledges and indeed stresses that "perspective cannot and need not claim to represent the world 'as we see it'" (Gombrich 1980: 209); the crucial point he makes is that perspectival representation, and in particular the photograph, provide objective information in a way a non-perspectival hand-made image definitely does not (cf. Gombrich 1980: 211).

4. The Moving Image

As I indicated above by way of introduction, single static images can plausibly conjure up a scene, or correctly depict a given view, but they trivially cannot convey what the state of affairs is they show; they cannot convey statements. In Wittgenstein's famous formulation (1958 [1953]: 11e): "Imagine a picture representing a boxer in a particular stance. Now, this picture can be used to tell someone how he should stand, should hold himself; or how he should not hold himself; or how a particular man did stand in such-and-such a place; and so on." The picture of course becomes unequivocal once it is complemented by a caption. But it can be disambiguated also by making it into an item in a series of pictures – a series can tell the story a single image cannot. Comics typically combine picture sequence with bits of text – speech bubbles. Other conventional graphic elements – for instance, speed lines – are also added. And note how easily even very young children understand these conventions. It can be shown how such conventions actually emerge from real visual phenomena. On the way speed lines emerge (cf. Kennedy 1982: 591–593).

Animated picture sequences are especially well suited to convey unambiguous narratives. And film and video – all possibilities of technical manipulation notwithstanding – are the ultimate carriers of mediated pictorial truth. Let me just come back to Cavell. Asking the question "What is film?", he begins to formulate an answer by quoting two theorists he finds particularly important: "Erwin Panofsky puts it this way: 'The medium of the movies is physical reality as such.' Andre Bazin emphasizes essentially this idea many times and in many ways: at one point he says, 'Cinema is committed to communicate only by way of what is real'" (Cavell 1979: 16).

5. Image and Metaphor

In his introduction to the volume (Johnson 1981), the editor quotes the following passage from the famous essay "On Truth and Falsity in Their Ultramoral Sense" by Friedrich Nietzsche: "A nerve stimulus, first transformed in a percept! First metaphor! The percept again copied into a sound! Second metaphor!" (Johnson 1981: 15). In the original German it is the word "Bild" – picture, image – that stands for "percept". Transposed meaning, Nietzsche suggests, is not a primarily linguistic phenomenon. A bodily feeling might give rise to an inner visual image, which in turn might become translated into a verbal formula. Nietzsche's essay was published posthumously in the early 1900s; I believe to detect a faint echo of it in Titchener's hypothesis that words are grounded in kinaesthetic images (Titchener 1909: 176–177). Titchener of course strongly influenced Arnheim. Significantly, there is an early paper by the latter in which he writes: "we speak without hesitation of a 'soft tune', thus applying a quality of touch to sounds, or of a 'cold color', thus relating temperature to an optical phenomenon. [...] words like 'cold', 'sharp', 'high', 'dark' have partially lost their specific perceptual connotation for us... this linguistic phenomenon itself bears witness to the fact that it is natural for man to rely on qualities that different senses have in common. These similarities [...] provide the bases of metaphoric speech in poetry" (Arnheim [1948] 1966: 275).

In the same paper Arnheim refers to Murry ([1927] 1931) and Brown (1927). "Metaphor", Murry wrote, "is as ultimate as speech itself, and speech as ultimate as thought." Quoting a familiar metaphor, Murry stressed that that metaphor was *necessary*, "because we find that there is no way of saying what we want to say [...] save by this metaphor or one of its variations", there is an "absence of genuine alternatives", indeed the quality here conveyed "could not have been perceived without the metaphor". Thus "metaphor appears as the instinctive and necessary act of the mind exploring reality and ordering experience. It is the means by which the less familiar is assimilated to the more familiar, the unknown to the known". To "attempt a fundamental examination of metaphor would be nothing less than an investigation of the genesis of thought itself". Through an apt new metaphor, we discern "resemblances between the unknown and the known" (Murry [1927] 1931: 1–2). What Murry next wants to argue for is that there is merely "a formal difference between metaphor and simile and image", "metaphor is compressed simile". However, he points out, not every image is a "visual image"; we should reject "the suggestion that the image is solely or even predominantly visual". "The image may be visual, may be auditory, may refer back to any primary physical experience" – Murry here specifically mentions those "metaphors which describe the process of thought itself as a grasping or apprehension" (Murry [1927] 1931: 3–4). Partly under the influence of Murry, but assembling a great many other sources, too, Brown (1927) by contrast indeed focuses on the role of the visual/pictorial. As he puts it, metaphor amounts to an "imported image coming vividly before our mental vision, while the notion which is the real subject of the discourse momentarily fades into the background, and is seen only through the image" (Brown 1927: 50). To recall Nietzsche: specific mental images can be construed as visual metaphors, with those images standing for physical/motor responses to physical stimuli. Verbal metaphors, for their part, essentially rely on mental images. It is this latter insight of which Brown is clearly a proponent.

6. Word and Image

Another passage by Brown takes me to the end of this paper. "The use of metaphor [...] involves no sacrifice of truth. But I think we may go further and say that it may express a portion, or at least an aspect, of the truth which would not otherwise find expression" (Brown 1927: 73). I believe metaphor, functioning as metaphor, functions because it conjures up images. Metaphoric language cannot be reduced to non-metaphoric language because the visual foundations of thinking actually cannot be eliminated. Sacrificing images would amount to sacrifice truth. As I have suggested by way of introduction, it is the image that serves as the fundamental vehicle of truth. And not only is it the case that, ultimately, only images can convey truths; I would go further and say that in a sense images cannot be but veridical. Of course there are fictitious paintings, and of course there are manipulated photographs (and films and videos, as I have noted in sect. 3 above). But even these are made up of visual segments that reflect elements of reality. As to photography, the most dramatic formulations here are probably those by Roland Barthes (1981). The photograph, writes Barthes, attests that "what I see has indeed existed" (Barthes 1981: 82), photography "offers an immediate presence to the world" (Barthes 1981: 84). "No writing", Barthes goes on, "can give me this certainty. It is the misfortune [...] of language not to be able to authenticate itself" (Barthes 1981: 85). Barthes sides with the "realists" of whom, he writes, he is one and of whom he was already one when he asserted that the photograph was "an image without code" (Barthes 1981: 88). An image without code – is that not a felicitous formula for the idea of pictorial truth?[1]

References

Arnheim, Rudolf ([1948] 1966): Abstract Language and the Metaphor. In: Arnheim, Rudolf: *Toward a Psychology of Art: Collected Essays*. Berkeley: University of California Press. 266–282.

Arnheim, Rudolf (1986): *New Essays on the Psychology of Art*. Berkeley, CA: University of California Press.

Barthes, Roland (1981): *Camera Lucida: Reflections on Photography*. Transl. by Richard Howard. New York, NY: Hill and Wang.

Brown, Stephen J. (1927): *The World of Imagery: Metaphor and Kindred Imagery*. London: Kegan Paul, Trench, Trubner & Co.

Cavell, Stanley (1979): *The World Viewed: Reflections on the Ontology of Film*. Enlarged edition. Cambridge, MA: Harvard University Press.

Golomb, Claire (2004): *The Child's Creation of a Pictorial World*. Second edition. Mahwah, NJ: Lawrence Erlbaum Associates.

Gombrich, E. H. (1973): Illusion and Art. In: Gregory, R. L. – Gombrich, E. H. (eds.): *Illusion in Nature and Art*. London: Duckworth. 193–243.

Gombrich, E. H. (1980): Standards of Truth: The Arrested Image and the Moving Eye. In: Mitchell, W. J. T. (ed.): *The Language of Images*. Chicago: The University of Chicago Press. 181–217.

Heidegger, Martin ([1929] 1997): *Kant und das Problem der Metaphysik*. Bonn: Friedrich Cohen. English translation: *Kant and the Problem of Metaphysics*. Transl. by Richard Taft. Bloomington: Indiana University Press.

---

1 I am indebted to Petra Aczél, Júlia Sipos and Eszter Deli. On the occasion of one of the very first Visual Learning Lab monthly research seminars, in her talk "Visual Rhetoric" (May 5, 2010, see http://vll.mpt.bme.hu), Aczél referred to Barthes and the idea of uncoded iconic messages. Almost exactly six years later, on Apr. 6, 2016, both Sipos and Deli brought up in their VLL talks the topic Barthes on the veracity of photographs, these two latter papers have been published as Sipos–Deli (2016).

Heidegger, Martin (1927/1962): *Sein und Zeit*. Jahrbuch für Phänomenologie und phänomenologische Forschung vol. VIII. Halle a. S.: Max Niemeyer Verlag. English translation: *Being and Time*. Transl. by John Macquarrie & Edward Robinson. Oxford: Basil Blackwell.

Johnson, Mark (1981): Introduction: Metaphor in the Philosophical Tradition. In: Johnson, Mark (ed.): *Philosophical Perspectives on Metaphor*. Minneapolis: University of Minnesota Press. 3–47.

Kennedy, John M. (1982): Metaphor in pictures. *Perception* 11: 589–605.

Murry, John Middleton ([1927] 1931): *Countries of the Mind: Essays in Literary Criticism*. Second series. London: Humphrey Milford / Oxford University Press.

Nyíri, Kristóf (2014): *Meaning and Motoricity: Essays on Image and Time*. Frankfurt am Main: Peter Lang Edition.

Nyíri, Kristóf (2016): Towards a Theory of Common-Sense Realism. In: Benedek, András – Veszelszki, Ágnes (eds.): *In the Beginning was the Image: The Omnipresence of Pictures: Time, Truth, Tradition*. Series Visual Learning, Vol. 6. Frankfurt am Main: Peter Lang Edition. 17–27.

Nyíri, Kristóf (2017): Wittgenstein as a Common-Sense Realist. *Conceptus* 42/101–102: 51–65.

Sipos, Júlia – Deli, Eszter (2016): Képi reprezentáció és hitelesség a 21. századi médiatartalom előállításában / Új ecset, új vászon: A modern képkorszak lehetőségei és kihívásai. In: Benedek, András – Nyíri, Kristóf (eds.): *Visual Learning Lab Papers* 2016/1. Budapest: BME GTK Műszaki Pedagógia Tanszék. 3–30.

Titchener, Edward Bradford (1909): *Lectures on the Experimental Psychology of the Thought-Processes*. New York: Macmillan.

Wittgenstein, Ludwig (1958 [1953]): *Philosophical Investigations*. 2nd edition. Transl. by G. E. M. Anscombe. Oxford: Basil Blackwell.

Wittgenstein, Ludwig (1977): *Remarks on Colour*. Ed. by G. E. M. Anscombe. Transl. by Linda L. McAlister and Margarete Schättle. Berkeley: University of California Press.

István Danka

The Pictorial, the Virtual and the Trivial. On Pictorial Realism and Relativism[1]

1. Introduction

This paper argues that an examination of pictoriality and virtuality as philosophical themes can provide ammunition for common-sense realism in its fight against extreme forms of relativism. Based on Kristóf Nyíri's recent work on the issue, three arguments will be provided to support that claim. The first will argue that a recent common sense realist argument against relativism is insufficient. The second will provide a replacement for that claim, applying visual metaphors. The third will provide a supplement to the replacement on metaphors from virtuality. These together can serve as a ground for a realism that is permissive enough to allow trivial relativism on the one hand, but excluding extreme forms on the other.

2. Common-Sense Realism and Relativism

Common-sense realism (CSR) claims reality to be in accordance with common sense, based on no mediation but a direct, and at least partly visual, perception of reality (Nyíri 2015a: 2). It builds on an *epistemological* claim that direct perception results in knowledge, and goes on to make an *ontological* claim that reality is in accordance with how we humans perceive it. This has been a *ratio cognoscendi* presentation of CSR though (Siegel 2011); a *ratio essendi* explanation should start with reality as it is (Sider 2009), and takes it to be the ground for our veridical perception. Reality is *thus and so* not because we *make it* be so by perception (as some forms of constructivism claim – cf. Hacking 1999) but the other way around: we perceive it thus and so because it *is* thus and so.

CSR is an uncomplicated view. Because of its purity, it is sometimes claimed to be naïve. However, from the purity of the position CSR holds does not follow the simplicity of its philosophical work-out. CSR has been challenged from several directions, common counter-arguments including problems with illusions, non-veridical perception, everyday experience vs. scientific explanations, experience

1 A support from the Hungarian Scientific Research Fund is acknowledged (OTKA K-109456/K-116191).

from different perspectives, etc. (Nyíri 2014, 2015a, 2015b). It *needs* to be supported by sophisticated philosophical argumentation (Boghossian 2006).

2.1 An Anti-Realist Argument: Perspectivism

Let me focus on the latter only: the buzzword *perspectives* (Kölbel 2004; Brogaard 2007; Hales 2014). Relativism is all about perspectives: it takes everything relative to some perspectives. Given that from different perspectives, things appear differently, a plurality of appearances occurs. Let us call this view *perspectivism*. Perspectivism should be no problem for the realist: appearances can differ if they reflect on one and the same unity of reality. But relativism concludes to the contrary: if perspectivism is right, so it says, there is no unique access to the sort of unity required by realism. Appearances from different perspectives are often in an apparent conflict. Hence, either we humans do not have access to reality as it is, or reality as such is relative to perspectives. Either way, realism is lost.

2.2 A Response: the Triviality Thesis

Common sense realists respond to this by recalling the 'Triviality Thesis'. It claims that what is true about relativism is trivial, what is non-trivial about relativism is nonsense (Haack 1996; Nyíri 2015a; cf. also Margolis 1991). How does the Triviality Thesis help the realist avoid problems with perspectivism? It makes her stop in perspectivistic claims where their triviality ends. Can things be seen differently from different perspectives? They trivially can. Can therefore perspectives determine how we see reality? They trivially can. Is therefore reality relative to perspectives? Well, *this* is not trivial: why not take differences in experience from different perspectives to be, for example, a characteristic *of the perspectives themselves* rather than that of the observable? The latter is not trivial, since the former is a *prima facie* viable option at the very least. Hence, a realist will take the latter untrue. Her reason to do so is a strategic one: anything non-trivial can be avoided by choosing another alternative (and there is always an alternative to something non-trivial; that is what non-triviality means). Given that a victory of relativism is the worst that can happen to realism, realists will always rightfully choose any option to a non-trivial relativist choice.

3. Pre-Pictorial CSR

The Triviality Thesis offers serious advantages for CSR: it allows the realist to accept what is undeniable from relativism without forcing her to accept what is unacceptable from it. Thereby trivially true relativist objections do not apply to realism accepting the Triviality Thesis. But it also offers disadvantages: difficulties arising from an unclarity of the trivial vs. non-trivial distinction. By letting trivial relativism in, CSR sometimes opens the door for extreme relativism, too.

3.1 The Compatibility Criterion

A criterion for trivializing relativism (partly) is what I shall call *Compatibility Criterion*. It claims that realism allows there to be different descriptions for the same perceptual phenomenon *as long as* they are compatible with each other. Therefore, the criterion allows different descriptions made in accordance with seeing things from different perspectives. Here a piece of non-naïvety of CSR can be caught: a naïve realism would disallow any plurality of descriptions as it is *prima facie* dangerous for a unity of reality. But it is the relativist who makes implications from the nature of descriptions to the nature of reality; to realism, as said, a *ratio essendi* explanation applies. Reality is unified, regardless of descriptions.

However, to make our understanding of reality also unified, compatibility among items of that understanding is required. This is why descriptions must be compatible with each other, constituting a minimalist requirement for how realism is to be defended against problems deduced from perspectivism. As Susan Haack puts it, "[c]ompatible descriptions may be combined in a longer, conjunctive description, which will be true just in case its conjuncts are; incompatible descriptions, however, cannot be jointly true" (Haack 1996, 304). If two descriptions are incompatible, only one of them can be true. This clearly goes against the non-trivial relativist claim that everything can be true from some perspective.

3.2 Two Objections

The Compatibility Criterion suffers from (at least) two possible relativist objections. The first is to be called the *Insufficiency/Unnecessity Objection*, the second the *Irrelevance Objection*. The first argues that the Compatibility Criterion is not good enough in trivializing relativism for realist purposes. The objection offers a dilemma for the realist, and whether she accepts the line or not would imply the criterion to be either insufficient or unnecessary.

The objection takes a *pseudo-realist meta-position* about perspectives (cf. Kaplan 1989; Kölbel 2004). It is pseudo-realist insofar as its realism is a methodological tool for defending relativism. Its position is a meta-position because realism is accepted at a meta-level as introduced by the objection; and the reason for introducing that meta-level is defending relativism *at the ground-level*. That is why the objection is dangerous for the realist: it *pretends* to be realist in order to go relativist at the end of the day.

The line goes as follows.

(1) *A* is true from perspective *P*.
(2) *Non-A* is true from perspective *R*.
(3) If $P \neq R$, then (1) and (2) are *compatible*.

The argument is delusive because it refers to *statements* at a ground-level and *perspectives* at a meta-level. *A* and *non-A* are in contradiction; they are simultaneously unacceptable for the realist. But the objection transfers the contradiction into a relation between *perspectives:* in the context of *P*, *A* is not necessarily in contradiction with *non-A* in the context of *R*. The only exception is if the two contexts are *exactly* the same. Since the majority of contexts at least slightly differ from each other, *A* and *non-A* can almost always be held together: compatibility and contradiction can be satisfied at the same time. So from the realist's Compatibility Criterion allowing trivial relativism, a most extreme relativism of *anything goes* follows.

What can the realist respond to this objection? Accepting the line makes the Compatibility Criterion *too weak*. If extreme relativism is allowed, the criterion is insufficient for defending realism. Rejecting the objection makes the Compatibility Criterion *too strong:* it would also imply rejecting trivial relativism as the objection starts with a trivial form. In this case, the criterion is unnecessary (and also undesirable). Hence, the objection demonstrates the Compatibility Criterion to be either insufficient or unnecessary.

The Irrelevance Objection, on the other hand, takes descriptions A, B, C, D … all true and having no inferential relation among them. The objection claims there to be no *unity* in their (however compatible) set; and a disunified reality is no reality. Perhaps a strong coherence of closely connected items is not a requirement for CSR as a warranty for unity; but something stronger than non-contradictoriness certainly is. A mass of unconnected descriptions makes a unified and ordered world as supposed by realism, no more accessible than an 'anything goes' relativism. Hence, the realist should have to provide a criterion *stronger than* the Compatibility Criterion, while also taking care of the consequences of the first objection: avoiding extreme relativism but not for the price of disallowing trivial relativism.

4. Pictoriality and Virtuality

In order to find a strong enough but not too strong criterion, first I shall provide a *replacement* for the Compatibility Criterion called *Overlap Criterion*. Second, I shall provide a *supplement to* it called *Connectivity Criterion*. The two may be sufficient separately but they seem to work better in a combination. They are not claimed to be the only possible solution(s) for the problems mentioned above but they are certainly among the candidates.

4.1 Support from the Pictorial: The Overlap Criterion

Kristóf Nyíri argues that "[i]t is not through the mediation of words we make contact with reality, but through direct perception, with visual perception playing the definitive role" (Nyíri 2015a: 2; cf. also esp. Nyíri 2001). Taking directness of perception seriously, a common sense realist must take visual thinking to be prior to verbal thinking (as applied to perception at least). Insofar as recent relativism mostly takes a form of a linguistic/conceptual issue (Davidson 1974; Rorty 1991), visuality can serve as a master argument to support realism: if visual thinking is prior to linguistic thinking, and relativity arises from language, visuality can warrant access to non-relativistic reality. Rejecting the priority of linguistic to visual thinking, linguistic relativism is untenable.

But there is a good reason why the buzzword *perspective* has been chosen to characterize relativism. Perspective is, eventually, a *visual* metaphor: seeing things from one perspective or another has nothing to do with language. Even in a pre-linguistic situation, things are *seen* differently from different perspectives. For example, a cylinder seems to be a rectangle from some perspectives and a circle from others but no single perspective allows *seeing* the cylinder as a whole. What can be seen is a set of mutually incompatible shapes similar to rectangles and circles.

However, all of this implies *trivial* relativism. From the majority of perspectives, a cylinder is neither a rectangle nor a circle, but some sort of a *combination* of their abstract images. This suggests a possible way of understanding them as *overlaps* of real attributes of a cylinder. Seeing the cylinder from all perspectives together provides a *unity* of the cylinder out of the overlapping parts.

The Overlap Criterion provides, accordingly, a criterion for perspectives that does not require compatibility (literally, nothing can be circle-like and rectangle-like at the same time) but nonetheless requires some sort of unity that is hardly put into words but can be visualized if a cylinder is imagined. All the same, it *weakens* the Compatibility Criterion that has been aimed to get stronger, so some additional criteria may be in order.

4.2 Support from the Virtual: The Connectivity Criterion

Taking metaphors of virtuality into account can provide some compensation for weakening the Compatibility Criterion by the Overlap Criterion. Kristóf Nyíri takes thinking to be describable in terms of computer networks or, perhaps more precisely, networked web pages of meaningful, multimedia content (cf. esp. Nyíri 2005). The WWW does have some sort of unity, even though its content certainly lacks coherence and compatibility. But it has a unique way of connections that makes content items unified. Unity in this model lies in the homogeneity of *connections* rather than the homogeneity of *items:* items do not have to share the characteristic of being true but they share the characteristic of being connected to each other via a complex network of hyperlinks.

Let me introduce connectivity as a *generalized form* of compatibility. In this approach, compatibility is an *instance* of a general connectivist theory of unity: the latter is a requirement that fails to apply to perspectivism in realism because even if its motivations and direction are correct, its actual form is over-specified. A more general theory of unity in terms of connections may help solve this problem.

Compatibility requires homogeneous connections because compatibility is a truth-preserving conjunction relation. If an item A is connected via compatibility to an item B, this connection establishes how their truth values can relate to one another. For instance, if A implies B, then B cannot be false if A is true (but not *vice versa*). This is how compatibility is normally understood.

If connectivity is a generalized form of compatibility, two incompatible items can serve as a unity if they are connected appropriately in ways *other than* compatibility. The only criterion is that they must comply with *some* rules, in a way analogous to inferential relations in the case of compatibility.

What these rules can and cannot be is another issue. Applying virtuality to the issue as one possible way takes connection to be a hyperlink-relation that is well describable in terms of transitivity, symmetry, and reflexivity. For being hyperlinked, connection is a requirement but compatibility is not. Different starting points and different routes define different 'perspectives' arriving at different descriptions, just as trivial relativism implies. A series of content items accessed through different routes can even contradict other series, but nevertheless, they are on the same map of a network, constituting a unity.

5. Conclusion

Connectivity as having access from one perspective to another, along with an overlap of routes, seems to be sufficient for warranting the sort of unity required by CSR. Perhaps it is strange for some realists that contradiction is allowed. But the benefit of this allowance is taking trivialities of relativism warranted but extremities of it rejected. Having some superficial contradictions is better than having a chaos of 'anything goes', and it is also better than naïvely disregarding perspectivistic thinking. If the overlap-plus-connectivity criteria are right, contradictions are at least restricted to the way how we approach things rather than how things themselves are.

References

Boghossian, Paul (2006): *Fear of Knowledge.* Oxford: Oxford University Press.

Brogaard, Berit (2007): Moral Contextualism and Moral Relativism. *The Philosophical Quarterly* 58: 385–409.

Davidson, Donald (1974): On the Very Idea of a Conceptual Scheme. *Proceedings and Addresses of the American Philosophical Association* 47: 5–20.

Haack, Susan (1996): Reflections on Relativism: From Momentous Tautology to Seductive Contradiction. *Nous* Vol. 30. *Supplement: Philosophical Perspectives* 10: 297–315.

Hacking, Ian (1999): *The Social Construction of What?* Cambridge, MA: Harvard University Press.

Hales, Steven (2014): Motivations for Relativism as a Solution to Disagreements. *Philosophy* 89: 63–82.

Kaplan, David (1989): Demonstratives: an Essay on the Semantics, Logic, Metaphysics, and Epistemology of Demonstratives and other Indexicals. In: Almog, Joseph – Perry, John – Wettstein, Howard (eds.): *Themes from Kaplan*. Oxford: Oxford University Press. 481–566.

Kölbel, Max (2004): Indexical Relativism Versus Genuine Relativism. *International Journal of Philosophical Studies* 12: 297–313.

Margolis, Joseph (1991): *The Truth About Relativism.* Oxford: Blackwell.

Nyíri, Kristóf (2001): The Picture Theory of Reason. In: Brogaard, Berit – Smith, Barry (eds.): *Rationality and Irrationality*, Vienna: öbv-hpt. http://hunfi.hu/nyiri/krb2000.htm [16. 03. 2017].

Nyíri, Kristóf (2005): *The Networked Mind.* http://www.hunfi.hu/nyiri/Nyiri_Networked_Mind_London_2005.pdf [16. 03. 2017].

Nyíri, Kristóf (2014): Visualisation and the Horizons of Scientific Realism. In: Nyíri, Kristóf: *Meaning and Motoricity.* Frankfurt am Main: Peter Lang. 11–34.

Nyíri, Kristóf (2015a): *Towards a Theory of Common-sense realism.* URL: http://www.hunfi.hu/nyiri/Nyiri_TTCSR.pdf [16. 03. 2017].

Nyíri, Kristóf (2015b): Wittgenstein and Common Sense Philosophy. In: Benedek, András – Nyíri, Kristóf (eds.): *Beyond Words: Pictures, Parables, Paradoxes.* Series Visual Learning, Vol. 5. Frankfurt am Main: Peter Lang. 231–243.

Rorty, Richard (1991): *Objectivity, Relativism, and Truth: Philosophical Papers* 1. Cambridge: Cambridge University Press.

Sider, Ted (2009): Ontological Realism. In: Chalmers, David - Manley, David - Wasserman, Ryan (eds.): *Metametaphysics*. Oxford: Oxford University Press.

Siegel, Harvey (2011): Epistemological Relativism: Arguments Pro and Con. In: Hales, Steven (ed.): *A Companion to Relativism*. Oxford: Blackwell. 201–218.

Orsolya Endrődy-Nagy

Images and Iconography in Cross-Cultural Context

1. Overview

Visual analysis can help researchers to understand information and social relations encoded in images (Kress – Leuween 2006). This paper focuses on the different ways people "read" images in East and West as a result of their diverse cultural, social, gender and religious backgrounds. The main research question is if there is any visual analysis method which may be useful for any researcher regardless of ethnicity, religion, gender, time, and space. The paper presents a quick overview of an interdisciplinary research project: a visual analysis of Japanese and European paintings and woodblock prints between the 16th and 19th centuries, regarding the conceptions of childhood. The analysis method below is based on Panofsky (1984), Bouteaud (1989), and Collier (2010).

The research objectives are the following:

1. to introduce possible Visual Analysis methods for a qualitative research methodology;
2. to introduce new sources for History of Childhood, Childhood Studies and Education;
3. to understand the differences of Conceptions of Childhood in Japan and Europe between the 16th and 19th centuries.

2. Theoretical Issues

An interdisciplinary research project, such as the present one, should focus on several related fields with the admission that they are only some of the possible fields and there could be other perspectives, narratives, and fields depending on the researcher's aims. This article only focuses on aspects of Childhood Studies, Visual Studies, and Cross-cultural Studies. Religious and ideological problems will be discussed in a future report.

2.1 Childhood Research

Childhood research focuses on a stage of life when we are vulnerable and dependent on adults. Childhood research includes several sub-disciplines such as

Childhood History, Contemporary Analysis, and Comparative Pedagogy. The first English book on Japanese childhood was written by Chaplin (1901), with a special focus on toys. In the Western literature Aries (1960), DeMause (1974), and Shorter (1976) were the first researchers to codify the primary paradigm about Childhood analysis. They believed that there had been major changes in the attitudes to and treatment of childhood over time. A new paradigm was created by Linda Pollock (1983), based on diaries. Shahar (2000) points out that parents always loved their children in history. Current childhood conceptions should never be compared with previous ones as they are always built on the contemporary social and mentality history of the period under review (Endrődy-Nagy 2016). According to Hendrick (2000), children should never be compared to adults although they are social actors, too. For decades, childhood historians mostly analyzed textual documents such as letters and diaries to recreate childhood history. Researchers used pictorial documents only to illustrate their theses, except Aries and his followers.

As a new branch of educational sciences, I shall introduce Iconography in Childhood Studies and Iconography in Education. Since the beginning of the 21st century, some researchers have focused not only on textual but also on visual documents as sources of education and childhood history, e.g. Grosvenor (1999), Depaepe – Henkens (2000), Mietzner et al. (2005). These works are based on photographs as possible sources of education history. At the same time, there are new analysis methods of other possible visual documents to understand attitudes towards children, in different periods such as the renaissance or the Early Modern Era, when photographs did not exist yet. In such periods, we must analyze other visual documents, such as paintings, illuminated manuscripts or woodblock prints. This raises the question what kind of documents can be the sources of education and childhood history?

2.2 Visual Research

The present author agrees with Nyíri (2009) in that pictures can convey information that cannot be coded in any other way. On the other hand, we need contemporary works from each period which we would like to study. Using micro historical perspectives, we can explore and understand several situations and aspects of everyday life and mentality (Endrődy-Nagy 2016). If we would like to find some universal visual analysis methods, we should discuss the possible iconographic traditions. These traditions were originally based on religious aspects, both in

Europe and in Asia. The meanings of the expected movements, gestures, and colors were coded traditionally, based on the teachings of Buddhism or Christianity. There are also differences in image philosophy and in the writing/reading system. People read and write from left to right in Europe but they do so traditionally from right to left in Japan. The way we encode pictures is probably also different (cf. *Figure 1*). This print shows men walking from right to left, which indicates a different story as they would walk from left to right.

Figure 1: Katsushika Hokusai: 冨嶽三十六景　深川万年橋下, Under the Mannen Bridge at Fukagawa (Fukagawa Mannenbashi shita), from the series Thirty-six Views of Mount Fuji (Fugaku sanjūrokkei), ca. 1830–32, polychrome woodblock print; ink and color on paper, 10 1/8 × 15 3/16 in. (25.7 × 38.6 cm), Metropolitan Museum of Art, New York

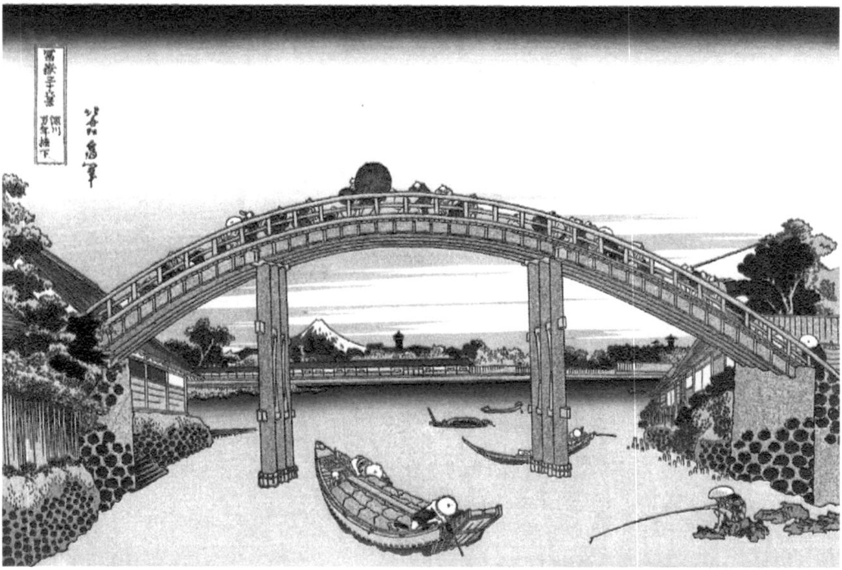

To be able to talk about the process of reading images, we need to discuss the decoding process as a hermeneutic approach (cf. *Figure 2*). According to Gadamer, we are able to read messages coded in pictures by first blending and then by reading. In the hermeneutic approach, we are able to understand the coded message but all encounters with the language of art is an encounter with an unfinished event (1989: 99). When it comes to decoding, there is always something more to be said (Davey 1999: 15), there is no unlimited experience, and probably there is no objective analysis method. What matters is always the researcher's intuition and intention, i.e. whatever he/she is looking for.

According to Assmann (2011), the visual was first and then it was followed by the textual. The human brain could build a visual reference earlier and then it invented textual references. We also need visual references to understand the textual. Such visual references are based on our experiences and mental images (Nyíri 2016). Writing systems were first repetitive and ritualistic, and there were parallelisms, so understanding was difficult. According to Davey (1999) and Kulcsár-Szabó (2005), reading images could also be distracting due to the multiple meanings so we need valid analysis methods independent of time, space, ethnicity, and gender. Bal (2006) points out that the coding schema is related to our cultural identity, so if we need a valid analysis method, as mentioned above, we must identify some contextual information about the creator and viewer of the visual document.

Figure 2: The hermeneutic process (based on the works of Gadamer 1998, Kulcsár-Szabó 2005, Bal 2006)

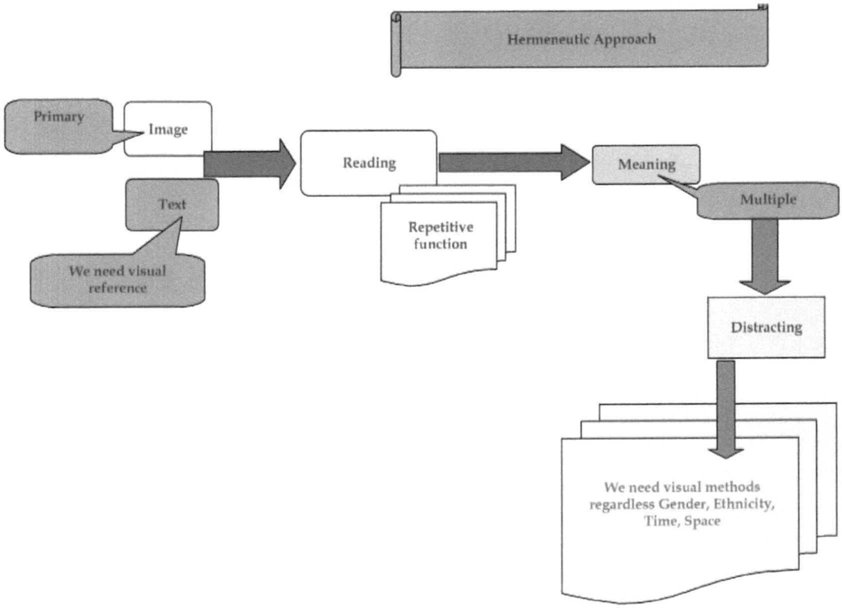

3. Possible Research Methods: Iconography as a Research Method in Childhood Studies

Interdisciplinary research enables us to understand the contextual information encoded in images. Iconography as a research method in childhood history and studies allows us to enrich our understanding within any society or era about the attitudes toward children. Now let us discuss the following problems:

1. How to classify the analyzed documents?
2. Are European analysis methods valid in Asia and vice versa?

As regards the first question of how to make groups by technique and topic (this research covers the same technique, ukiyo-e print), we chose thematic groups related to childhood issues, such as play, parenting, schooling, care, sickness, and mortality. As for the second question, we should compare analysis systems from Europe and Asia by trying them on the same corpus. So far we have tried the methods of Panofsky (1972), Bouteaud (1989), and Collier (2010) on the corpus. The results of the analysis mentioned below are based on these methods. Panofsky has a three-step method, based on the coded symbols in visual documents: 1. Pre-iconographical description, 2. Iconographical analysis 3. Iconographical synthesis (Endrődy-Nagy 2016). The French scholar Bouteaud invented an analysis system based on technical issues. In his search for the connections between the textual and visual elements, he stated that the meaning always depends on the period in which the analysis was made (Bouteaud 1989). Collier's method is a serial visual analysis, based on the researcher's intuition, by making notes and lists of the emerging thoughts from the very beginning of the analysis (Collier 2010). His method is considered among visual anthropological ones.

Addis has a very important work about the reading of Japanese images and art itself (Addis 1996), but it is not a complex analysis system. At the same time, without it, we would not understand technical and cultural related elements of the woodblock prints.

4. Description of the Corpus

In making the corpus, we should consider the following aspects. We need to find pictures related to the importance of play so we can compare the similarities and differences between toys and the use of everyday objects as toys. We must focus on everyday situations and parenting practices. Ukiyo-e (浮世絵 – Japanese woodblock prints) are really easy to observe as there are free on-line open databases. In the golden age of Ukiyo-e, in the 17th to 19th century, there was no censorship regarding these prints so we can find images of every aspect of human nature and life, including several topics that are taboo in Europe (e.g. sexuality, giving birth and mortality), and images of each stage of life from early childhood to old age. As there are special terms for the various topics, it is easy to search for special image groups, e.g. *Bijin-ga* 美人画 – beauty of woman, *Shun-ga* 春画 – sexuality. Originally prints about children were related to bijin-ga type of prints (Inagaki – Kami 1998).

The corpus consists of over 600 prints so far, all related to childhood and children. The Kumon Institute of Education, Osaka, and the Hopp Ferenc Far East Museum, Budapest, allowed us to use their archives for research, and Ukiyo-e Search, which is also a useful tool for such purposes. The corpus can be analyzed in a wider context, in comparison with the collection of The Smithsonian Institution, Washington DC, and the Museum of Fine Arts, Boston.

5. Results

The analysis of the prints mentioned above has led to several conclusions:

5.1 Rule Nature versus Admire Nature

As regards religion and ideology, such as Confucianism, Buddhism, and Shinto traditions (Emmanuel 2016), it seems that children in Japanese prints never rule nature but are in harmony with it. By contrast, European visuals made in the same period show children playing with animal intestines, picking flowers or trying to rule the natural elements, as it were. In sum, the former admire cherry blossoms, and the latter play with a pig's bladder (*Figure 4*).

5.2 The Importance of Play

The visuals show similar toys. We need further research to understand the importance of play. Similar toys were used in Europe and in Japan. In both regions there are tops and hoops (*Figures 3–4*), beanbags or stuffed balls, and wooden dolls but there are also different toys, such as kendama (けん玉, a traditional wooden toy in Japan) as opposed to kolf, a hockey and golf-like game played in Europe/the Low Countries during winter (Endrődy-Nagy 2015).

Figure 3: Utagawa Hiroshige II & Utagawa Toyokuni III, Boasting of Edo's Thirty-Six Pleasures: Nihonbashi – First Bonito of the Season and Hoop rolling, 1864, Kumon Institute, Japan

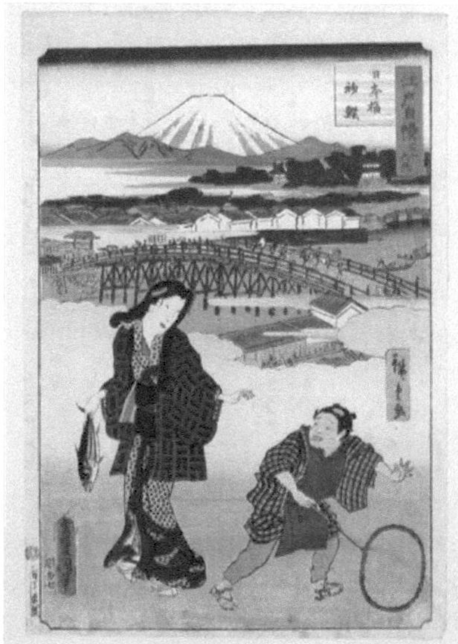

Figure 4: Pieter Brueghel the Elder, Children's games, 1560, Kunsthistoriches Museum, Vienna, detail

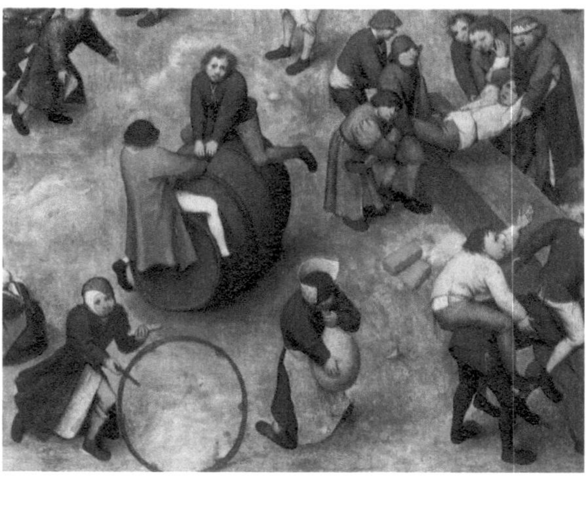

5.3 A Patron of Children in Both Cultural Regions

In Japanese tradition, Hotei is a patron of children (Getty 1998; Bunce 2001), often depicted among them playing, having fun, marching loudly and singing gaily while holding flags. In other pictures he is holding a child on his shoulder to help him or her cross a river or keep walking despite fatigue. In the Christian tradition, St. Christophe is a patron of children who, legend has it, helped Jesus cross the river by holding him on his shoulder.

5.4 Trauma and Problems Caused by Disease and Death

In both regions there are worrying mothers and everyday situations such as a ukiyo-e with a child frightened by a nightmare, metaphors of death and symbols, e.g. pictures of skeletons.

5.5 Differences of Parenting Practices

Several types of ukiyo-e prints are related to parenting: caretaking, bathing, feeding and breast-feeding. However, the Virgin Mary is depicted when breast feeding the baby Jesus as an iconographic type coming from the Christian canonical traditions. In Japanese genres, this very intimate situation is depicted more widely as a mother-child bond of humans. Some titles also state that children are a present for the parents, e.g. *kodakara* 子宝 'treasure children' (Inagaki – Kami 1998).

5.6 Problems in School

In both regions, we can find caricatures of school and school masters. It seems that in Japanese *terakoya* 寺子屋 'temple', elementary school masters and village school masters in the Low Countries, Europe, equally suffer from the naughty, playful, and nosey children (*Figures 5–6*).

Figure 5: Utagawa Hiroshige, Hiroshige's Caricature: Mischievous Boys at Terakoya (Schoolhouse of the Edo Period) 1839–1844, Kumon Institute, Japan

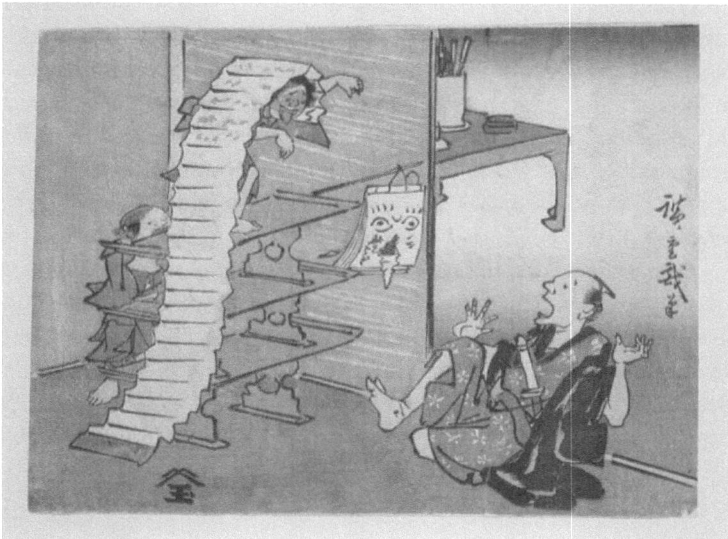

Owned by Kumon Institute of Education

Figure 6: Jan Steen: Village school, cc.1670, oil, National Gallery of Scotland, Edinburgh

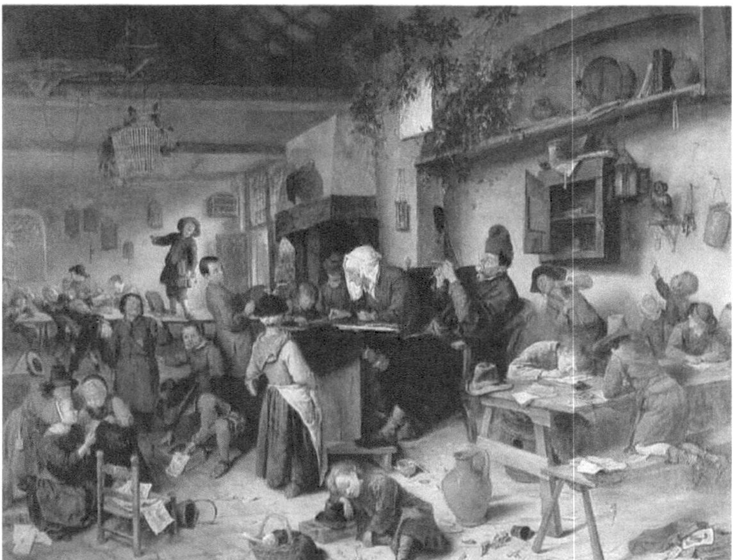

6. Possibilities in Iconographic Research. Conclusions

It seems reasonable to shorten the period under review. It would make sense to focus on a period of transition when everything is changing with examples of past and future practices. It is definitely difficult to do such delimitation but if we first look at a longer period, we can identify a shorter one later. As a closing remark, we should consider the viewpoints that determine the way of coding and reading images. Religious views could determine topics and depiction. We always need to keep in mind the artist's background. Pictures could be coded texts; their conservative function helps us to break the silence regarding the attitude towards children both in Japan and in Europe. Ukiyo-e, Japanese prints, help researchers gain a day-to-day experience of childhood in Japan's Edo era to create a possible narrative of childhood in such period. The conception of childhood shows nosey and playful children who are sometimes naughty, but adored by their parents, and taken care of by their mothers. We also recognized the ideological influence of Confucian traditions about admiring nature, i.e. living in harmony with it, not ruling it.

References

Addis, Stephen (1996): *How to Look at Japanese Art*. New York: Harry N. Abrams.

Aries, Philippe (1960): *L'Enfant et la vie familiale*. Paris: Libraire Plon.

Assmann, Jan (2011): *Cultural Memory and Early Civilization: Writing, Remembrance, and Political Imagination*. Cambridge UK: Cambridge University Press.

Bal, Mieke (2006): *A Mieke Bal reader*. Chicago – London: The University of Chicago Press.

Boutaud, Jean-Jacques (1989): *Application des recherches en iconographie publicitaire à la pédagogie de l'expression en I.U.T.* Lille 3: ANRT.

Bunce, Fredrick William (2001): *A Dictionary of Buddhist and Hindu Iconographic – Illustrated*. New Delhi: D. K. Printworld

Chaplin, Matilda Ayrton (1901): *Child-life in Japan and Japanese child stories*. Boston: D. C. Heath & Co.

Collier, Malcolm (2010): Approaches to Analysis in Visual Anthropology. In: Leeuwen, Theo van – Jewitt, Carey (eds.): *Handbook of Visual Analysis*. Los Angeles – London – New York: Sage. 35–61.

Davey, Nicholas (1999): The Hermeneutics of Seeing. In: Heywood, Ian – Sandywell, Barry (eds.): *Interpreting Visual Culture. Explorations in the Hermeneutics of the Visual*. London – New York: Routledge. 3–30.

DeMause, Lloyd (1974): *The History of Childhood.* New York: The Psychohistory Press.

Depaepe, Marc – Henkens, Bregt (2000): The History of Education and the Challenge of the Visual. *Paedagogica Historica* 36: 10–17.

Emmanuel, Steven M. (2016, ed.): *A Companion to Buddhist Philosophy.* UK–USA: Willey Blackwell.

Endrődy-Nagy, Orsolya (2015): *A reneszánsz gyermekképe. A gyermekkép reneszánsza 1455–1517 között Európában, ikonográfiai elemzés.* Budapest: ELTE Eötvös Kiadó – TEPA.

Endrődy-Nagy, Orsolya (2016): Paintings and Illuminated Manuscripts as Sources of the History of childhood: Conceptions of Childhood in the Renaissance. In: Benedek, András – Veszelszki, Ágnes (eds.): *In the Beginning was the Image: The Omnipresence of Pictures.* Frankfurt am Main: Peter Lang. 91–103.

Gadamer, Hans-Georg (1998): *Truth and Method.* London: Sheed and Ward.

Getty, Alice (1988): *The Gods of Northern Buddhism. Their History and Iconography.* New York: Dover.

Grosvenor, Ian (1999): *Silences & Images: The Social History of the Classroom (History of Schools and Schooling).* Frankfurt: Peter Lang.

Hendrick, Harry (2000): The Child as a Social Actor in Historical Sources – Problems of Identification and Interpretation. In: Christianssen, Pia – James, Allison (eds.): *Research with Children: Perspectives and Practices.* Oxford: Routledge Falmer, Taylor & Francis Group. 36–57.

Inagaki, Shinichi – Kami, Shoichiro (1998): *Children represented in Ukiyo-e.* Osaka: Kumon Institute of Education.

Kress, Gunther – Leeuwen, Theo van (2006): *Reading Images. The Grammar of Visual Design.* London – New York: Routledge, Taylor & Francis Group.

Kulcsár Szabó, Zoltán (2005): *Hermeneutikai szakadékok.* Debrecen: Csokonai Kiadó.

Mietzner, Ulrike – Meyers, Kevin – Peim, Nick (2005) (eds.): *Visual History: Images of Education.* Frankfurt: Peter Lang.

Nyíri, Kristóf (2009): Gombrich on Image and Time. *Journal of Art Historiography* 1: 9–32.

Nyíri, Kristóf (2016): Towards a Theory of Common-Sense Realism. In: Benedek, András – Veszelszki, Ágnes (eds.): *In the Beginning was the Image: The Omnipresence of Pictures.* Frankfurt et al.: Peter Lang. 17–29.

Panofsky, Erwin (1979): *Studies in Iconology, Humanistic Themes in Art of the Renaissance.* Oxford: Westview Press, Perseus Book Group. 3–33.

Pollock, Linda (1983): *Forgotten Children: Parent-child relations from 1500 to 1900.* Cambridge: Cambridge University Press.

Shahar, Shulamith (1992): *Childhood in the Middle Ages.* New York: Routledge.

Shorter, Edward (1976): *The Making of the Modern Family.* London: Collins.

Diagrammatic, Visual, Practical

Amirouche Moktefi

Diagrams as Scientific Instruments[1]

1. Reasoning with Diagrams in Mathematics

Diagrams have long been used in science. Although it is not easy to precisely define what a scientific diagram stands for, we will take it in the following to refer to any diagram used in scientific activity, regardless of the extent to which it contributes to discovery or proving practices (Allamel-Raffin – Moktefi 2011). In mathematics, diagrams have often been dismissed and are said to play no non-redundant role in proofs. This ban of diagrams from mathematical proofs has become a common practice since the beginning of the twentieth century (Rota 1997: 183). Within this "suspicious view" (Giardino 2013), proofs need to be formal. Hence, diagrams are held to play no role in proofs. They are rather viewed as useful pedagogical devices which, yet, "*prove* nothing" (Brown 2008: 26).

However, a trend in diagram studies has been developed since the 1990s, viewing diagrammatic logics as formal languages. A breaking work in this direction was Sun-Joo Shin's *The Logical Status of Diagrams* (Shin 1994), which rigorously defined the syntax and semantics of two diagrammatic systems. Two decades later, many more diagrammatic systems with sound and complete inference rules have been published. This trend has produced fertile and rich results in terms of expressiveness, inference, and diagram drawing (Allwein – Barwise 1996; Moktefi – Shin 2013; Stapleton 2014). This "formal view" claims the possibility of making inferences with diagrams that would not save undesired properties. As such, diagrams might be used for proof purposes and shall not be limited to discovery and heuristic settings. This view argues that diagrams can be formalized and that it is possible to construct rigorous formal proofs with diagrams.

Both the suspicious and the formal views of diagrams have raised criticism. It has been argued that in actual practice, mathematicians do not construct such ideal (formal) proofs. Research journals and university textbooks rather contain practical (acceptable) proofs, *i.e.* proofs that are expressed in such a way as to convince mathematical readers that a certain claim is true and that a formal proof, if desired, could justifiably be constructed (Hamami 2014; Larvor 2016). Reuben Hersh explains that there are two meanings of proof in mathematics:

1 This research benefitted from the support of ERC project "*Abduction in the age of uncertainty*" (PUT 1305, Principal Investigator: Prof. Ahti-Veikko Pietarinen).

> The trouble is, "mathematical proof" has two meanings. In practice, it's one thing. In principle, it's another. We *show* students what proof is in practice. We *tell* them what it is in principle. The two meanings aren't identical [...]
> Meaning number 1, the *practical* meaning, is informal, imprecise. *Practical mathematical proof is what we do to make each other believe our theorems.* It's argument that convinces the qualified, skeptical expert [...]
> Meaning number 2, theoretical mathematical proof, is formal [...] It's transformation of certain symbol sequences (formal sentences) according to certain rules of logic (Hersh 1997: 49).

Since real proofs are not formal, diagrams do not need to be formalized in order to play a role in mathematical proving practices. In recent years, a significant movement has developed, aimed at approaching mathematics from the standpoint of practices. As such, it pays prominent attention to the actual practices of mathematicians (Van Kerkhove – Van Bendegem 2007; Mancosu 2008; Giardino et al. 2012). An *Association for the Philosophy of Mathematical Practice* was founded in 2009 to promote this new approach in the philosophy of mathematics. Contrary to the "formal view", where diagrams are used as pictures of abstract objects that are ruled to make derivations, the "practical view" considers diagrams as tools that are used within a specific practice for problem-solving. As such, they should always be interpreted within a particular context of use.

Formalists are accused of forcing diagrams to fit within a framework to which they do not 'naturally' belong (Giardino 2013). We do not make derivations with diagrams. We rather use imagination, not rules, to manipulate diagrams in order to solve problems. The formalist mode would be the realm of symbolic demonstrations alone. When it comes to diagrams, the strategy is different: we work *with* diagrams (as tools), rather than *on* diagrams (as objects). However, it is not clear within the practical view how diagrams are supposed to be efficiently manipulated. Some supporters of this trend argue that the ambiguity of diagrams is productive as it allows manipulative imagination (Grosholz 2007). Yet, it is necessary to inquire as to what makes a reliable manipulation in proving practices. In the next sections, we will argue that diagrams may be viewed as technical artifacts, and thus, the reliability of a diagram may be translated in terms of technological reliability.

2. Diagrams as Instruments

Notations are essential to mathematical practice. We may consider "as mathematical notations all that mathematicians write down as a cognitive aid in *stable* and *shared* practices" (De Toffoli 2017: 161). The association of such notations (both symbolic and diagrammatic) with technical artifacts is naturally old. Symbolic notations have long been viewed as shortcuts that allowed mathematicians to handle complicated expressions and to save labor. In the early years of symbolic logic, Hugh MacColl praised symbolic methods for their aid to the logician, as follows:

> Symbolical reasoning may be said to have pretty much the same relation to ordinary reasoning that machine-labour has to manual labour. In the case of machine labour we see some ingeniously contrived arrangement of wheels, levers, & c., producing with speed and facility results which the hands of man without such aid could only accomplish slowly and with difficulty, or which they would be utterly powerless to accomplish at all. In the case of symbolical reasoning we find in an analogous manner some regular system of rules and formulae, easy to retain in the memory from their general symmetry and interdependence, economizing or superseding the labour of the brain, and enabling any ordinary mind to obtain by simple mechanical processes results which would be beyond the reach of the strongest intellect if left entirely to its own resources (MacColl 1880: 45).

Unlike many other technologies that extend our physical aptitudes, notations rather extend our cognitive capabilities. Catarina Dutilh Novaes has recently offered a theoretical framework to study formal languages as cognitive technologies. Formal languages are said to be technologies in the sense that they are devices used to solve particular problems. As such, they are not methods properly but rather tools to implement certain methods. Also formal languages are said to be cognitive in the sense that they give rise to new patterns of reasoning and extend our cognitive scope (Dutilh Novaes 2012). This framework incorporates diagrams as long as one views them as instruments for problem-solving.

In brief, philosophers of technology tell us that technical artifacts are objects that have been subject to a process in order to perform a specific function. This function consists of transforming an undesired state into a desired one. A coffee machine, for instance, transforms beans into a coffee-drink. Naturally, artifacts can have accidental, possibly harmful, functions beyond those prompted by their designers (De Vries 2005). Diagrams amply fit within this description and, hence, may legitimately be viewed as technical artifacts. Accordingly, we would expect the philosophy of technology to provide insights on diagrams (and notations in general). Indeed, mathematical notations are subject to the same dynamics that face other technical artifacts. For instance, the evolution of mathematical notations in history can be viewed as a problem in technological change. One has then to search for the conceptual, social and aesthetical factors that contribute to the choice, the circulation, the adoption or the resistance to new notations (Cajori 1928–1929; Durand-Richard – Moktefi 2014).

Also, the construction of a diagram can be viewed as a problem of design. We are told that technical artifacts have a dual nature: physical and functional. It is, then, the business of the designer to conceive what physical properties would enable the desired functions. When users face an artifact, they also try to understand this dual nature in order to figure out the usage that can be made of an artifact. Similarly, mathematical notations are constructed in order to fulfill specific functions and evolve through history depending on the use that is made of them. Even simple figures such as Euler circles which are commonly held to derive their force from their 'naturalness' can be shown to be the subject of complex constructions, where the representing and the represented objects influence each other (Moktefi 2015).

If we accept to view diagrams as technical artifacts, it does not take long to consider the diagrams used in mathematics as a specific type of artifacts, namely scientific instruments (Boon 2009). Instruments are not stranger to modern mathematics, notably with the development of experimental mathematics (Avigad 2008; Borwein – Bailey 2008; Sørensen 2016). It has been argued that prior to the introduction of computers, "mathematics was practically the only science not to use any instruments. Unlike their lab-coated colleagues, mathematicians only required a blackboard and some chalk to make their science progress" (Dowek 2015: 124). This is disputable as mathematical instruments have certainly been in use among mathematicians in older times (Bennett 2011), as is famously depicted in the sixteenth century Flemish paining "The Measurers". It might be objected that those instruments were applications of mathematics rather than instruments for the benefit of mathematicians. However, the latter also have used instruments such as rulers, compasses, geometrical models, and calculating machines.

For our purpose, we claim that mathematical notations (including diagrams) can also be viewed as mathematical instruments. In doing so, we merely expand Gottlob Frege's famous passage where he stated that the relation of his ideography to common language was comparable to that of a microscope to the eye (Frege 1879: v). Also, our approach is similar to Ursula Klein's study of Berzelian chemical formulas as "tools on paper" or "paper tools"" (Klein 2001), with the slight difference that we do take notations to be scientific instruments in a *literal* rather than mere *metaphorical* sense. If diagrams are scientific instruments, then the reliability of a diagram can simply be restated as the reliability of a scientific instrument.

3. On the Reliability of Instruments and Diagrams

Even though figures might provide useful insights, it is commonly feared that they possess undesired properties that would mislead the mathematician and lead to undue generality. Such fallacious reasoning occurs in classrooms and justifies the caution as to the manipulation of diagrams, especially in geometrical proofs.

Mathematicians are familiar with the famous geometrical proof that every triangle is isosceles (Ball 1905: 38–39). The main difficulty with diagrams is that, contrary to a symbolic variable that might stand as an abstraction for an infinite number of individuals, reasoning with diagrams always requires the appeal to a particular figure standing for a general type, whether mentally constructed or drawn in ink on paper (Giaquinto 2007). For instance, while we reason in geometry on triangles in general, we can only draw a finite number of such triangles. Hence, it is necessary to ensure that what is discovered through the manipulation of those particular triangles holds for every triangle that might be considered and is not consequent to an undesired property of the particular triangles used in the proof. The generality problem can also be found if we attempt to diagrammatically prove an arithmetical theorem. We necessarily use a figure where a particular number of individuals is represented (for instance, by dots) and it is, then, necessary to secure that the result is not biased by that particular number. It must be added that the lack of generality should not be confused with lack of rigor. It simply imposes the determination of the extent to which our diagrams hold and apply. It is only when diagrams are used beyond their scope that they entail a lack of rigor (Azzouni 2013).

Natural scientists also face uncertainty and need to reduce factors that might mislead them during experiments. In particular, they need to secure the appropriate working of their instruments to avoid experimental biases. To reduce this uncertainty, they appeal to epistemological strategies that have been thoroughly studied by philosophers of science. Allan Franklin identified many such strategies which he described as follows:

> [T]here is an epistemology of experiment, a set of strategies that provides reasonable belief in the validity of an experimental result. These strategies distinguish between a valid observation or measurement and an artefact created by the experimental apparatus [...] I will show that these strategies can be incorporated, quite naturally and plausibly, within a Bayesian approach to the philosophy of science. This satisfies an important criterion for a good philosophy of science, that it explicates in a reasonable way the accepted good practice of science. As the examples will illustrate, these strategies are used by practicing scientists (Franklin 1990: 103–104).

Although Franklin's list of strategies has been criticized for being an ad-hoc construction (Hon 2003), it certainly accounts for experimental practices that are widely found in the natural sciences. One may wonder if such strategies are to be found in mathematical practice as well. Two specific strategies identified by Franklin can be of interest for our purpose: calibration and inter-instrumentality.

Calibration, as understood in the natural sciences, covers mainly the experimental checks that are made to secure the reliability of the experimental apparatus.

It might be achieved by checking the reproduction of results that are previously known or artifacts that are known to be present (Franklin 1990: 104–105). For instance, to calibrate a weighting scale, one might first check whether it accurately measures the weight of an object whose weight is known in advance. If a bias is detected (extra-weight for instance), this observation should be considered in subsequent measures. Calibration, if successful, reinforces the reliability of the apparatus and the results that it provides (Soler et al. 2013). Inter-instrumentality consists of confirming the validity of an experimental result by the use of a different experiment rather than to repeat the same experiment: "the fact that the same phenomenon was observed under very different conditions makes it extremely unlikely that it is an artifact created by the experimental apparatus [...] Thus, if we wish to know the correct time, it is better if we compare watches than if either of us looks at our own watch twice" (Franklin 1990: 107–108). Hence, the concordance of observations and measurement that are found by different instruments makes scientific results more robust (Allamel-Raffin 2005).

These strategies observed in natural sciences can also be met with when we construct and manipulate diagrams in mathematics. To apply calibration and inter-instrumentality strategies would increase the reliability of diagrammatic proofs. If a diagram is viewed as a scientific instrument, the need to calibrate it is immediately felt in order to check that it does not hold undesired properties that would undermine the proof. It might be similarly said that providing different proofs of mathematical theorems "bolster(s) confidence not only in the particular results that are proved, but in the overall structure and coherence of mathematics itself" (Dawson 2006: 281). From this standpoint, diagrams ought to be viewed as an instrument in proving practices that contributes to the robustness of the results. Checking with a diagram a result that was symbolically processed is a familiar practice in mathematics. Hence, different instruments of proof are not redundant or rival. They rather collaborate to shape and confirm the result.

4. Conclusion

We identified three distinct views on diagrams in mathematics: the suspicious, the formal, and the practical. The first bans diagrams from proofs on the ground that proofs are formal while diagrams are not. The second "formalizes" diagrams to include them in proofs thanks to rigorous rules of construction and manipulation. The third claims that diagrams do not need to be formalized in order to play a role in proving practices. It views diagrams as instruments that we use in specific contexts of problem-solving. However, it was not clear how this practical view accounts for rigorous diagrammatic reasoning.

In this paper, we explored the idea that diagrams are *literally* scientific instruments. Accordingly, we considered the applicability of epistemological strategies that are widely used in the natural sciences, where visual elements contribute to the robustness of results. This framework needs further analysis but it can already be said that it offers a new perspective on the role and reliability of diagrams in proving practices. It is hoped that future research will prove it to be a fruitful direction in diagram studies.

References

Allamel-Raffin, Catherine (2005): De l'intersubjectivité à l'interinstrumentalité. L'exemple de la physique des surfaces. *Philosophia Scientiæ* 9/1: 3–30.

Allamel-Raffin, Catherine – Moktefi, Amirouche (2011) (eds.): *Définir l'image scientifique*. Special issue of *Visible* (8). Limoges: Presses Universitaires de Limoges.

Allwein, Gerard – Barwise, Jon (eds.) (1996): *Logical Reasoning with Diagrams*. Oxford: Oxford University Press.

Avigad, Jeremy (2008): Computers in Mathematical Inquiry. In: Mancosu, Paolo (ed.): *The Philosophy of Mathematical Practice*. Oxford: Oxford University Press. 302–316.

Azzouni, Jody (2013): That we *see* that some diagrammatic proofs are perfectly rigorous. *Philosophia Mathematica* 21: 323–338.

Ball, W. W. Rouse (1905): *Mathematical Recreations and Essays*. 4th ed. London: Macmillan.

Bennett, Jim (2011): Early Modern Mathematical Instruments. *Isis* 102/4: 697–705.

Boon, Mieke (2009): Instruments in Science and Technology. In: Olsen, Jan Kyrre Berg – Pedersen, Stig Andur – Hendricks, Vincent F. (eds.): *A Companion to the Philosophy of Technology*. Oxford: Wiley-Blackwell. 78–83.

Borwein, Jonathan – Bailey, David (2008): *Mathematics by Experiment: Plausible Reasoning in the 21*st *century*. Second edition. Wellesley, MA: A. K. Peters.

Brown, James Robert (2008): *Philosophy of Mathematics: a Contemporary Introduction to the World of Proofs and Pictures*. Second edition. New York: Routledge.

Cajori, Florian (1928–1929): *A History of Mathematical Notations*. 2 vols. La sale, Illinois: Open Court.

Dawson, John W. Jr. (2006): Why do Mathematicians Re-prove Theorems? *Philosophia Mathematica* 14/3: 269–286.

De Toffoli, Silvia (2017): 'Chasing' the diagram – the use of visualizations in algebraic reasoning. *The Review of Symbolic Logic* 10/1: 158–186.

De Vries, Marc J. (2005): *Teaching about Technology: an Introduction to the Philosophy of Technology for Non-philosophers*. Dordrecht: Springer.

Dowek, Gilles (2015): *Computation, Proof, Machine: Mathematics Enters a New Age*. New York: Cambridge University Press.

Durand-Richard, Marie-José – Moktefi, Amirouche (2014) : Algèbre et logique symboliques: arbitraire du signe et langage formel. In: Béziau, Jean-Yves (ed.) : *La pointure du symbole*. Paris: Pétra. 295–328.

Dutilh Novaes, Catarina (2012): *Formal Languages in Logic: a Philosophical and Cognitive Analysis*. Cambridge: Cambridge University Press.

Franklin, Allan (1990): *Experiment, Right or Wrong*. Cambridge: Cambridge University Press.

Frege, Gottlob (1879): *Begriffsschrift*. Halle: Verlag von Louis Nebert.

Giaquinto, Marcus (2007): *Visual Thinking in Mathematics: an Epistemological Study*. Oxford: Oxford University Press.

Giardino, Valeria (2013): A Practice-based Approach to Diagrams. In: Moktefi, Amirouche – Shin, Sun-Joo (eds.): *Visual Reasoning with Diagrams*. Basel: Birkhäuser.

Giardino, Valeria – Moktefi, Amirouche – Mols, Sandra – Van Bendegem, Jean Paul (2012) (eds.): *From Practice to Results in Logic and Mathematics*. Special issue of: *Philosophia Scientiae* 16/1. Paris: Kimé.

Grosholz, Emily R. (2007): *Representation and Productive Ambiguity in Mathematics and the Sciences*. Oxford: Oxford University Press.

Hamami, Yacin (2014): Mathematical Rigor, Proof Gap and the Validity of Mathematical Inference. *Philosophia Scientiae* 18/1: 7–26.

Hersh, Reuben (1997): *What is Mathematics, really?* Oxford: Oxford University Press.

Hon, Giora (2003): The Idols of Experiment: Transcending the "etc. list". In: Radder, Hans (ed.): *The Philosophy of Scientific Experiment*. Pittsburgh: University of Pittsburgh Press. 174–197.

Klein, Ursula (2001): Paper Tools in Experimental Cultures. *Studies in History and Philosophy of Science* 32/2: 265–302.

Larvor, Brendan (2016): Why the naïve derivation recipe model cannot explain how mathematicians' proofs secure mathematical knowledge. *Philosophia Mathematica* 24/3: 401–404.

MacColl, Hugh (1880): Symbolical Reasoning. *Mind* 5/17: 45–60.

Mancosu, Paolo (2008): *The Philosophy of Mathematical Practice*. Oxford: Oxford University Press.

Moktefi, Amirouche (2015): Is Euler's Circle a Symbol or an Icon? *Sign Systems Studies* 43/4: 597–615.

Moktefi, Amirouche – Shin, Sun-Joo (2013) (eds.): *Visual Reasoning with Diagrams*. Basel: Birkhäuser.

Rota, Gian-Carlo (1997): The Phenomenology of Mathematical Proof. *Synthese* 111: 183–196.

Shin, Sun-Joo (1994): *The Logical Status of Diagrams*. New York: Cambridge University Press.

Soler, Lena – Wieber, Frédéric – Allamel-Raffin, Catherine – Gangloff, Jean-Luc – Dufour, Catherine – Trizio, Emiliano (2013): Calibration: a Conceptual Framework Applied to Scientific Practices which Investigate Natural Phenomena by Means of Standardized Instruments. *Journal of General Philosophy of Science* 44: 263–317.

Sørensen, Henrik Kragh (2016): 'The End of Proof?' The Integration of Different Mathematical Cultures as Experimental Mathematics Comes of Age. In: Larvor, Brendan (ed.): *Mathematical Cultures: the London Meetings 2012–2014*. Basel: Birkhäuser. 139–160.

Stapleton, Gem (2014): Delivering the Potential of Diagrammatic Logics. In: Burton, Jim – Choudhury, Lopamudra (eds.): *DLAC 2013: Diagrams, Logic and Cognition*. Series CEUR Workshop Proceedings (1132). 1–8. http://ceur-ws.org/Vol-1132/ [16. 03. 2017]

Van Kerkhove, Bart – Van Bendegem, Jean Paul (2007) (eds.): *Perspectives on Mathematical Practices: Bringing Together Philosophy of Mathematics, Sociology of Mathematics, and Mathematics Education*. Dordrecht: Springer.

András Benedek

Visual Learning and Open Content Development (OCD)

1. Introduction

Developed by the end of the 20th century, "modern" learning materials have remained unchanged in terms of verbal and image communication, linear structure, written text dominance, and static image conveyance. Although electronic learning resources and multi-media e-learning representations include more dynamic (flash, podcast, video) transfers of content, the "logic" of building up learning materials has changed little—in fact, visual content is only a completion to verbal communication. In community based learning resource development, teacher training may offer outstandingly good conditions for visual learning; we prove this statement by introducing our experimental data. Developing Open Learning Resources (OLR) with the participation of students means a potential of content and methodology that is capable of surpassing traditional, school and notebook based teaching through pilot curriculum developments like the SysBook (W1) and the applied info-communication technology (ICT), open source and commercial learning management systems (LMS), memory independent management of complex visual elements and the flexible management of micro-contents. This chapter presents the OCD research concept, formed in conjunction with our activities in the Visual Learning Lab (VLL), set up in 2009 at the Budapest University of Technology and Economics (BME) (W2), and its internationally distributed results are well summarized in the Visual Learning Series (W3).

2. Theoretical Background

The history of our Visual Learning Lab (VLL) from 2009 until today represents how modern educational theories have "overtaken" the slowly spreading, century-old paradigm of traditional learning. Kristóf Nyíri's image theoretical philosophy, summarized in a detailed study in 2016 (Nyíri 2016), exerted a strong impact on this process. The conceptual background is Rudolf Arnheim's seminal work, *Visual Thinking*, which highlights the importance of the interplay between thinking and visual images, and hence gave strong impetus to education and learning (Arnheim 1969). Accordingly, in a relatively wide multidisciplinary framework, the VLL continuously made efforts to study cognitive metaphor theory. The other important characteristics are the fact that BME is a polytechnic university and a set of pedagogical features in vocational education and training (VET) with a history of one and a half centuries. Influenced by ICT, our theoretical and practical perception of learning took a significant and impulsive turn, recognizing the role of networks and relying on the classical schools of psychology and philosophy, such as behaviorism, constructivism and the latest one, cognitivism.

Prior to our current research, in the early 2010s, we looked at the effects of the digitization of traditional learning resources as well as the possibilities of open content development in an ICT environment at university and secondary school levels (Benedek – Molnár 2011, 2017). Our main finding was that the closed learning material structures built of sequences face two basic problems in our days. On the one hand, in structures that are closed and difficult to manage, educational content can hardly be changed, updating is irksome, and professional motivation is low. On the other hand, pupils and young students who gain network knowledge in a variety of ways in today's ICT environment are not sufficiently motivated to learn and elaborate traditional learning materials. This finding is especially important as young people's communication practices, including communication amongst themselves, using the services offered by community applications (e.g. Facebook), reading news or blogs, etc., are dominated by image messages. At the same time, a look at the list of educational tools based on teachers' opinions since 2007 (W4) clearly shows that YouTube has been on the lead in recent years, and the most popular forms of communication are software that allows the transmission and creative editing of image information (PowerPoint, Prezi, and Powtoon).

While a basic element of the traditional classroom is the blackboard, where everyone can see the process of image making (writing and drawing), most of our educational materials include only few image elements. A practical reason for this, in addition to learning material design traditions that rely on text dominance, is the limited nature of students' books as well as the difficulties of handling images and colors in press work and its cost increasing effect. Some students' books are indeed visually attractive, but this is rarely the case today given the differentiating nature of educational structures and the rapid changes of content, which is typical in VET.

While electronic learning materials regularly include media elements, more dynamic and interactive media applications often face the limits of internet bandwidth and the necessary storage capacities. At this point, it is worth repeating the above mentioned source (W2): the programs supported by cloud services (like Google Docs, Google Search or Dropbox) are increasingly popular in education programs. The growing demand for the spread and use of network learning and the underlying learning materials that are formed in complex (non-linear) network structures clearly show the need for cloud services in education and learning material development. These realizations prompted us to look at open content development as a way to manage visual content elements in education since 2016.

Education and training content is in constant change. This is especially true of VET, where rapid technological and accelerated labor market changes bring about imperative modifications. This topic is strongly linked to VET (Gessler – Herrera 2015) and is partly connected to endeavors to shape the alternatives of traditional VET curricula in a learning environment determined by modern ICT and that require interactivity not only in the learning process but also in curriculum design (Colons – Halverson 2009).

For community curriculum development, teacher training can provide especially good conditions, as is suggested by our research data. Developing Open Educational Resources (OER) with students' participation means a potential of content and methodology and the applied ICT solutions (open source and ICT supported Learning Management System [LMS], memory independent management of complex visual elements, and the flexible management of micro-contents) are capable of surpassing traditional, school- and notebook based teaching. Only two decades have passed since the introduction of the Open Access principle, and its adoption in a wider context of practice has stirred up pedagogical thinking, which means that the trend of opening education was born (Das 2012; Santos – Punie – Muñoz 2016). We have focused on the current methodological renewal, and we wish to introduce the construction process in the course of which we moved from our theoretical presumption through the first empirical surveys to the creation of our OCD model.

3. The OCD Project

The new four-year project (Open Content Development, OCD) to be implemented between 2016 and 2020 focuses on developing content, methodologies and services related to vocational education, on the current structural changes originating in practice and on meeting the challenges of a visually enriched society (W5). The project is rooted in the idea that the strategic goals of the VLL presume, from its very beginning, the continuous development of teacher quality and excellence. These developments may be foreseen as a potential in the activation of students who are moving from the traditional quantitatively oriented curricula towards new ones representing a contributing approach. Learning activities in the web 2.0 environment are characterized by collaborative skills, innovation, creativity, and ICT supported communication for network relationships (Molnár 2012). At the same time, proactivity, reflective and critical thinking, intercultural sensitivity, and problem solving skills are also important for community based content development.

As a form of Open Content Development, our research focuses on applying visual learning within this approach; we can fully utilize its potentials in creating development opportunities for those who want to transmit knowledge and those who wish to acquire it. Its core is to involve students (future vocational teachers) in the process of developing learning resources as well as to transmit them methodological knowledge offering good grounds in terms of the continuous improvement of active learning and community based content development using visual elements.

By today, the descriptions of Learning Outcomes have become important input factors in formal education. The new type of these descriptions connects to the requirements of the European Framework for Qualifications, and it is easy to achieve their operationalization at the itemization level. The "input" competencies and motivations of learners/students attending the given course are also of great importance and must be treated with the necessary diversification; these factors can greatly contribute to success in education. The innovation skills of the affected teachers are also input factors since their active and proactive participation is a key component of the successful development of the OCD model.

Especially in a period dominated by constructivist learning theories, Learning Outcomes were built on well-constructed curricula and the determination of the adequate duration of teaching. This was clearly reflected by the terms *seat-time learning* and *time-based teaching*. The main component of this model (*Figure 1*) was end-of-course assessment in the form of examinations with the related certification. The model of competency-based learning has created a new order. The description of competencies, which increasingly includes a detailed description of Learning Outcomes, has become the main component.

Figure 1: Inputs and outputs of the OCD

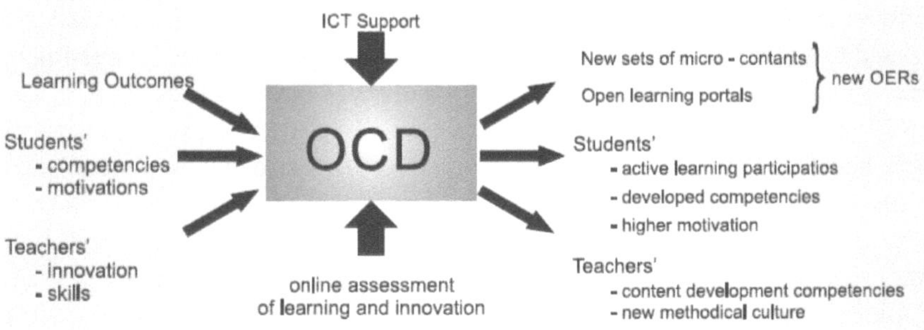

(source: diagram created by the author)

According to these inputs and outputs, our network concept, which is characterized by active student contribution, encouraged the development of new educational content. The result of these activities integrated the original OCD model to formulate a real open environment where information exchange is organized into an informal network. Our hypothesis states that knowledge elements, especially the visual ones interlinked at the level of micro-contents, could form a complex curriculum. The creation of open curricula with rich visual contents has become an important direction for content development. This process is typically characterized by constructive learner contributions.

4. Practical Considerations

In 2015 and 2016, we undertook to elaborate a new complex curriculum as a framework for a general course on system theory analysis, and a possibility for students to prepare case studies to participate in the development of the course curriculum. We followed the general rules of OER development, and in the autumn of 2015, we started teaching the "System Theory" course to a major group of our respondents. We also made an e-learning resource for the course, administered in the Moodle system together with the solutions of the exercises.

Our research on didactics essentially focused on content development by vocational teachers and students, and on the application of new educational methods and processes. According to this approach, the curriculum developers created a new e-learning textbook in the fall semester in 2016 (subject: Vocational Education Systems) with the SysBook platform (*Figure 2*) linked to the learning material; it makes, in terms of openness, the thematic connections more colorful and perhaps even raises them to a higher level of visual and mathematical connections and complex examples. This possibility is, of course, also dependent on the vocational interest and the previous competences of the users of the resource.

Figure 2: Illustration from SysBook – Different explanations of harmony (W6)

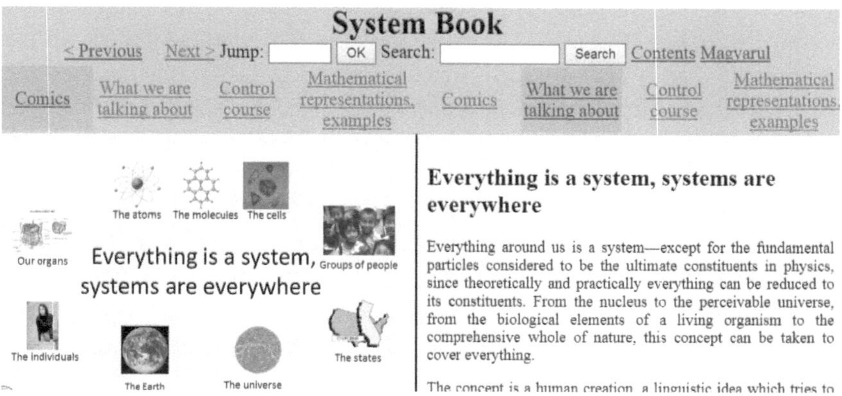

Concerning inputs, the Learning Outcomes database is an input service for users of the system, which offers both orientation and information on the existing sources. This solution does not only allow the filtering of theoretically possible recurrences, but the topics contained in the actual educational requirements, although lacking learning resources (this is, unfortunately, often true of VET in Hungarian these days), can also be described more precisely. In fact, this is a divided database produced by developers to help the description of innovation objectives, as a service for those interested. Open for the participating students/learners and educators, the system is accessible through the research web page (W5); the page also contains BYOD (Bring Your Own Device) proposals that serve the methodological support of the innovations implemented within the open system. The SysBook platform (W6) connects to the OCD model and introduces the open learning resource elaborated in relation to a certain comprehensive topic ('About systems and management for everyone'). This platform (W7) also presents students' innovations and serves as a space for publishing the development results after expert evaluation.

Another essential element of the ICT environment is the university Learning Management System (LMS), which allows joining the process of learning resource development as well as the documentation, assessment and further utilization of the development results through the BME–Moodle system. In fact, this is an open source code system that makes the automatic organization of activities possible even in our case of a high number of planned participants, and is also capable of meeting the rules of archiving. Actually, our Moodle system that serves educational objectives at BME possesses the features of the Cloud systems: eight independent educational systems, the two biggest covering 18,248 and 10,728 students and teachers, and 386 courses managed within the LMS.

When we looked at the content and image characteristics of the newly developed learning material units in open content development, we found it reasonable to provide a general orientation in the first phase. The experimental framework was provided by the subject called 'System Theory'. The task was to describe and present a system, introduce the input and output variables, and system functions and controllability. A further aspect in developing the micro-content was to prepare, considering the age group specificities of the pupils (15–18 years), a micro-content that demonstrates the given system or process and to make sure that the elaborated learning material unit can be applied at a classroom lesson, taking into account its time frames (45 minutes). In this phase, we surveyed the attitudes of the participating students and the visual nature of the content solutions developed.

The students' work was supported by a learning material, the students' e-learning book, which presented the theoretical information and comprehensive case studies. This material, however, was clearly a professional book of a traditional linear sequence. Further help was offered by the SysBook platform that introduced the systems from the perspective of philosophy, science history, mathematics and engineering, and in a most general way. In addition to the texts, it also offered comic-like graphic explanations. One example for this is a SysBook-page on dynamic relations (*Figure* 3; W8).

Figure 3: Illustration from the SysBook (W9)

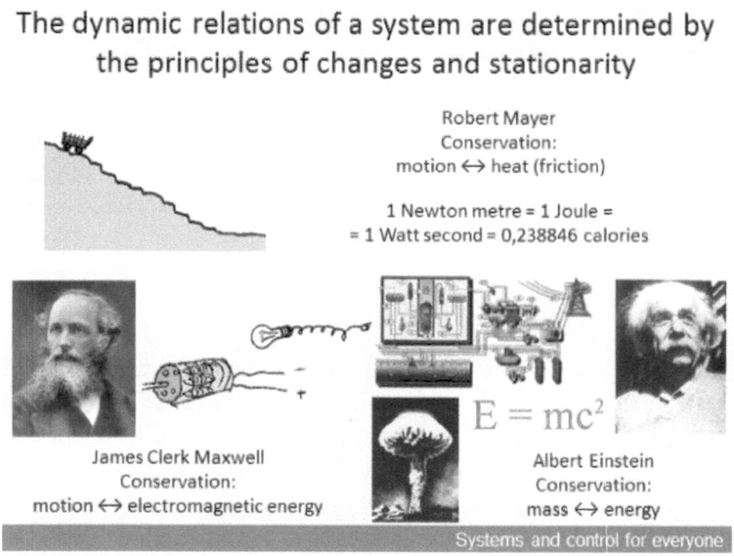

Students' work contain many approaches as the innovative results of the authors, such as the evolutionary interpretation of complex system problems, or the demonstration of how to handle the various possibilities of implementing systems with the general tools of deep mathematical and physical thinking. This approach seems to be interesting and successful; it has to be continued with the teachers' and the students' enthusiastic participation, although in a more professional manner. As is shown by *Figure* 5, this is an experiment to enhance the possibilities of an e-book, which is still an amateur work. The aim was to show that a systemic view is important for everyone and that systems and control are all around us as parts of our everyday lives. Accordingly, the form is also amateurish, some of the pictures professional, but many of them chosen from enormous picture galleries. The presentation is also based on conventional methods.

Figure 4: Students' job – Audio system

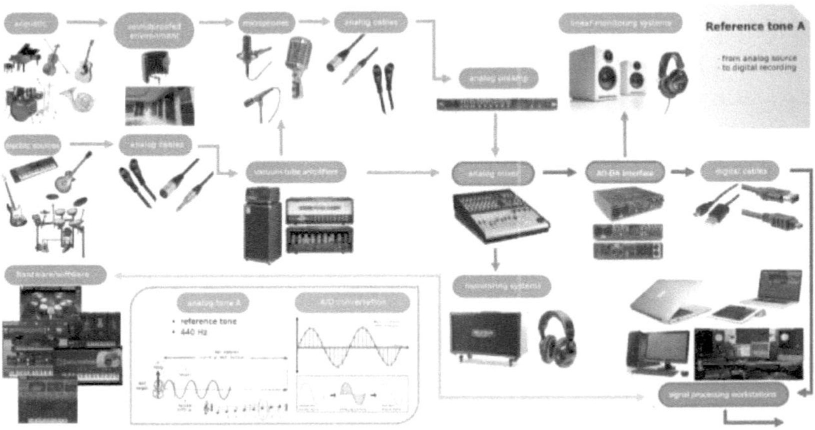

(source: part of a student's work; author: István János Kishonti, Budapest University of Technology and Economics, 2016)

First generation student works that did not include content requirements besides the general thematic frameworks clearly indicated that visual characteristics were much stronger than text-based descriptions in the content elements developed. The applied graphical solutions were static, the students did not strive to embed videos and flash-like media elements, and they thought that the learning material units sufficiently met the requirements of demonstration. This was also indicated by the construction process of the SysBook portal developed with a professional developer background. The experts also found it difficult to prepare a mathematical description for each phenomenon. It is worth mentioning that in this case, as well, mathematical representation was partial, in many cases the professionals failed to describe the main interconnections with mathematical formulas. This deficiency was also present in the students' work. In general, they undertook to present complex phenomena and systems and referred to the mathematical interrelations when demonstrating their theoretical background. However, our main finding was that the students' spontaneous content development work, the micro-contents gave a convincing proof of the demand for and possibility of visual knowledge transfer. In addition, exact measurements must be made in terms of their motivation to develop and perform independent construction tasks improved. They did not only learn the knowledge content of the given topic but also gained capabilities and competencies that would considerably enhance their teaching efficiency in the future.

In summary, this project encouraged teacher training institutions to "learn" in an environment where content development, especially visualization organized into an IT based informal network, plays an increasingly important role. The core point of the OCD concept is participation in the network and access to information as well as to software packages that are able to interpret information in various contexts, and promote cooperative and self-organized learning.

References

Arnheim, Rudolf (1969): *Visual Thinking*. Berkeley – Los Angeles: University of California Press.

Benedek, András – Molnár, György (2011): The Empirical Analysis of a Web 2.0-based Learning Platform. In: Paleologu, Constantin – Mavromoustakis, Constandinos – Minea, Marius (ed.): *ICCGI 2011*. The Sixth International Multi-Conference on Computing in the Global Information Technology, Luxembourg, June 19–24. 56–62.

Benedek, András – Molnár, György (2017): Open Content Development in ICT Environment. In: Gómez Chova, L. – López Martínez, A. – Candel Torres, I. (eds.): *INTED2017. Proceedings: 11th International Technology, Education and Development Conference.* 1883–1891.

Collins, Allan – Halverson, Richard (2009): *Rethinking Education in the Age of Technology*. New York: Teacher College Press.

Das, Anup Kumar (2008): Open Access to Knowledge and Information: Scholarly Literature and Digital Library Initiatives & the South Asian Scenario. *Journal of the American Society for Information Science* 49/6: 507–516.

Gessler, Michael – Herrera, Lázaro Moreno (2015): Vocational Didactics: Core Assumptions and Approaches from Denmark, Germany, Norway, Spain and Sweden. *International Journal for Research in Vocational Education and Training* 2: 152–160.

Grenfield, Patricia (2009): Technology and informal education. What is taught, what is learned. *Science* 323: 68–71.

Molnár, György (2012): Collaborative Technological Applications with Special Focus on ICT based Networked and Mobile Solutions. *WSEAS Transactions on Information Science and Applications* 9: 271–281.

Nyíri, Kristóf (2016): Elfelejtett képelméletek. In: Benedek, András – Nyíri, Kristóf (eds.): *Képi Tanulás Műhelye Füzetek* 3: 3–55.

Santos, Andreia Inamorato – Punie, Yves – Muñoz, Jonatan Castaño (2016): Opening up Education: A Support Framework for Higher Education Institutions. *JRC Science for Policy Report*, EUR 27938 EN doi:10.2791. 293–408.

W1 = SysBook. http://sysbook.sztaki.hu/sysbook6.php?lang=en

W2 = Műszaki Pedagógia Tanszék. www.mpt.bme.hu

W3 = Series Visual Learning. Facebook page. https://www.facebook.com

W4 = Tools for Learning. http://c4lpt.co.uk/top100tools/top-200-tools-for-learning/

W5 = OCD. www.ocd.bme.hu

W6 = SysBook. http://sysbook.sztaki.hu/sysbook6.php?page=2&lang=en&left=intro&right=text

W7 = SysBook. http://sysbook.sztaki.hu/studentarea.php

W8 = SysBook. http://sysbook.sztaki.hu/sysbook6.php?page=31&lang=en&left=intro&right=text

W9 = SysBook. http://sysbook.sztaki.hu/sysbook6.php?page=60&lang=en&left=intro&right=text

György Molnár

How Digital and Virtual Life Trapped in Visuality and New Media Systems Affect Teaching and the Learning Process

1. Introduction

In modern times, visuality, what is more, virtual reality and cyberspace appear to provide a really impressive and beneficial way of life for digital citizens both in everyday life and in special fields, such as education. It allows people to study at their own discretion online. This particularly favors those who are motivated to learn on their own. The three-dimensional virtual reality empowers people with positive experiences. The most advanced ICTs, such as virtual classrooms (Google Class), gamification (Classcraft), digital, interactive curriculum, and several VR systems (goggles, gloves) are at hand now. Further examples include Facebook Oculus and Samsung Gear VR systems. If the learning process is located in a 3-dimensional virtual reality enhanced space, the experience is almost the same as in real life, while time, money and energy can be saved, not to mention the risks that can be avoided. The process of understanding – under special circumstances – can be measured and analyzed with special ICT tools. The Tobii system, for example, can follow and track eye movement, monitor brain activity, and present them on a heat map. This paper first introduces the theoretical and technical background, and then presents the results of an empirical survey conducted on 100 subjects in spring 2016.

Owing to the rapid development of ICT (Information and Communication Technologies), we have experienced a variety of social and economic changes in different kinds of phenomena, and a shift in roles and our ways of life. Today almost all inhabitants of the Earth have mobile devices and subscriptions as there are around 6 billion mobile phone subscriptions all around the world. This comes as a great potential for development. There has never been a greater enhancement in any field with a bigger effect on society and culture than ICT. The industrial revolutions (especially the last two) have altered our everyday life and made it more energetic, dynamic, and active. This shift has been labeled as the "digital culture" and is represented by online presence. The effects of the Internet have been of great importance since the individual can run errands anytime and anywhere. Also, this supports the human-machine interface that has opened its doors toward the dimensions of the so-called augmented or virtual reality (Molnár 2013; Szűts – Yoo 2014). Images are particularly inspiring in understanding (Nyíri 2012). As a result, on the one hand, the set of values and activities of the traditional world have shifted towards digital culture. On the other hand, the technical development has tripled life expectancy. In information based societies with a digital environment, gathering and using and information are as easy as they were never before (Okumura - Oku – Ishikawa 2012). At the same time, we have come the farthest from physical reality and our real lives (Molnár 2016). All of these have had and will have an impact on human interactions, consequently on education and training, especially on creating values, developing the problem-solving and reflective or critical thinking, and prompt us to have our own reflective thinking. These all are the aims of education and are on the opposite side of the over-emphasized digital culture and phenomena.

1.1 A Shift in the Learning Environment and a New Way of Life

Our learning environment has been altered in the past few years. The constant development of ICT requires the sequential development of our technical skills that were found by the new technological advancements. This is understandably true of processes at different levels such as elementary, secondary and higher education (Dukán – Kővári 2013). These three stages should intertwine in the field of mastering and developing digital competences. However, the truth is that these stages are not intertwined. Besides the importance of visuality, virtual reality and cyberspace society can provide their citizens with a fruitful and desirable way of life both in social and in learning aspects since students of these environments attend these courses only when they want to or have the time for it. This notion is especially true for the digital native generations (Benedek 2016a, 2016b).

The rapid technical and technological development changed the learning environment, which resulted in the expansion of digital learning and, in parallel, changed learning forms and fundamental theories (Benedek – Novák 2007; Benedek – Horváth 2016). This shift can be traced back primarily to the overwriting of the classical learning-teaching methods, the redefining of the learning environment, and the alternation of general roles. The effects of these are tangible in our lives but show great differences among generations. That is the reason why they all emphasize the importance of generation studies and more research in the differences between generations (Prensky 2000).

According to the generation theories (Prensky 2001), the younger actors of our modern times who are present in education belong to digital natives. Their attributes include that they:

- were born into the world of technology,
- use multimedia sources,
- live in the world of parallel information processing,
- like random, hyperlinked data as their dominant search algorithm,
- learn last minute or just-in-time as part of a network,
- require instant and interactive feedback, and
- are interested in relevant information and trivia only.

According to another well-known generation theory (Howe – Strauss 2000), in the higher education stage the members of Generations Y and Z are the most prominent students. Generation Y adults:

- were born between 1980 and 1994 therefore they are 23–37 years old, belong to the active workforce, and are on the verge of starting their own families;
- are open-minded, tolerant, able to learn, hard-working thus they value themselves a lot;
- have their own Internet personalities and propose a new-wave communication style to differentiate themselves from their parents;
- are stubborn, brave, quit situations easily so they are not attached on an emotional level but are a bit oversensitive;
- live a dual life: they have virtual and real social relationships;
- value individual freedom and a formality-free world;
- are qualified with less factual knowledge but are better at finding information with the help of technology;
- need to go through reversed socialization: they teach the older generations;
- value free time, and
- are the perfect consumers.

The following image illustrates the paradigm shift in the learning environment as the traditional environment transformed into a digital, network-based one.

Figure 1: Paradigm shift from the traditional to the digital environment

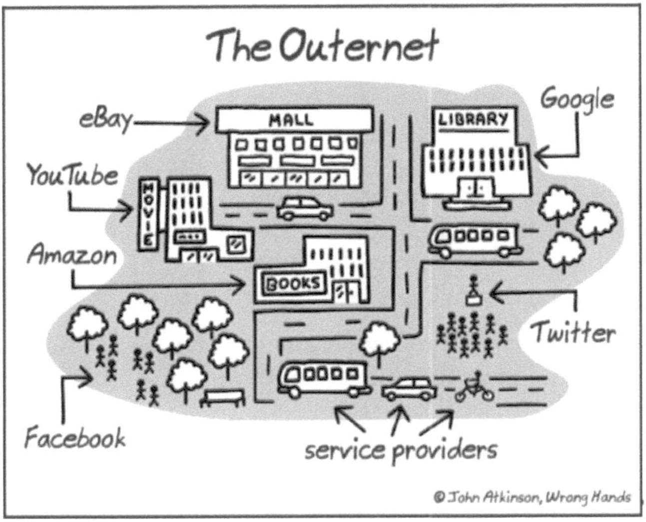

(source: W2)

1.2 The Role of Virtual Reality in Today's Society

Virtual reality means a computer-generated artificial, non-real world in which the user tries to live through virtual phenomena. If we consider the original English expression, *virtual reality* means computer applications used to create a discoverable and accessible three-dimensional world (Benedek – Molnár 2014). Virtual reality is an interaction in which a dynamic, reactive and computer-generated environment affects different senses and body parts. Its aim is to stimulate the user's senses in a way that is equal or the closest to them (Sikné 2003; Batty 2010).

Augmented Reality, or AR for short, is a technology for expanding the real physical environment with virtual elements. Such elements can be a three-dimensional model, an animation or a video clip. While there are multiple definitions, the most widely accepted one was created by Ronald T. Azuma, by which augmented reality happens in real time and it interactively transforms the real world and virtual reality, registered in 3D (Azuma 1997; Veszelszki 2016). The new division can be found between the real and virtual dimensions (Gere 2006).

Virtual reality is an evident reality that can be traced everywhere. The next figure (*Figure 2*) shows the stages of virtual and augmented reality development in a chronological order. That is also the path that leads from the HDM system to today's Oculus and HTC goggles (Geron 2011).

Figure 2: Milestones in the history of virtual reality

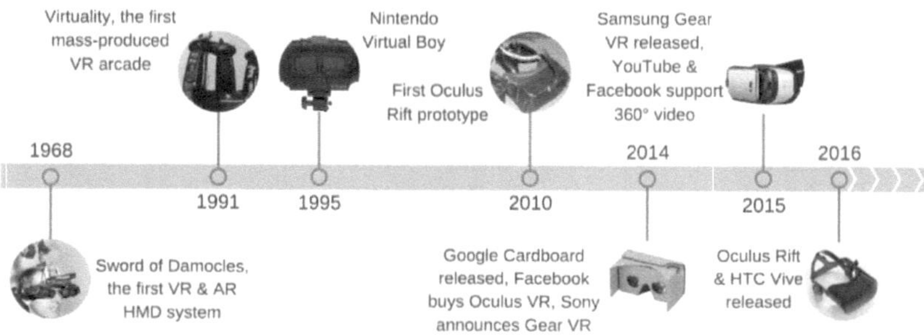

(source: Story Hunter [W1], August 25, 2016)

According to the latest statistics by statista.com, the number of virtual reality users will reach 90 million worldwide by 2017, a figure which shows the development of these systems (*Figure* 3). Consequently, it seems that virtual reality will become inevitable in the future.

Figure 3: The number of virtual reality users between 2014 and 2018

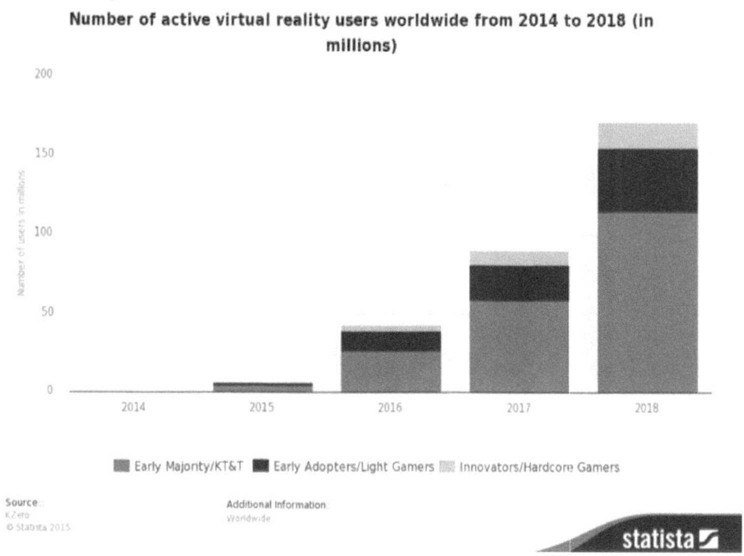

(source: W3)

2. Virtual and Digital ICT Devices Used in Education

With the use of modern digital and info-communication technologies offered by ICT devices, learning and teaching progress can be made more experience-like as opposed to the traditional methods. It is capable of attaching and keeping learner awareness. For these reasons, the virtual learning environment (VLE) and augmented reality (AR) offer notable examples (Bíró 2016).

The already mentioned new methodological approach and the concept of BYOD (Bring Your Own Device) are considered as great potentials as it is worth using the mobile devices that are hiding in students' pockets. This methodological innovation is framed here but even this brief mention is enough for further practice (Szűts – Jinil 2013).

While the different barcode technologies are not new under the sun, they can be motivating for Gen Y & X students. A case in point is the QR code, which uses a two-dimensional coding algorithm. QR is an abbreviation for Quick Response, which comes from the two dimensions. Its creation and display is easy. The following example code stands for the text "Message coding visual with the help of QR codes" and is displayed when we scan the picture with a proper camera of a mobile phone that is capable of decoding it. The QR code is one of the simplest displays and uses of augmented reality (*Figure 4*).

Figure 4: QR code

(source: the author's screenshot)

Apart from coding texts, the QR code is also a perfect tool for coding URL links, telephone numbers, text messages, business cards and short, 160-character messages. From an educational point of view, it could manage a website of learning materials or lecture notes in a picture format. With the help of this method, the QR code is also suitable for sharing the date and location of the next assessment. There are many websites for decoding information but one of the most popular generators is the following tool: http://qrcode.kaywa.com/. *Figure 5* shows the display of this site where we can create our own QR code free of charge in a static way (creating a dynamic code needs registration).

Figure 5: Ways of creating a QR code

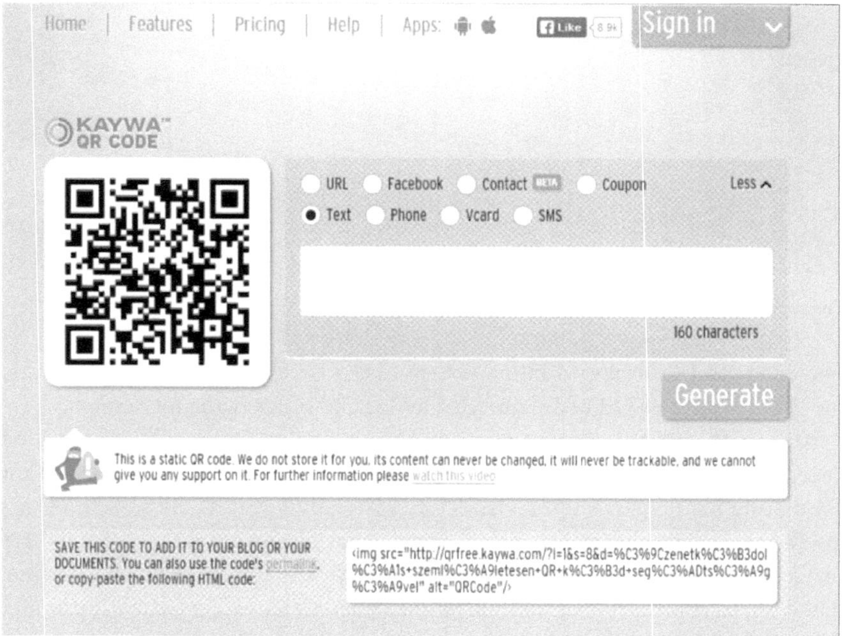

(source: the author's screenshot)

Figure 6 represents the beginning of a university lecture. In accordance with the Evocation, Realization of Meaning, Reflection model, the use of the QR code can be seen when the students scan the code with their mobile phones and answer the question audibly so that their peers can hear it. Then the correct answer is displayed and students need to figure it out with the help of the device to check their ideas. All of this happens in the first phase of the lesson for motivation purposes.

Figure 6: A QR code used in a university lecture

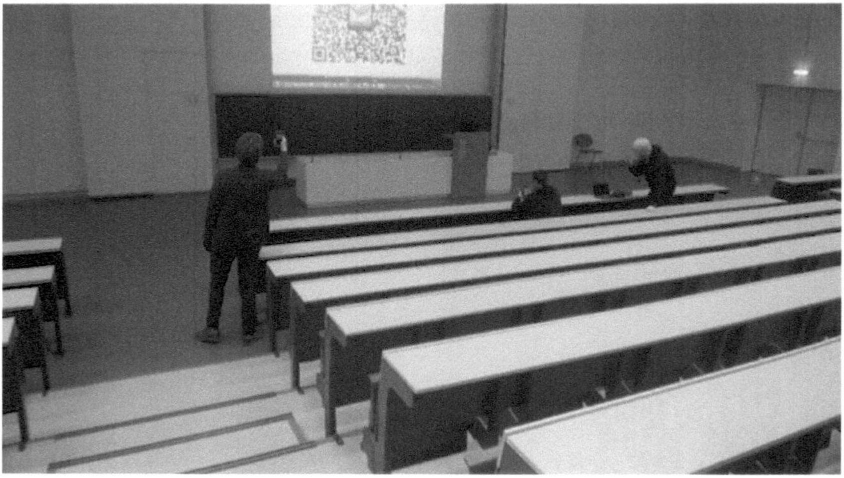

(source: the author's own photo)

The code can be developed into a system that is capable of displaying dynamic movements such as QR codes decoded by the algorithm made for Scratch.

One of the newest developments aims to virtualize Facebook and is called Facebook Oculus. For a real-like sense, all we need is a console, a skin-sensation simulating haptic glove and a visor (virtual-reality goggles). Besides the Oculus Rift, many manufacturers offer virtual-reality headsets, like the HTC Vive or Google Cardboard. In 2016 a promising system appeared on the market: the wireless, computer-free, mobile phone operated Samsung Gear VR product (*Figure 7*).

Figure 7: Gear VR

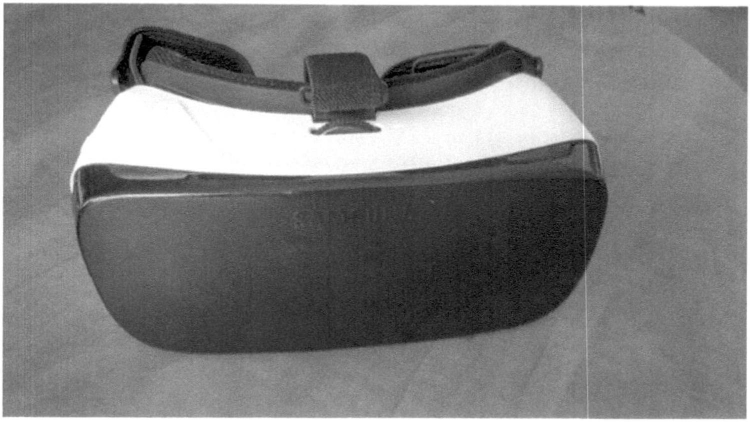

(source: the author's own photo)

One of the finest examples of AR (besides the QR code) is the Aurasma Studio application, which is supported by both Android and Apple. This program allows for converting two-dimensional objects into a three-dimensional picture, leaving the paper-based two dimensions behind. The online client allows us to organize an Aurasma collection. The next photo (*Figure 8*) shows the homepage of its website.

Figure 8: Aurasma Studio homepage

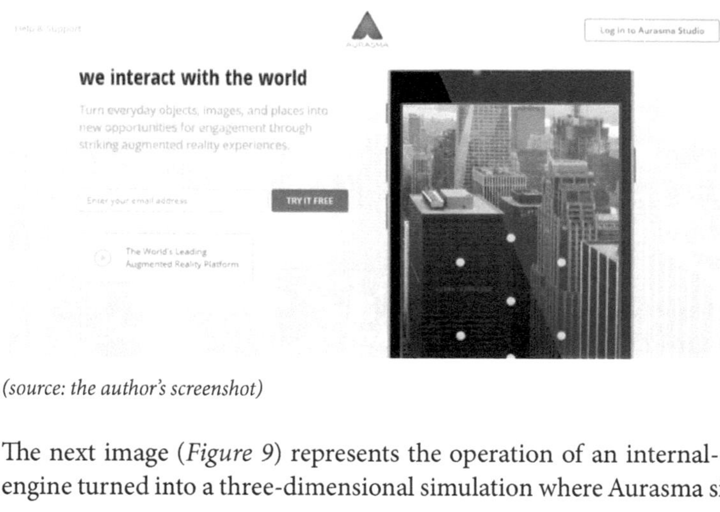

(source: the author's screenshot)

The next image (*Figure 9*) represents the operation of an internal-combustion engine turned into a three-dimensional simulation where Aurasma simulates the operation of an engine in the programmed environment. Seeing it in motion and in three-dimensions, the students can better understand the system's operation and spatial localization. This only requires a free mobile phone application and an inbuilt camera.

Figure 9: A developed program of four-cycle engine by Aurasma Studio

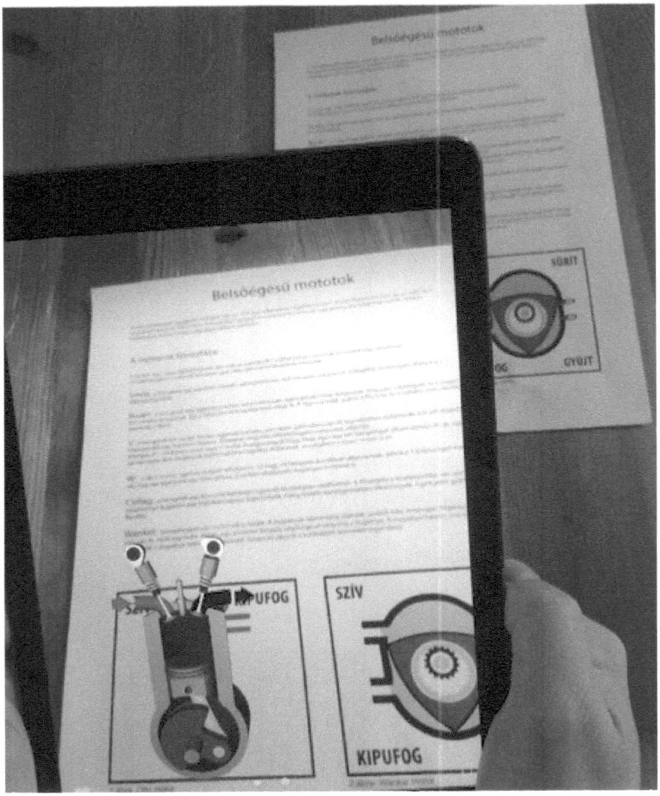

(source: the author's screenshot)

3. An Attitude Survey about the Use of Virtual and Digital Devices

Maintaining and developing the level of infrastructure is a prerequisite for sustainability. ICT is a phenomenal catalyst for pedagogical innovation, especially when we consider network-based and mobile-enhanced pedagogical methods. However, these can function only in a learning environment where there are not only proper and usable ICT devices but both the teachers and the students are open to the new methods.

To prove this point, we conducted an empirically based micro-survey. The survey included 100 respondents in the autumn of 2016. We clearly found that university students are in favor of virtual reality and its use as a learning environment. Also, students are open and eager to participate in such environments. Sampling was random and simple in different learning groups among engineering students aged 18–23. The survey methodology consisted of a questionnaire and a quiz. Our instruments came from pedagogy and we used services that are common in teaching and instant online surveying. One of the instruments was the website called *kahoot.it*, while the other was *mentimeter.com*, both capable of collecting real-time data from the audience via their mobile phones, tablets or personal computers.

In accordance with the survey's objective function, and due to the limitations of its scope, only the biggest group results are published, and solely the more interesting and informative data are evaluated in diagrams and written explanations. This bigger group consisted of 51 respondents.

Figure 10: Age range of the biggest survey group

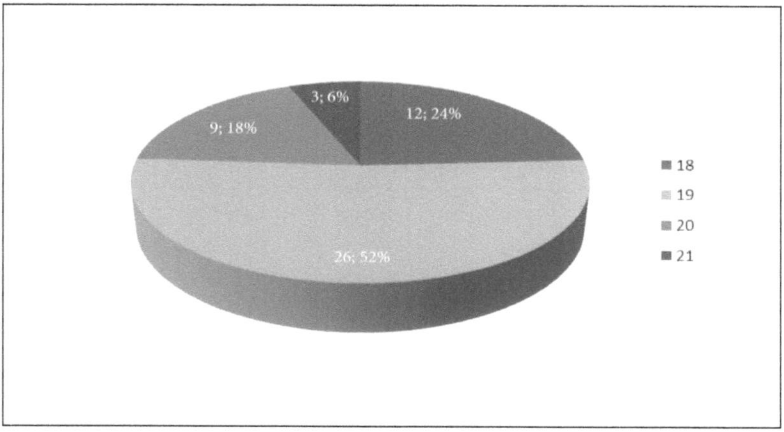

(source: the author's own diagram)

The diagram (*Figure 10*) clearly shows that most respondents belonged to Generations Y and Z so they are in their "university student age" range.

Figure 11: Range of openness towards new and interactive teaching methods

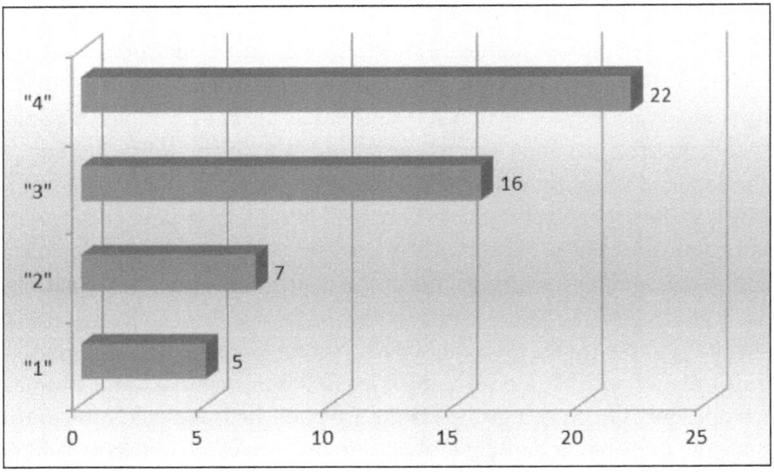

(source: the author's own diagram)

Figure 11 shows how open the respondents are to new, modern and virtual teaching methods. The scale ranges from 1 to 4 and it is notable that almost half of the surveyed university students chose 4, which means that they are positive receivers of VR teaching methods.

Figure 12: Proportion of smart phone owners

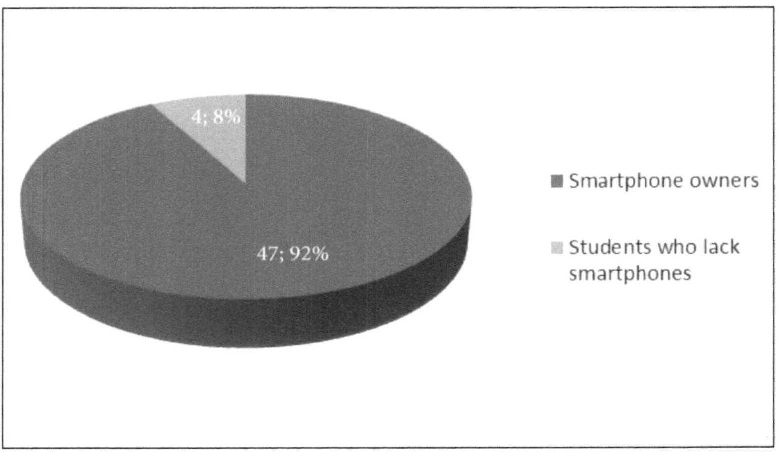

(source: the author's own diagram)

Figure 12 indicates that 92% of the surveyed students own smartphones which they keep in their pockets during every lecture, seminar or laboratory practice.

Figure 13: Number of Facebook profiles

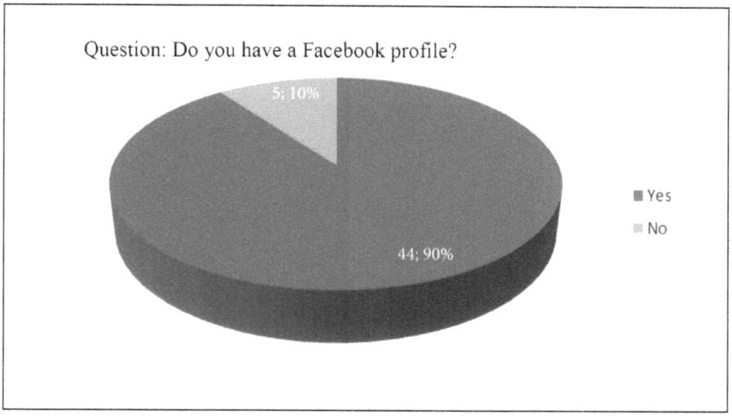

(source: the author's own diagram)

Figure 13 depicts the social network use among the surveyed students. It seems that they are confident users of Facebook.

Figure 14: Attitudes to mobile phone application downloads

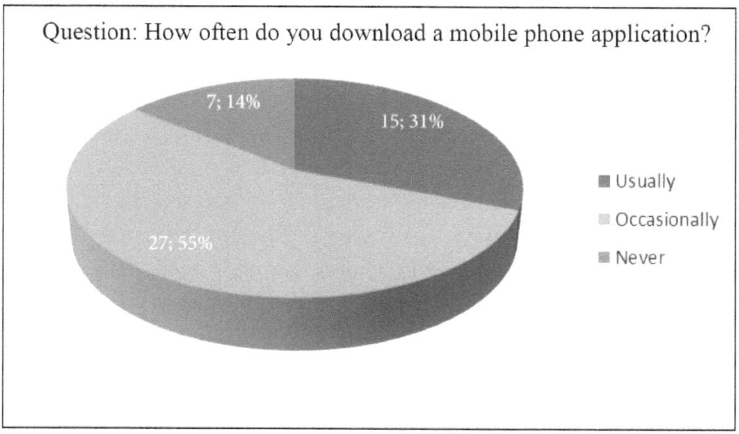

(source: the author's own diagram)

The answers suggest that 27 respondents (55%) occasionally download applications, while 31% of them do so usually. Only 14% said they are opposed to this idea (*Figure 14*). One of the reasons for these data is clear when considering the most popular mobile phone operational systems and their application support. On the other hand, students tend to download programs which they consider useful and are mostly free of charge.

Figure 15: Openness to the innovative methods of AR

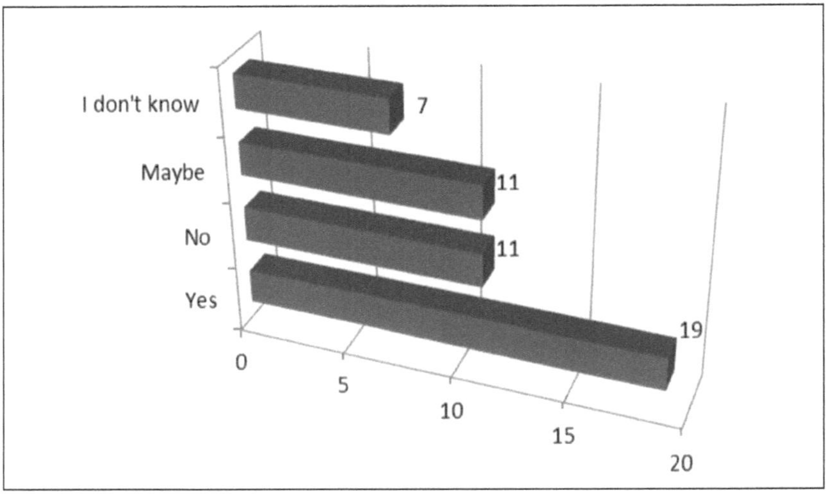

(source: the author's own diagram)

Figure 15 presents the answers to the following question: *Would you like to try student experiments within the lectures by using an application similar to Pokémon Go?* The distribution of the answers indicate that almost half of the respondents are open to trying augmented-reality or virtuality-based teacher or student lectures and experiments. Pokémon Go is seemingly popular among the surveyed students, and rightly so. It offers a kind of augmented reality that fits into the students' own world and is fun for the users. For these reasons, students feel that it should be included in the lectures.

4. Summary

Today's statistical data concerning the digital era as well as the openness of the digital generations to modern digital and virtual systems are key indicators of potential opportunities. This is also highlighted by the new way of thinking, environmental changes and the connected new behavioral patterns. Moreover, our micro-survey has revealed the general open-mindedness and a need for new up-to-date technological and methodological solutions. Such opportunities are provided by the aforementioned digital, mobile-based, augmented or virtual reality programs and models which can be used by students highly effectively, even in virtual or mobile environments. Generations Y and Z are in favor of such technologies. The main reason is that the new methodologies fit better their generational attributes, lifestyles and learning styles thus resonate more with their general needs. The most prominent positive effect is the maintaining of their motivation, with the note that it meets the frames and rules of lectures and modules. What is more, these modern devices can be used effectively at the beginning of each course as evocation or in the end as a reflection or feedback.

Based on the results, the demand for new-generation teaching methods explicitly signals and assigns the tactical and strategic way of them as well as the methodological reforms. In order to satisfy these needs, research methods must be fine-tuned. Also, the survey should be expanded to include all generations and training forms. In accordance with the latest research, literature review and our own survey, we can surely claim that the individual characteristics must be considered and the students' own devices must not only be utilized in teaching, but should also be turned into supporting tools for teaching (as we can see in the BYOD teaching style).

The appreciation of visuality is assisted by virtual and augmented reality spaces. Cyberspace, which houses both, offers a promising and beneficial way of life to digital citizens in both public life and learning as they attend courses only when they wish or have the time. Obviously, in order to be successful in it, they must use digital devices constantly and acquire self-driven and informal learning.

References

Azuma, Ronald (1997): A Survey of Augmented Reality. *Presence: Teleoperators and Virtual Environments* 355–385.

Batty, Michael (2010): Web 2.0 and the GIS revolution. *Annals of GIS* 16: 1–13.

Benedek, András – Nováky, Erzsébet (2007): Tanulás és tudás a digitális korban: A jövőről a jelenben. *Magyar Tudomány* 168/9: 1159–1162.

Benedek, András (2016a): Új tanulási és tanítási módok a XXI. század első felében. In: Tóth, Attiláné – S. Gubik, Andrea (eds.): *Magyarország 2025-ben és kitekintés 2050-re: Tanulmánykötet Nováky Erzsébet 70. születésnapjára.* Budapest: Arisztotelész Kiadó. 133–142.

Benedek, András (2016b): Sysbook as a Visual Learning Frame. In: Benedek, András – Veszelszki, Ágnes (eds.): *In the Beginning was the Image: The Omnipresence of Pictures: Time, Truth, Tradition.* Series Visual Learning, vol. 6. Frankfurt am Main: Peter Lang Internationaler Verlag der Wissenschaften. 161–170.

Benedek, András – Horváth Cz., János (2016): New Methods in the Digital Learning Environment: Micro-contents and Visual Case Studies. In: Moreira Teixeira, António – Szűcs, András – Mázár, Ildikó (eds.): *Re-Imaging Learning Environments: Proceedings of the European Distance and E-Learning Network 2016 Annual Conference.* Budapest: European Distance and E-Learning Network (EDEN). 27–34.

Benedek, András – Molnár, György (2014): ICT in Education: A New Paradigm and Old Obstacle. In: Leist, Arno – Pankowski, Tadeusz (eds.): *ICCGI 2014: The Ninth International Multi-Conference on Computing in the Global Information Technology*. Sevilla, IARIA. 54–60.

Bíró, Kinga (2016): *Augmentált tanulási környezetek a természettudományos tantárgyak támogatására.* Manuscript, National Conference of Scientific Students' Associations.

Dukán, Péter – Kővári, Attila (2013): Felhő alapú számítástechnika: Virtualizációs metodológiák biztonsága. *Dunakavics* 1/4: 25–32.

Gere, Charlie (2006): *Art, Time and Technology.* Bloomsbury: Berg Publishers.

Geron, Tomio (2011): Viewdle's SocialCamera App Tags And Learns Your Friends' Faces. *Forbes* 4/27/2011.

Howe, Neil – Strauss, William (2000): *Millennials Rising: The Next Great Generation.* Knopf Doubleday Publishing Group.

Molnár, György (2013): Challenges and Opportunities in Virtual and Electronic Learning Environments. In: Szakál, Anikó (ed.): *SISY 2013: IEEE 11th International Symposium on Intelligent Systems and Informatics proceedings.* Budapest: IEEE Hungary Section. 397–401.

Molnár, György (2016): Pillanatképek az IKT-szakképzésben alkalmazható megoldásairól – avagy kételyek és jó gyakorlatok az innovatív pedagógiai módszerek útján. Visszatekintés az EDU elmúlt időszakára. *Edu Szakképzés és Környezetpedagógia elektronikus szakfolyóirat* 6/2: 7–18.

Nyíri, Kristóf (2012): Visualization and the Horizons of Scientific Explanation. In: Benedek, András – Nyíri, Kristóf (eds.): *The Iconic Turn in Education.* Series Visual Learning, vol. 2. Frankfurt: Peter Lang Internationaler Verlag der Wissenschaften. 127–150.

Okumura, Kohei – Oku, Hiromasa – Ishikawa, Masatoshi (2012): *Lumipen: projection-Based Mixed Reality for Dynamic Objects.* IEEE International Conference on Multimedia and Expo. http://www.k2.t.u-tokyo.ac.jp/members/okumura/pdf/okumura_icme2012.pdf [20. 03. 2017].

Prensky, Marc (2001): Digital Natives, Digital Immigrants. *On the Horizon* 9/5: 1–6.

Sikné Lányi, Cecília (2003): *A virtuális valóság és alkalmazásai*. Egyetemi jegyzet. Veszprém: Pannon Egyetem.

Szűts, Zoltán – Yoo, Jinil (2013): A kiterjesztett valóság térhódítása. *Információs Társadalom: társadalomtudományi folyóirat* 2013/2: 58–67.

Szűts, Zoltán – Yoo, Jinil (2014): Interactivity and Reception. The Question of Hypermedial, Geo-Spatial and Augmented Literature. *World Literature Studies* 2014/4: 13–26.

Veszelszki, Ágnes (2016): Egy sziget körülhajózása. *Képi Tanulás Műhelye Füzetek* 2016/3: 56–62.

W1 = https://www.vrs.org.uk/virtual-reality/history.html.

W2 = https://wronghands1.com/gallery-3/the-outernet-3/.

W3 = statista.com.

Social, Visual, Digital

James E. Katz, Daniel Halpern

Image Self-Involvement and Romantic Relationships: The Case of Selfies

1. Perspective

Since the advent of the mobile phone, no other technology-based practice has altered public space or affected public performances as much as has the selfie. The pursuit of the selfie has become commonplace at quotidian events ranging from standing in line to dining in a restaurant, and even to political campaigns (Villacorta 2014). Their creation seems to be a feature of most every dramatic event from funerals to festivals. Pursuing a good selfie can be a dangerous practice, as many passengers of driving services such as Uber may have witnessed. Beyond minor risks and eccentricities, the pursuit of the selfie has led to tragic consequences, including fatal accidents while executing daring stunts, car accidents, and even plane crashes (Frantz – Nottingham 2015).

The fantastically speedy and widespread adoption of the selfie-taking, exchange and curation are to our knowledge completely unforeseen by futurists and other prognosticators. This may not be surprising, given that self-portraits were created by artists since at least the renaissance, and the first photographic-like selfies were taken in the 1840s, using Daguerreotypes, followed by Polaroid technology from the 1940s. So the next step in technological progress, the digital camera, when paired with a mobile phone, might not have seen so dramatic. Yet the ready availability of the camera meant that quite remarkable has been the adeptness of selfie takers, who are able to practice their craft in an astonishing variety of circumstances, ranging from scrambling out of crashed airplanes to being able to capture themselves with a selfie while marching in a blindfolded group.

This change in the proliferation of selfies and their creative achievement is one side of the fascinating coin of everyday practice. As such it has attracted a variety of analyses from scholars' perspectives, and was explored in the previous volume of this collection and numerous other scholarly outlets as well.

The other side of the coin, the side that is but little explored, is how these seemingly individual practices spill-over to affect dyadic relations and the larger social order. This larger social order of course encompasses the relationship between members of a romantic couple and their setting within a complex mediated environment of other social ties, both existing and potentially waiting to be created.

Given the possible ramifications of such activities they are of compelling interest at sociological, psychological and policy levels. Yet, these aspects of selfies are much harder to tackle empirically, which may be one reason why less attention has been directed towards them. Perhaps another reason is that it is more subtle and indirect, and thus would not immediately strike a researcher as a topic to investigate.

Selfies, as with other types of social media, may be negatively affecting the quality of personal relationships. In particular, earlier work on Facebook found rising divorces associated with the spread of that technology. Could the same be true of selfies? In this study, a longitudinal panel of Chileans in a romantic relationship was surveyed at a one-year interval to see if their involvement with selfies was associated with a directional change in paired evaluations of the quality of their relationships.

2. Logic of Inquiry

Let's look at the rationale behind the study. The first element is that it appears that a sense of co-presence is a necessary predicate for a strong, stable, and mutually satisfying romantic relationship (Roberts 1982). That said, it is not mere presence, whether virtual or physical, that is the key. Rather, more important than merely being in each other's presence, is the degree to which the pairs of actors in a significant romantic relationship focus on each other (Davis 1985).

The second element is that many factors in the use of technology can serve to undermine this predicate. In explaining why social media in particular may be harming romantic relationships, the literature has explored two main reasons. In this chapter we offer a third one. We are going to start with the first one, which is based on the idea of constant availability. In fact, there is a new word, *pphubbing*, which may be useful to explain this phenomenon. *Pphubbing* is the short word for "partner phone snubbing" (Roberts & David, 2016). We know that we are phubbed when in close proximity to someone else who, instead of communicating with us, decides to attend his/her cell phone. Partner phubbing (pphubbing) is when the above takes place in the company of our significant other. This story here is simple: more than a decade ago Katz and Aakhus coined the term *perpetual contact* to underscore how individuals strain toward connectedness with each other. The problem is that in the last 10 years, research has also shown that conflicts between romantic partners are been triggered by this perpetual availability (Hall – Baym 2012; Duran – Kelly – Rotaru 2011; Miller-Ott – Kelly – Duran 2012; Valkenburg – Peter 2007): individuals are constantly receiving notifications through their phones, and as they are notified, they also have to struggle with so many opportunities to be in touch, and the way they handle these requests appears to affect their relationships.

The second line of research explains that affordances presented in social media have the potential to be harming relationship quality (Hudson et al. 2015; Utz – Beukeboom 2011). Valenzuela, Halpern and Katz (2014) explain how these social platforms can create an environment with potential situations that may evoke feelings of jealousy between partners, harming the quality of their relationship (Elphinston – Noller 2011). Research has shown that Facebook, for instance, facilitates users reconnecting with a variety of people with whom they have had a past relationship (Ellison – Steinfeld – Lampe 2007), creating the potential for jealousy in current relationships. Valenzuela et al. (2014) also explain how social media capabilities in general and Facebook's affordances in particular, make cheating easier. If someone is trying to find another person, it is possible to search in Facebook by name, email address, company/workplace, or common friends, and even get narrow results by indicating only hometown or school, making it still easier to find, for example, an ex. Similarly, with the "event" invitations feature, it is easy for users to monitor and determine if a certain person of potential interest will be attending a particular event. And finally, Facebook allows users to have multiple profiles: a person could have a Facebook profile for family and friends which lists them as married but also a secondary profile which lists them as single and being interested in forming relationships. This tool makes it easy for those so inclined to cheat. From a theoretical perspective, Kendall (2011) explains that when people manage more information about others and it is easy to search for partners after marriage, the expected benefit from a new match may outweigh the cost of dissolving the old one, which increases the divorce rates.

However, in this paper we also postulate that a third reason may be given to explain the negative effect of social media on romantic relationships: following research published in a previous article (Halpern – Katz – Carril 2017), we believe that specific uses of SNS – and not necessarily the affordances per se – may be also affecting romantic relationships. For this purpose we explored in more than 400 individuals in a romantic relationship how the numbers of "selfies" that they take, which are being used transversally across these platforms, may affect their relationships. Why did we focus on selfies? Because this form of self-presentation gives picture-takers a vast array of ways to portray themselves by customizing and projecting an individual's image by the same individual (Katz – Crocker 2015). Consequently, given this individualistic form of SNS usage, where users focus on how they want to be seen by others from their own perspective, and that quality in a romantic relationships depends on the degree to which the pairs of actors focus on each other (Davis 1985), there is an argument to be made that if this is done recurrently, it will affect negatively their relationships.

Thus, we wish to focus on how selfie production and consumption can contribute or, more likely, harm this sense of commitment and focus. Regarding the mechanism through which this process can occur, we explore two different avenues: jealousy and self-idealization.

2.1 Jealousy

It has already been amply demonstrated that social networking sites (SNS) offer an easily accessible interpersonal communication medium, with an immense variety of potential third party threats (Elphinston – Noller 2011). The literature reveals that these threats, whether acted upon or not by an actor, can lead to a response by the actor's partner. These responses fall along three axes as follows:

i. Hypervigilance for relationship threats;
ii. Jealousy-related suspicions, and
iii. Surveillance behaviors in a person's romantic relationship.

Moreover, as explained above, social media platforms such as Facebook facilitates users reconnecting with a variety of people with whom they have had a past relationship (Ellison – Steinfeld – Lampe 2007), creating the potential for jealousy in current relationships. Similarly, Facebook also supports users' maintenance of relationships that may otherwise be only transitory, but could become a source of conflicts when juxtaposed to the marital relationship. Elphinston and Noller (2011) explain that exposing one's partner to all of these individuals, many of whom may be unknown to the partner, may increase the potential for jealousy and suspicion. Valenzuela et al. (2014) also mention research that has corroborated empirically this jealousy-provoking information between partners using Facebook (Muise – Christofides – Desmarais 2009): as users see activities related to their partners, it creates a feedback loop whereby heightened jealousy leads to increased surveillance of a partner's Facebook page, causing even more suspicion between the parts, which ultimately affects negatively the relationship. Based on this line of reasoning, we argue that individuals develop feelings of jealousy when their partners:

i. take more selfies, and
ii. make / receive comments associated to the sharing of their personal images.
iii. Feelings of jealousy will arise as a result of their online activities.

In this way, we believe that partners may begin to question the volume of photographs, statuses and other activities shared by their significant others. The partner might begin wondering why there is such a desire for the partner to share more broadly with others something that is reasonably viewed as "theirs." And the feelings of jealousy that could arise from this situation would most probably cause partners to respond with even more jealous thoughts and engagement in surveillance behaviors, harming the comity of the relationship.

2.2 Ideal Self

Self-presentation and identity formation have become key functions of young people's personal photography (Mendelson – Papacharissi 2010). Contemporary technology yields the potential to select, curate and digitally manipulate one's self-image. This allows the selfie to become a powerful tool for identity formation (Katz – Crocker 2015).

Research shows that in social media, self-affirming profiles offer a positive and desirable form of self-presentation. A necessary corollary of this process is the presence of an audience able to observe and evaluate users' profiles, which in turn motivates individuals who put their material online to put their best face forward (Kim – Lee 2011; Toma – Hancock 2013).

Next, previous studies have also demonstrated that a significant element in determining self-construction is the public nature of the self-presentation (Gonzales – Hancock 2008). In this regard, the social psychology literature has revealed that one's awareness of an audience, or sense of publicness, augments the effect of self-presentation on identity (Kelly – Rodriguez 2006). Hence, when people behave in particular ways, they shift their self-beliefs to correspond to their behaviors.

We reason that as users share their selfies, they may create a fantasy of themselves based on the "ideal persona" they construct online, thus causing a conflicting view of oneself vis-à-vis the partners' view. We argue that when this change in self-perception meets the eyes of a partner, supposedly the person who knows the other best, this illusion could cause dissonance between what partners know about picture-takers and what picture-takers believe about themselves, which would increase the conflicts between romantic partners in SNS (Halpern et al. 2017).

To learn more about this topic and test out our theorizing, we used a two-wave panel survey of a previously created group of volunteers. Working on the assumptions that the people using today's communication technology are likely to be similar, no matter their nationality, and because we had access to a sample of users in Chile, we elected to study users there. (But even if they are different in their behavior from those of other countries due to national differences, that would be interesting, too. In other words, it is useful to know what is going on in Chile whether or not they are similar to the rest of the world. That said, it is not yet known whether Chileans are similar to or different from users in the EU and USA, hence that constitutes a worthy research question.) So our sample was of Chileans, about 49% male and 51% female, and in terms of age distributions, mostly young (18–34: 55%; 35–44: 20%; 45–64: 22%; 65+: 3%). Using email invitations, 1225 responded out of 8840 solicitations, and 717 of those individuals were in a romantic relationship in this first wave. After one year, we invited them to participate in a second survey. Out of those 717, 410 responded but 105 were no longer in a relationship anymore, leaving 305 cases for further analysis. More details can be found in Halpern et al. (2017).

3. How We Measured these Questions

We used several scales to measure these concepts. In terms of instrumentation, we used data from the first wave to measure frequency of posting selfies, jealousy and the creation of the online ideal persona and data from the second wave to measure SNS photo-related conflicts and perceived relationship quality.

Perceived relationship quality. Five components of relationship quality such as a happiness and strength perception of the relationship (e.g., "We have a very healthy relationship") were asked and respondents registered their degree of agreement (M = 4.3, SD = .69, = .906) with Likert-scale statements on a 5-point scale ranging from 1 (absolutely disagree) to 5 (absolutely agree).

Photo related conflicts. We wanted to know how often they had argued with their significant others about pictures they had seen or posted on social media, comments posted on others pictures, or comments posted by other users on their pictures (M = 1.9, SD = .77, = .89). We used these four questions for that purpose ranging from 1 (never) to 5 (always).

Jealousy. We asked participants about the feelings of jealousy they have experienced after their significant others posted pictures, or received comments from other users about the pictures posted. We used the same 5-points scale of frequency, from never to always (M = 2.63, SD = .92).

Online ideal persona. Eight items measured a) the projection of an ideal self (e.g. "Selfies always have to show your best face") and b) the impact that users seek to create in others through selfies (e.g. "I share selfies to increase my exposure to others"). Respondents answered their degree of agreement with this set of variables (M = 2.3, SD = 0.82, α= 0.809) with Likert-scale statements on a 5-point scale ranging from 1 (absolutely disagree) to 5 (absolutely agree).

Selfies. How often they had taken a picture of themselves for sharing on a 7-point scale during the year, from never to everyday (M = 3.1, SD = 1.7).

Selfies with partners. To avoid potential selfies that may improve the perceived quality in a relationship instead of negatively affecting it, we controlled for selfies they had taken with their partners.

4. Results: What We Learned from the Investigation

Confirmatory structural equation modeling (SEM) was used to test the mediation of the variables. First, the results showed that frequency of posting selfies was related positively to jealousy in SNS between romantic partners (b = .088, SE = .032, p < .01) and the ideal persona that users construct online (b = .122, SE = .03, p < .001). Moving to the second part of the proposed model, we found that both mediators, jealousy in SNS and the ideal persona, were related positively to photo-related conflicts. Notably, a significant effect was found between photo-related conflicts and perceived quality in the relationship between romantic partners, (b = -.232, SE = .056, p < .001), showing that these variables are linked negatively, as the model in *Figure 1* shows. Furthermore, data analysis revealed a significant indirect effect of both variables: whereas the indirect effect of jealousy through selfies associated conflicts was strong (effect = -.073, SE = .023, p < 0.01 [95% bias-corrected bootstrap CI -.128, -.04]), the indirect effect of the fantasy persona, though less robust, was still significant (effect = -.031, SE = .018, p < 0.05 [95% bias-corrected bootstrap CI -.074, -.01]). As it is reported in Halpern et al. (2016), both indirect effects were statistically different from zero, as revealed by a 95% bias-corrected bootstrap confidence interval, indicating that selfies-related conflicts mediate the relationship between both mechanisms and perception of lower quality in the relationship between romantic partners. Overall, we found an indirect effect between taking selfies and lower perceptions of relationship quality by romantic partners, which was mediated by two main mechanisms: *jealousy and an ideal self.*

Figure 1: Structural model predicting Perceived Relationship Quality

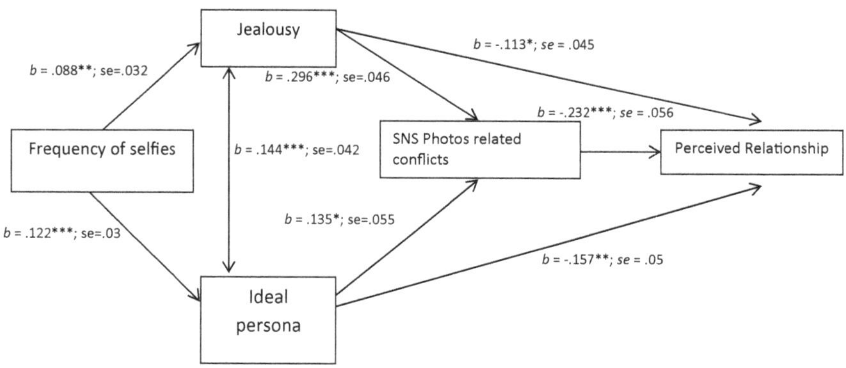

Note. Age, sex, time partners have been in the relationship and taking selfies with partner, were entered in the model as control variables. *p < 0.05; **p < 0.01; ***p < 0.001

4.1 Jealousy

According to Muise et al.'s (2009) "jealousy effect" on Facebook, SNS jealousy operates in a feedback loop:

i. Spending more time on social media increases exposure to information about one's partner that may arouse jealousy.
ii. Jealousy, in turn, increases the amount of time spent on SNS in search of relationship-relevant information.

We extended these findings by showing that jealousy was not an inevitable consequence of SNS use, but rather could also be predicted by a specific use, such as *taking selfies.*

4.2 Ideal Self

We elaborated notion of selective self-presentation, originally developed to refer to the textual elements of online self-presentations, to selfie production in SNS. We discerned that individuals not only create an image that reflects their aspirational social selves, but they also shift their self-beliefs to correspond to their perceived public. The problem is that when this change in self-perception meets the eyes of a partner, the person who knows the other best, this illusion causes dissonance between what partners know about picture-takers and what picture-takers believe about themselves, which would affect negatively the relationship.

4.3 Limitations

It needs to be said that like all studies of this nature, there are many limitations and reasons why the results may not be accurate. And the scope of questions, including dealing with psychological backgrounds, was limited and the sample was relatively small. Future research should be able to address these aspects in order to extend these findings.

5. What We Concluded

Bearing these limitations in mind, we can tentatively conclude that certain kinds of uses of selfies did appear to negatively affect romantic relationships. In terms of implications, the power of self-image is far-ranging indeed, long before the invention of the cell phone, and certainly much more in today's world. One of the unintended consequences of the selfie revolution is to promote self-regard. A possible extension of this consequence goes to the heart of concern over the stability of romantic relations in terms not only of personal fulfillment but also child-raising and socialization. Here the power of technology in interpersonal relationships to both raise expectations and reduce the incentive to make the effort to meet them can spill over to erode comity and stability in these relationships. As such, there is an unfortunate side-effect of selfies that go to the heart of virtual and veridical, two themes of this year's conference.

References

Davis, Keith E. (1985): Near and dear: Friendship and love compared. *Psychology Today* 19: 22–30.

Duran, Robert L. – Kelly, Lynne – Rotaru, Teodora (2011): Mobile phones in romantic relationships and the dialectic of autonomy versus connection. *Communication Quarterly* 59: 19–36.

Ellison, Nicole B. (2007): Social Network Sites: Definition, History, and Scholarship. *Journal of Computer-Mediated Communication* 13/1: 210–230.

Elphinston, Rachel A. – Noller, Patricia (2011): Time to Face it! Facebook Intrusion and the Implications for Romantic Jealousy and Relationship Satisfaction. *Cyberpsychology, Behavior, and Social Networking* 14/11: 631–635.

Fantz, Ashley – Nottingham, Shawn (2015): NTSB: Taking Selfies Likely Caused Fatal Colorado Plane Crash. February 4, 2015. CNN.com. http://www.cnn.com/2015/02/03/us/selfie-plane-crash/ [09. 05. 2017]

Gonzales, Amy L. – Hancock, Jeffrey T. (2008): Identity Shift in Computer-mediated Environments. *Media Psychology* 11/2: 167–185.

Hall, Jeffrey A. – Baym, Nancy K. (2012): Calling and Texting (too much): Mobile Maintenance Expectations, (over)dependence, Entrapment, and Friendship Satisfaction. *New Media & Society* 14/2: 316–331.

Hudson, Michael B. – Nicolas, Sylis C. – Howser, Molly E. – Lipsett, Kristen E. – Robinson, Ian W. – Pope, Laura J. – Hobby, Abigail F. – Friedman, Denise R. (2015): Examining How Gender and Emoticons Influence Facebook Jealousy. *Cyberpsychology, Behavior, and Social Networking* 18/2: 87–92.

Halpern, Daniel – Katz, James E. – Carril, Camila (2017): The Online Ideal Persona vs. the Jealousy Effect: Two Explanations of why Selfies are Associated with Lower-quality Romantic Relationships. *Telematics and Informatics* 34/1: 114–123.

Katz, James E. – Crocker, Elizabeth T. (2015): Selfies and Photo Messaging as Visual Conversation: Reports from the U.S., U.K., and China. *International Journal of Communication* 9: 1861–1872. http://ijoc.org/index.php/ijoc/article/view/3180/1405.

Kelly, Anita E. – Rodriguez, Robert R. (2006): Publicly Committing Oneself to an Identity. *Basic and Applied Social Psychology* 28/2: 185–191.

Kendall, Todd D. (2011): The Relationship between Internet Access and Divorce Rate. *Journal of Family and Economic Issues* 32/3: 449–460.

Kim, Jung-Hyun – Lee, Jong-Eun R. (2011): The Facebook Paths to Happiness: Effects of the Number of Facebook Friends and Self-presentation on Subjective Well-being. *CyberPsychology, Behavior, and Social Networking* 14/6: 359–364.

McAndrew, Francis T – Shah, Sahil S. (2013): Sex Differences in Jealousy over Facebook Activity. *Computers in Human Behavior* 29/6: 2603–2606. DOI: 10.1016/j.chb.2013.06.030.

Mendelson, Andrew L. – Papacharissi, Zizi (2010): Look at Us: Collective Narcissism in College Student Facebook Photo Galleries. In: Papacharissi, Zizi (ed.): *The Networked Self: Identity, Community and Culture on Social Network Sites.* Routledge. 251–273.

Miller-Ott, Aimee E. – Kelly, Lynne – Duran, Robert L. (2014): Cell Phone Usage Expectations, Closeness, and Relationship Satisfaction between Parents and their Emerging Adults in College. *Emerging Adulthood* 2/4: 313–323.

Muise, Amy – Christofides, Emily – Desmarais, Serge (2009): More Information than You Ever Wanted: Does Facebook Bring Out the Green-eyed Monster of Jealousy? *CyberPsychology, Behavior and Social Networking* 12/4: 441–444.

Roberts, M. (1982): Men and Women: Partners, Lovers and Friends. *Advances in Descriptive Psychology* 2: 57–78.

Roberts, James A. – David, Meredith E. (2016): My Life Has Become a Major Distraction from my Cell Phone: Partner Phubbing and Relationship Satisfaction among Romantic Partners. *Computers in Human Behavior* 54: 134–141.

Toma, Catalina L. – Hancock, Jeffrey T. (2013): Self-affirmation Underlies Facebook Use. *Personality and Social Psychology Bulletin* 39/3: 321–331.

Utz, Sonja – Beukeboom, Camiel J. (2011): The Role of Social Network Sites in Romantic Relationships: Effects on Jealousy and Relationship Happiness. *Journal of Computer-Mediated Communication* 16/4: 511–527.

Valenzuela, Sebastián – Halpern, Daniel – Katz, James E. (2014): Social Network Sites, Marriage Well-Being and Divorce: Survey and State-level Evidence from the United States. *Computers in Human Behavior* 36: 94–101.

Valkenburg, Patti M. – Peter, Jochen (2007): Online Communication and Adolescent Well-being: Testing the Stimulation versus the Displacement Hypothesis. *Journal of Computer-Mediated Communication* 12/4: 1169–1182.

Villacorta, Natalie (2014): The Politics of the Selfie. *Politico.com*. http://www.politico.com/story/2014/03/selfies-politics-104910 [09. 05. 2017]

Rachel A. Katz[1]

All About Image: Development of Visual Literacy through American Dating Apps

I hate photos that show off toned bodies. It creates a sense that there isn't anything else to that person.

Only photos of himself drinking on his profile? I would hope he has more of a personality than just that!

All your photos are selfies? One selfie of yourself at a party is fine, but if all your pictures are selfies that tells me that you have no friends or are a raging narcissist.

1. Digital Dating

When discussing profile pictures, these comments by dating app users indicate that image cues in profile pictures hold great meaning for viewers. This symbolic communication becomes critical for image-based dating apps (IBDA) such as Tinder. Studying how people create and assimilate dating app profiles yields new understandings of image-based communication. Specifically, in this chapter I argue that IBDA contribute to, and even help structure, a new visual literacy. The visual format of profile images takes precedence over text on profiles as a communication method to potential matches. Visual literacy in the site of dating apps is predicated on discourses of authenticity within images, as opposed to ambiguity within images. In this context IBDA are considered critically distinct from web-based alternatives because they are so heavily image-based and mobile, with little in the way of text and no website platform.

1.1 Digital Courtship: Images Trump Algorithms

To contextualize my argument, I examine the background of computer dating. A generation ago, computer dating services promised to help singles beat the numbers game and find a soulmate by using algorithms. This invocation of the language of rationality remains successful; current popular online dating websites such as eHarmony and OKCupid purport to use science to match people up. But in a comprehensive review of over "80 years of scientific research about dating and

1 Orcid identifier: orcid.org/0000-0002-3521-8291.

attraction", Finkel *et al.* (2012) were "unable to prove that computers can indeed match people together" (Bilton 2014; Finkel et al. 2012). In other words, there is no basis to believe that computer algorithms promote better romantic outcomes than conventional offline dating (Finkel et al. 2012).

The idea that images are of vast importance has found support in research. Christian Rudder, co-founder of the dating website OKCupid (I consider OKCupid a dating website since although it now has an app in addition to its website, it has features of dating websites such as the opportunity for extensive text and the use of algorithms), conducted a study from a nationally representative data set of thousands of OKCupid users in the United States and concluded that profile text constitutes only 10% of what people look at on a profile (Rudder 2014). Images matter far more than profile text when it comes to receiving romantic interest in online dating. Commenting on his research, he summarizes that when it comes to online dating, "your picture *is* worth that fabled thousand words, but your actual words are worth… almost nothing" (Rudder 2014). Supporting Rudder's conclusions is De Vries's finding that photographs were equally, if not more, important in generating young people's interest in online profiles (De Vries 2010: 538). Thus scholarly evidence concerning online dating websites is that dating compatibility algorithms are ineffective, while images matter greatly.

Dating apps are different from online dating, but they inherit the legacy of online dating as the modern way to date via technology. The success of image-oriented dating apps such as Tinder, which forgo the capability of displaying large amounts of text, seems to offer yet more validation for the critical role visual communication plays in arousing partnering interest. Hence it is unsurprising that dating with technology has moved from questionnaire-based online dating to mobile image-based dating apps which rely on users to make matches themselves through images.

1.2 Conceptual Background

An interpretive sociological framework is employed to understand how risk plays into dating app behaviors such as rejection of certain profiles and selection of profile pictures. Risk is perceived as a potential future that is a result of human action (Couch et al. 2012: 669; Zinn 2008; Hall 2001; Lupton 2006), and some have theorized that it "should be controlled through personal responsibility" (Couch et al. 2012: 669). In their investigation of perceived "dangers of online dating" (Couch et al. 2012: 697), they found that "all participants believed that online dating was risky in some way" (Couch et al. 2012: 697). Concern over risk is a vestige from online dating that may influence dating app practices; how is risk mitigated? Risk applies to theorizing ambiguity in dating app images, later addressed in section 3.

Additionally, Anthony Giddens's *The Transformation of Intimacy* provides a framework for conceptualizing romance that extends to communication taking place on the romantic sites of dating apps. He argues that modern romantic intimacy is based on conceptualizations of authenticity and incomplete self-identity. Intimacy in a relationship relies on "mutual disclosure" (Giddens 1992: 6) so that the authentic incomplete selves generate "psychic communication" (Giddens 1992: 45). This mental connection means that "the other, by being who he or she is, answers a lack… directly to do with self-identity: in some sense, the flawed individual is made whole" (Giddens 1992: 45). In other words, intimacy in romantic love is fostered primarily through closeness with the mind of the other and the mind of the self, selves that are incomplete. It is only once these selves meet that each partner's identity become complete. Intimacy, and therefore the ideal romantic love, stems from a need for another fully realized identity to complete one's self-identity through authentic interaction. Giddens's theory is helpful for thinking about how notions of romance and authenticity are sustained as a result of dating app technologies.

2. Data Sample

To better contextualize Giddens's framework, I undertook a qualitative interpretive sociological study of young people. Using a mixed-methods data collection strategy, I conducted an online survey with follow-up interviews via Skype. The population parameter was that potential participants had to have been living in America for at least six months of the past four years. The consent form and questions made clear that participants were being asked specifically about their experiences of dating apps in America. The sample was geographically limited to New York City and its surrounding area. This of course limits the generalizability of any findings.

The sample's ages ranged from 18 to 29 years old, despite the survey being available to anyone over 18. Yet this range reflects the typical user of these apps. As Smith points out, "22% of 18- to 24-year-olds now report using mobile dating apps, a more than fourfold increase from… 2013" (Smith 2016). Therefore that age group of "young adults are now more likely than any other age group to use mobile dating apps" (Smith 2016). 86 people responded to the survey; 74 met the conditions to participate. Six interviews were also conducted with two women, three men, and one non-binary individual. All information was anonymized by the researcher; any names used in subsequent reports are aliases.

The survey sample was skewed toward women (74.3% of respondents). There was a mix of sexualities, with the majority (61.6%) identifying as heterosexual. Most were students, with 75.7% currently enrolled in a university. 93% of survey respondents used the dating app Tinder, which is therefore the dating app primarily discussed in the analysis.

2.1 Data Collection

The final version of the Google Forms survey was distributed through snowball sampling with numerous entry points from March to May 2016. Discussed here are responses to the open-ended questions asked, such as how participants chose their profile images and what constitutes an ideal profile with which to match. They were also asked about what constituted bad profiles as well as the reasoning behind their choice of favorite dating app.

Six semi-structured interviews were conducted via Skype in May 2016 to supplement the questionnaire results and expand on themes. Conversations were manually transcribed from interview audio recordings. Statements were then thematically hand coded using grounded theory techniques (Gibbs 2007; Pfeffer 2014). Open-ended survey responses were also sorted according to similar thematic codes to those found in the interviews. Since survey responses were compared with the interviews in order to confirm themes, themes discussed in the analysis using interview quotes were therefore patterns also reflected in the survey data.

2.2 A Note on Limitations

It must be noted that the sample was limited demographically, and obviously the non-systematic recruitment of participants meant that the sample could not be construed as a random or statistically representative of any group. The fact that it was small and self-selecting further limits any claims to generalizability. Additionally, the data could have benefitted from quantitative analysis through statistical software. However, within the qualitative framework and short timeframe of the study, it was not possible to analyze correlative or other relationships among variables.

3. Findings and Issues

The data show that users describe themselves as being quite adept at reading image codes via mobile devices to determine aspects of identity, values, and personalities. In fact, it seemed so much so that it is arguably a novel form of visual literacy. This "image reading" differs from historical notions of codes in images and of representational conventions in art studies, where there was a decisive understanding of image based on a written scholarly code. Rather, this form of communication has developed socially and organically among users without a driving "correct" dictionary of codes developed by gatekeepers. Digital natives are constructing their own visual language through technology.

Notably, a dichotomy between authenticity and ambiguity marked user discourse on dating app profile images. Images were interpreted by users according to what they believed to be generally understood image codes in order to determine if authenticity or ambiguity was implied. Authenticity and ambiguity are useful examples of how "image readings," i.e., visual literacy, operates in dating app spaces.

3.1 Personal Safety and Concerns over Ambiguity

Concern over safety and fears over deception explain why ambiguous imagery alarms users and can help explain why visual literacy in this domain has developed. People within the sample age are digital natives, having grown up with mobile communication, social media, and the internet. They have therefore learned to seek cues of fake profiles and danger online. Use of networked technologies within dating apps, such as the incorporation of social media websites, appears to have an important role in establishing authenticity.

Tinder was among the first dating apps connected to Facebook. It establishes security through its link to Facebook, a feature for which users expressed appreciation. Tinder's anchor to Facebook means that the identities presented on Tinder are probably real, as it is difficult to make a fake Facebook profile. The only photos Tinder users can put up on their profile come from Facebook, doubling Tinder's appropriate content settings with Facebook's. Tinder does not allow for private sharing of photos, furthering its reputation as a secure place to interact with real people without fear of unsolicited sexual images.

The connection between social media networks and dating app social networks means Tinder's connection with Facebook contributes to security; users can trust identities presented, confident that they will not be bombarded with unwanted images in private chats.

Despite the Facebook connection, study respondents remain concerned over valid identities and are deeply attuned to ambiguous images, which are perceived negatively. When asked about safety, users express concern by describing ambiguous imagery. As Tina describes, "if like, some people only have photos of them doing things, but it's always from the back or in the distance, then that's a sign that they've got a bad face and they're hiding it." Essentially, this hiding of one's face is seen as a sign of deception. User responses did not find it understandable that some people would disguise their appearances if they did not consider themselves attractive. Ambiguous images were always value-laden with negative language and marked by users as "red flags." Other cues constituting ambiguous imagery include blurry images, group photos, incomplete profiles, and what users determined to be meticulously staged images. Users expected full disclosure of identity in their profiles, which is perhaps why Tinder, being anchored to Facebook, is their dating app of choice.

3.2 Authenticity in Profile Images

Authenticity is presented as the other feature to look for in images in contradistinction to ambiguity. Dating apps have been stigmatized as superficial due to their image basis ("Woman wears fat suit on Tinder date", W1). In this assumption, people are implying that Tinder users select matches based solely on their looks. However, the data show that people select their profile photos to reflect hobbies and other values—that is, their personality.

> *"I tried to use images that represented, like, some values that I have." (Milan)*

> *[I chose photos of myself] "traveling and cooking and I'm also like slightly on the political side so that's why I have a picture of the demonstrations." (Sanjay)*

The research reveals the care people take in selecting their own profile images and choosing other images to match with; superficial approaches were absent in self-descriptions. Rather, users make meaning through their attentive selection to profile images and choices of who to match with; generally, the meaning sought is to reflect authenticity.

Respondents displayed an emphasis on impression management. Milan, for example, expressed his concern about being as clear that his status was a medical student rather than a doctor: "I wanted to make sure that people knew exactly, like, in which position I was at the time." To do this, he made sure not to display any photos of himself on his profile of him at school wearing medical clothing. Such sentiment reflects how users deliberately anticipate how they will be perceived in terms of authenticity.

Users look for evidence of mutual interests, personality, and positive character in profile images, drawing on settings and activities presented. They consider their own dating app profiles reflections of their authentic selves and opt for disclosure of personality and realistic examples of their physical appearance through their choice of profile pictures. In the context of dating app romance, people want someone to like them for who they "truly," authentically are.

With the ability to take multiple digital photos instantly with a smartphone, users have unprecedented access to flattering images. Therefore, although people were concerned with looking attractive, they sought to do so within a more meaningful photo that captured an aspect of their personality or interests. The importance of authenticity is doubled; users want photos that accurately capture their appearance but also display an aspect of their authentic internal self. The data refute claims about divided digital selves, such as those advanced by Ansari and Klinenberg in their statement "the fact that your interactions on your phone can have such a profound effect on people's impression of you as a person makes it clear that you basically have two selves now—your real-world self and your phone self" (Ansari–Klinenberg 2015: 47). In fact, users express a genuine belief that their profiles reflect their inner sense of self and expect profiles of others to also be authentic.

4. Conclusion

This brief chapter can only sketch key points concerning the study's findings. First is that visual literacy is constructed through image codes created by the consumption and distribution of images, perhaps compounded by the use of multiple social media platforms. These image codes are noteworthy in that they structure people's notions of how to perceive and convey authenticity solely through images on their dating app profiles. They share a visual language, with codes and cues that mark identity and meaning.

Dating apps' image basis arguably fosters a new visual literacy based on communicating particular codes in profile images. Visual literacy plays out on both sides of dating app user interaction, as users embed codes in their selection of their own profile images and read them into others' profile images. The dichotomy of ambiguity and authenticity in dating app images illustrates how image codes operate in the development of visual literacy, potentially as a result of concern over risk.

I found that Giddens's theory of romance is partially upheld in my investigation of the modern media of dating apps. However, his point regarding incomplete selves does not appear to resonate with study participant experiences. Dating app users seemed to already feel that their authentic self-identities were very much whole and on-display for others to "take or leave," depending on whether or not people thought the images (and implied values) presented were compatible. They did not seek another person in order to have a sense of a complete self-identity. Nevertheless, his theory of romantic intimacy links authenticity and self-disclosure with romance, a connection reproduced in user discourse on dating app images. Authenticity was a driving value in communication through profile images for the purpose of connecting people/selves, and therefore a factor in romantic interaction.

Visual literacy potentially operates beyond dating apps like Tinder, such as in image-heavy social network technologies like Facebook, Instagram, and Snapchat. This study highlights how more academic attention needs to be paid to image-based dating apps specifically as opposed to grouping them together with studies of online dating. Dating app technologies have given new significance to the power of visual communication. Their contribution to everyday practices of interpreting visual images will be affecting not only any given person's life course, but additively, the larger picture of how society will operate in the future.

References

Ansari, Aziz – Klinenberg, Eric (2015): *Modern Romance*. Penguin.

Bilton, Nick (2014): Tinder, the fast-growing dating app, taps an age-old truth. *The New York Times*. https://www.nytimes.com/2014/10/30/fashion/tinder-the-fast-growing-dating-app-taps-an-age-old-truth.html [30. 03. 2017].

Couch, Danielle – Liamputtong, Pranee – Pitts, Marian (2012): What are the Real and Perceived Risks and Dangers of Online Dating? Perspectives from Online Daters: Health Risks in the Media. *Health, Risk & Society* 14/7–8: 697–714.

de Vries, Jan (2010): Impact of Self-descriptions and Photographs on Mediated Dating Interest. *Marriage & Family Review* 46/8: 538–562.

Finkel, Eli J. – Eastwick, Paul W. – Karney, Benjamin R. – Reis, Harry T. – Sprecher, Susan (2012): Online Dating: a Critical Analysis from the Perspective of Psychological Science. *Psychological Science in the Public Interest* 13/1: 3–66.

Gibbs, Graham R. (2007): Thematic Coding and Categorizing. In: *Analyzing Qualitative Data*. London: Sage. n.p.

Giddens, Anthony (1992): *The Transformation Of Intimacy: Sexuality, Love And Eroticism in Modern Societies*. John Wiley & Sons.

Hall, David (2001): The Sociology of Risk and Social Demographic Change. *PSC Discussion Papers Series* 15/12: 1.

Lupton, Deborah (2006): Sociology and Risk. In: Mythen, Gabe – Walklate, Sandra (eds.): *Beyond the Risk Society: Critical Reflections on Risk and Human Security*. Maidenhead: Open University Press.

Pfeffer, Carla A. (2014): "I Don't Like Passing as a Straight Woman": Queer Negotiations of Identity and Social Group Membership. *American Journal of Sociology* 120/1: 1–44.

Rudder, Christian (2014): *Dataclysm: Who We Are (When We Think No One's Looking)*. Random House Incorporated.

Smith, Aaron (2016): 15% of American Adults Have Used Online Dating Sites or Mobile Dating Apps. *Pew Research Center: Internet, Science & Tech.* http://www.pewinternet.org/2016/02/11/15-percent-of-american-adults-have-used-online-dating-sites-or-mobile-dating-apps/ [18. 05. 2017].

Zinn, Jens (2008): *Social Theories of Risk and Uncertainty: an Introduction.* Oxford: Blackwell Publishing.

W1 = Woman wears fat suit on Tinder date (2014): *Cosmopolitan.* http://www.cosmopolitan.com.au/love/ woman-wears-fat-suit-on-tinder-date-2473 [01. 05. 2017].

Ágnes Veszelszki

Verbal and Visual Aggression in Trolling

1. Introduction

Social media has become so pervasive in society that it is easy to forget that this form of communication became global only around 20 years ago. Myspace was launched in 2003, Facebook in 2004, Twitter in 2006, Instagram in 2010, Pinterest and Snapchat in 2011, and Periscope only in 2015. In other words, in 2017 even the oldest and most popular social networking website was less than 15 years old, and the youngest one was only a couple of months old (cf. Rampton 2016). Still, during these one and a half decades social networking websites have had a tremendous impact on society and on how people communicate and think. This paper deals with trolling as a new type of behaviour taking place in the internet, specifically, social media. Although trolls are not only present in social media (the first descriptions of trolls date back to the 1980s: Doyle 1898; Maddox 1989; cf. Hardaker 2013: 58), their activity presented here can be typically observed in social media.

According to Márton Petykó, who examined the identity and linguistic behaviour of trolls from a functional pragmatic aspect, "the process of identity construction is dominated by linguistic identity practices, as the use of non-linguistic tools (such as images) is restricted to the interacting participants, particularly commenters" (Petykó 2013: 281). My argument in this paper is that although internet trolling is indeed characterised by verbal identity construction, visual tools may also appear dominantly in it.

To analyse this, I will first outline the verbal and visual forms of online aggression, trolling as an online behaviour (troll types, trolling strategies and areas typically exposed to trolling). This will be followed by some examples of verbal and visual trolling, and finally a few ideas will be suggested for handling trolls.

2. Online Aggression

Considering the findings of international literature it can be assumed that quasi-anonymity and the lack or weakness of reprisals make computer-mediated communication harsher than offline communication and give more room to offensive, personal remarks (cf. Wallace 2006: 143; Hardaker 2013) which are difficult to handle, as there are no established language strategies, only suggestions for guidance (mainly for social marketing purposes).

Aggression is one of the most basic patterns of human behaviour. "It has been said that he who was the first to abuse his fellow-man instead of knocking out his brains without a word laid thereby the basis of civilisation" (Hughlings-Jackson 1879/1958: 179). Naturally, this does not mean at all that offence, abuse and verbal aggression are positive attitudes, but as they form part of our lives, we have to learn how to handle them.

Verbal aggression is "a form of verbal behaviour, a verbal act by which the speaker wants to directly or indirectly (but in any case deliberately) abuse, insult or offend another person with the content and/or quality [e.g. high volume] of the utterance" (Kegyesné Szekeres 2008: 61). Certain forms of verbal aggression are even criminalised (such as libel, defamation, blackmailing or hate speech). Milder, more ordinary types of verbal aggression which entail no or only social/psychological sanctions are the use of profanities or offensive language. Verbal aggression causes damage to the victim in the same way as physical aggression. "Examining the diversity of utterances, we find that any linguistic element, usage characteristic, manner of turn-taking organization [...] can become a vehicle for aggression. Aggression can take many forms, including volume, intonation, word choice, wording, irony or the interruption of the partner [...]" (Domonkosi 2008: 54).

Verbal aggression can be direct and indirect. Direct verbal aggression is usually taken to include mocking, taunting, teasing, cursing, making personal remarks to or verbally abusing the partner, and using profanities and foul language. In its indirect form verbal aggression includes lies, libel, malevolent gossip, intrigues, and even certain forms of jokes.

Technological development is constantly increasing the importance of transferring visual information in digital communication as well (cf. Veszelszki 2017). As opposed to verbal language with its conventionalized symbols permitting only linear decoding, visual language can be decoded quickly and simply. The perception of visual information differs from that of verbal information, which enhances its role in conveying offensive attitudes, further differentiating it from texts. Internet psychology expert Patricia Wallace analysed an escalating conflict in a series of emails where visual signs and emoticons were also used: when the tone of the emails was neutral, the emoticons softened the possible harshness of the utterances. "When the emoticons were added to really nasty messages, however, the smileys just made them look even more sarcastic" (Wallace 1999: 103).

There are relatively few research findings in this field of study. The most relevant research questions are the following: To what extent can visual (or audiovisual) information be offensive? Is it verbal or visual information that can be more offensive?

In digital communication offences are often "disguised", which makes them more difficult to identify. Quite commonly, particularly in online communication, aggressors do not admit or make explicit their awareness of being offensive or insulting. On the contrary, they expressly deny this by giving offensive remarks an appearance as if they were only jokes or humorous, ironic remarks. A troll can only obstruct a conversation until their behaviour is exposed by another participant of the conversation. The same seems to be true to cyberbullying[1]: a cyberbully can conceal their offensive behaviour for quite a long time pretending to be joking or bantering (which may also be considered as a strategy of manipulation). The question is when this behaviour reaches a point where it should be considered as an offence or bullying rather than bantering. Naturally, some situations are easier to identify, such as the ones where direct insults, foul language and swear words are used. However, in such situations it still remains a question whether a few swear words are the signs of offensive attitude or the markers of a group identity (such as the in-group verbal insults of Turkish youngsters living in Germany; cf. Günthner 2008: 64–69).

Although early studies in internet communication explained the increased presence of aggression with physical remoteness and anonymity (e.g. Wallace 2006: 160; Hardaker 2013: 59), social networking websites turned anonymous (or through nicknames: pseudo-anonymous) online presence to presence through digital identity where users use their real names (Veszelszki 2015a). Now many users can be identified, for example, through their Facebook profile, which includes their name, photo and (at least partly) public personal data, but verbal aggression is still present in comments to the same extent.

3. Troll as an Internet Role

In virtual communication involving multiple participants (e.g. on internet forums or social networking websites), a *troll*[2] is a person who intentionally causes disturbance and disagreement, a provocateur (Veszelszki ed. 2012), "a CMC user who constructs the identity of sincerely wishing to be part of the group in question [...], but whose real intention(s) is/are to cause disruption and/or to trigger or exacerbate conflict for the purposes of their own amusement" (Hardaker

1 Cyberbullying is the aggressive, intentional act or behaviour of harassing, bullying a person online by sending or posting mean, hurtful, threatening, or intimidating messages, usually anonymously.

2 On the basis of Donath (1999), Hardaker (2013: 58) distinguishes "the post (a troll), the individual (a troller), and the act (trolling)". In Hungarian "troll" means the actor and "trollkodás" (trolling) the act.

2010: 237). Trolls usually try to disturb communication with hateful or personal remarks, incomprehensible or irrelevant comments (Shin 2008). This destructive and deceptive behaviour is called *trolling*. "Online trolling is the practice of behaving in a deceptive, destructive, or disruptive manner in a social setting on the Internet with no apparent instrumental purpose" (Buckels – Trapnell – Paulhus 2014: 97). Sarah Jeong (2015) describes undesirable content on the internet as garbage which might be a spam, malware or a threat directed towards another user. Trolling belongs to this latter category.

The word "troll" is commonly derived from the name of a quarrelsome aggressive creature in Scandinavian mythology, fantasy literature and role playing games (W1). According to another theory, the word "trolling" refers to a fishing technique where the lure is slowly dragged from a moving boat (W2; Petykó 2013: 274).

Claire Hardaker (2010) uses the concepts deception/fraud, aggression, disorganisation and success to describe trolling from the perspective of linguistic politeness. However, trolling can also be related to other social phenomena, such as manipulation, insults, and taunting. Manipulation is a form of influencing where one person wants to influence the thoughts, opinion, emotions or behaviour of another person (generally without the latter becoming aware of it; cf. Van Dijk 2006). By throwing insults, the insulter can obtain a dominant position and/or make his/her existing or hypothetical dominant position more articulate. One of the main causes of insults is "the competition for power and dominance, the provocation of the insulted person, or simply the venting of negative emotions and frustration" (Heltai 2016: 2). By taunting, the speaker also tries to make the other person look inferior, discredit the other person and at the same time strengthen his/her own positive self-image. Showing contempt for somebody can also serve to express that the uttered words are not valid for the utterer (Batár 2007; Veszelszki et al. forthcoming).[3]

In trolling, humour and aggression intertwine. Humour is an umbrella term for non-serious, non-threatening playful communication activities which involve cognitive incongruence, some aggression, psychological relief, and "joke work" (Witzarbeit), as Freud put it (Freud 1905/1985; Brock 2008: 555). Several authors underline the power of surprise as well. Due to its multi-functionality, humour is a highly effective communication tool (Brock 2008: 555). Although there are several forms of humour, aggression theories hold that humour has an (at least mild) aggressive component (Norrick 2001: 1438). Aggressive humour is intentionally and usually malevolently directed at a victim: the direct recipient or a

3 On the rhetoric of trolling cf. Danka 2016.

third person, whether present or absent (Brock 2008: 551). Aggressive humour is especially effective in forming group identity (and excluding outsiders), and in expressing power and dominance.

3.1 Troll Types

Judit Rudas (2016) distinguishes two main types of trolls on the basis of their relationship with the communication partner(s). According to her, the "provocative troll" tries to get attention or disturb the conversation by posting a comment which can arouse passion (usually disguised as a serious statement or question). "Reactive trolls", on the other hand, pick specific users to insult, intentionally misinterpreting their words and sending them personal remarks.

To use and extend the categories of Rudas (2016; categories 1–6), the most typical trolling behaviours are the following: 1. "First trolls" usually post comments under YouTube videos with the single word "first". 2. "Aggressive trolls" post harsh, violent, and often obscene comments. They always express a negative opinion regardless of the topic and without considering counter-arguments. They only make personal remarks. They tend to type in all caps, which symbolises shouting (e.g.: *STUPID XD*). 3. There are trolls who press on with their political or religious views and come up with the same preferred political or religious issues in connection with any topic and refuse any counter-opinion. 4. The "know-it-all trolls" immediately reassure the community in the case of an information uncertainty that they can complete or correct what has been said. The comments of such trolls are characterised by irony and open sarcasm. 5. A sub-category of the know-it-all troll is the Grammar Nazi who directs attention to others' alleged or real spelling or grammatical mistakes in a sermonizing, sarcastic tone, less often with good intentions. 6. "Grammar trolls" specialise in provoking this type of users by "playing dumb", "which entails intentionally misspelling a word or a phrase in order to solicit reactions or corrections from those unable to tolerate faulty grammar, [...] known as Grammar Nazis" (W3). 7. The "meme propagator" is up to date with the latest memes (text, image or video) and will post them even if they are irrelevant to the subject. 8. The comments of "emoticon abuser trolls" are generally difficult to understand, as it does not make any meaningful contribution to the subject, only expresses a feeling or a mood, often laughing at the previous comment. 9. The "copy/paste troll" posts a series of events in an apparently authentic way, but as the narrative unfolds it turns out that it was taken from a film script or the lyrics of a song. 10. The "shocker" shocks the victims with pornographic or terrifying visual content. The list is naturally not exhaustive; it can be extended with many other troll types.

3.2 The Natural Habitat of Trolls

Trolls usually appear in multiparty online communication situations. Initially, the most exposed areas were internet forums, but now trolls prefer social media message walls and groups.

A former study on bereavement (Veszelszki – Parapatics 2016) showed that trolls can appear in unexpected situations and that nothing is "sacred" for them. This study analysed the forms of death announcements and grieving in social media. Negative comments may also appear, if rarely, on memorial pages both from real friends and posters with no real attachment (RIP trolls or memorial trolls; cf. Camber – Neville 2011). The trolls (sometimes using fake user names) post indecent or irrelevant comments to the death announcement or its commentary. As such comments are usually moderated (deleted), we did not find any specific example in our Hungarian corpus but we could deduct from certain reactions that they did exist. Inappropriate comments (sent by malevolent trolls) may become a source of conflict between grieving family members, sympathizing posters and illegitimate persons. In such cases, grievers use the option of moderation (deletion) and keep on posting their difficulties with processing the trauma.

3.3 Troll Strategies

Spotting trolls, i.e. identifying trolling as such, is not always easy.[4] Hardaker (2013: 62–64) argues that trolling happens in the "grey zone" between the reconstruction of speakers' intentions and the assumptions of listeners.[5] Users can never be sure (1) whether there is a real intention behind an apparently offensive comment or only the context or the readers' associations make it look so; or (2) whether a comment reflects real lack of knowledge or the apparent naivety (and misspelling) is a deliberate deception. The latter dilemma appears in the following comment of a Facebook user under the post (written about a completely different subject) of a well-known international lawyer who is also an active public figure in Hungary: *Maybe Mr X as an international lawyer could help forex debtors, couldn't he?* This comment received no responses, so the trolling was not revealed, still it looks suspicious.

---

4 More than 500 respondents completed the survey designed by Judit Rudas (2016) which prompted respondents to decide whether a given situation (with images) is subject to trolling. The method also raises the question whether lay language users or scientists with meta-linguistic knowledge are better in excluding (?) subjective factors and identifying trolls.

5 Cf. in this context on-record and off-record impoliteness strategies in politeness theories (Brown – Levinson 1978; Szili 2007: 10).

A revealed trolling case draws attention to this strategy of trolls. A special subcategory of trolls deceives users by pretending to be ignorant and so mocking ignorance, lack of education, and erroneous pseudo-scientific views and movements go viral on the internet. The post and series of related comments in *Figures 1 and 2* may be an example of this, where the commenter states that 11-year-olds have no kidney, as this organ only develops at puberty. The comment created a great stir and was shared by many users as an image which received loads of comments guessing whether the outrageous post was serious. The mystery was solved by a commenter who alleged she knew the poster personally and that he often posted messages with a similar content (factual errors) and form (typos).

Figure 1–2: Trolling

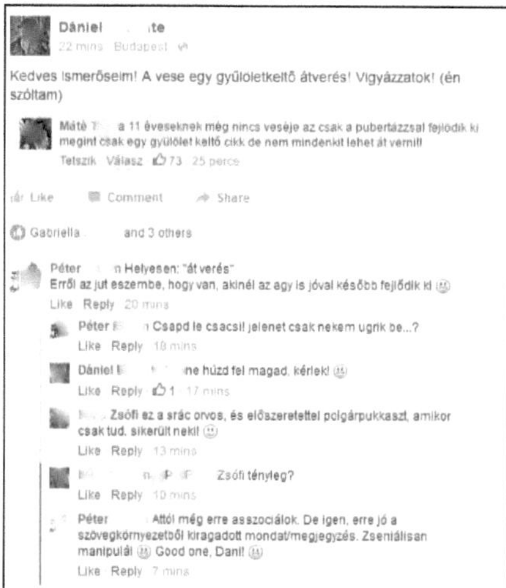

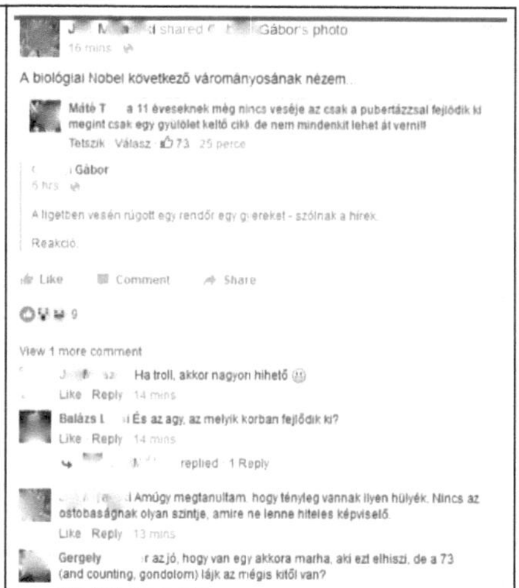

Post1:	**Post2:**
[user1] Dear Friends, The kidney post is a hoax designed to incite hatred. Beware! (I warned you) "An 11-year-old child has no kidney, it only develops at puberty. So this article is yet another instance of hate speech, but not everyone can be fooled!!"	[user4] And this year's Nobel Prize in Biology goes to: "An 11-year-old child has no kidney, it only develops at puberty. So this article is yet another instance of hate speech, but not everyone can be fooled!! »A boy was kicked on the liver by a police officer in Városliget, according to the news.«"

Comments:	Comments:
[user2] Correctly: "hox" This makes me think that certain people's brain also develops at a later stage. ☺ […] [user1] Just don't be upset. ☺ [user3] this guy is a doctor and loves to outrage people whenever possible. He succeeded. ☺ [user3] Really? [user2] […] But, indeed, this is what posts/ remarks without context are good for. Excellent manipulation! ☺ Good one, [user1] ☺	[user4] If he's a troll, he's convincing. ☺ [user5] And at what age does the brain develop? [user4] If there's one thing I've learned in life, it's that stupid people actually exist. Only two things are infinite: the universe and stupidity. [user6] I accept that there is a moron who bought this, but who on earth gave the 73 (and probably counting) likes?

(source: Facebook, July 2016)

Hardaker (2013) analysed a corpus of nearly 3,800 Usenet discourses (including more than 86 million words) focusing on the perception of trolls by other users and disregarding the intentions of the speakers. On the basis of the large corpus, Hardaker distinguished between six troll strategies: digression, (hypo)criticism, antipathising, endangering, shocking and aggressing. These strategies were placed on a scale from overt to covert (*Figure 3*).

Figure 3: Troll strategies on a scale

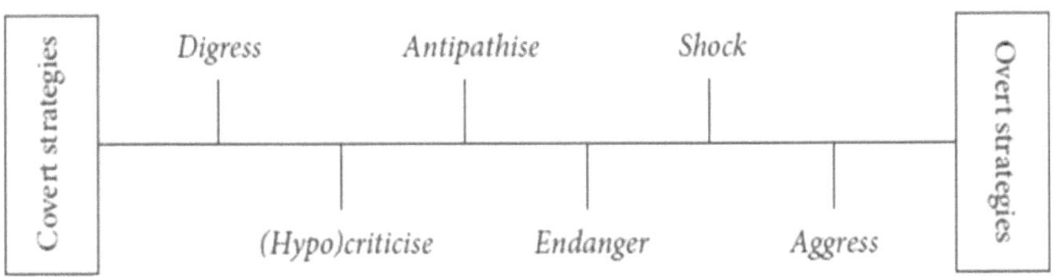

(source: Hardaker 2013: 80)

Due to the data collection method used, Hardaker's corpus only contained verbal elements and could not take into consideration visual troll strategies (and visual reactions to trolling). It would be reasonable to extend the discourse about trolling to include the aspect of visuality.

4. Trolls' Verbal and Visual Tools

In a Hungarian context, troll identity and linguistic behaviour was only analysed by Márton Petykó (2013) from a functional cognitive pragmatic aspect. Petykó summarises the characteristics of (political) trolls in three points, which are the result of relative anonymity, the casual character of the community and the linguistic character of the common activity: "1. The construction of identity is dominated by linguistic identity practices as the use of non-linguistic tools (e.g. images) is restricted to interacting participants, especially commenters [...]; 2. Identity manipulation is relatively easy through deception [...]; 3. The troll identity is typically casual, because when someone is identified as a troll in a given discourse, the discursive consequences will be restricted to the given discourse" (Petykó 2013: 281).

A look at troll properties identified by Petykó on a Facebook page (on the basis of empirical research on the Facebook page Trollfoci; cf. Veszelszki 2015b, 2015c) reveals that Facebook users, based on the website's rules and general practices in Hungary, registered with their real names (though obviously there are fictitious profiles), so relative anonymity is not applicable to Facebook discourses. The composition of the community is usually contingent, indeed, but on a Facebook page (such as the examined Trollfoci) it is only partly casual as troll campaigns take place repeatedly, although with a very large number of participants and with varying composition. Furthermore, Facebook (also) enables its users to share visual and video information in posts and comments, which primarily takes the form of memes. This way, the linguistic activity which excludes visual information, as referred to above, is not typical to this instance of discourse.[6]

The following section will present three possible examples of visual trolling.

If discourse is not restricted to a multi-party conversation, but is interpreted more widely, then the following example can be considered as visual trolling. Even a single viral photo conveying a negative message can create a communication crisis. In the summer of 2015, a customer of the fast food chain KFC shared a photo of a rat shaped piece of meat with the text that he was served deep fried rat at the restaurant. KFC was quick to react checking the piece of meat (kept by the customer as evidence) with the conclusion that it was an "unfortunately shaped" chicken. They expected the customer to apologise for damaging their corporate image, but this never happened. Although the allegation was not true, the grotesque story was shared by more than 22,000 times and even found its way to the

6 Petykó refers to this possibility as well (2013: 281, Footnote #6).

news, causing evident damage to goodwill, perhaps the most important asset of the food chain.

Image 4: Social media and complaint management: KFC customer alleges to receive deep fried rat instead of chicken in the restaurant

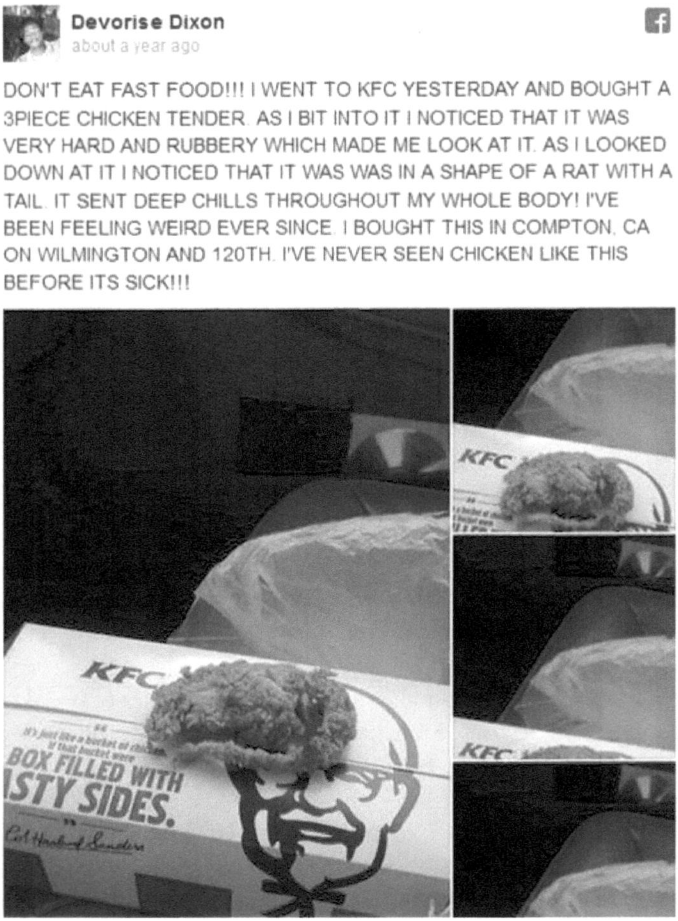

(source: screenshot by the author)

A narrower interpretation of the concept of discourse (cf. Tracy – Mirivel 2009) can be illustrated by the following example: Discourse can be killed by blocking communication between the administrators and followers of a page on a social networking website through overloading and troll campaigning. The users of Trollfoci, which is admittedly a hub for trolls, even used pictures to flood the Facebook page of a British football club with memes when Hungarian football player Bálint Bajner was transferred to the club. The images included variations of the well-known "*Keep calm and carry on*" poster (*Figure 5–7*).[7] By continuously posting the pictures (and hashtags related to the transfer and the footballer's name), the trolls virtually made the normal operation of the Facebook page impossible (for a detailed analysis cf. Veszelszki 2015b, 2015c). In this case making the act of trolling explicit could not prevent the effect due to the large number of trolls involved.

Figure 5–7: Three instances of the Keep Calm series

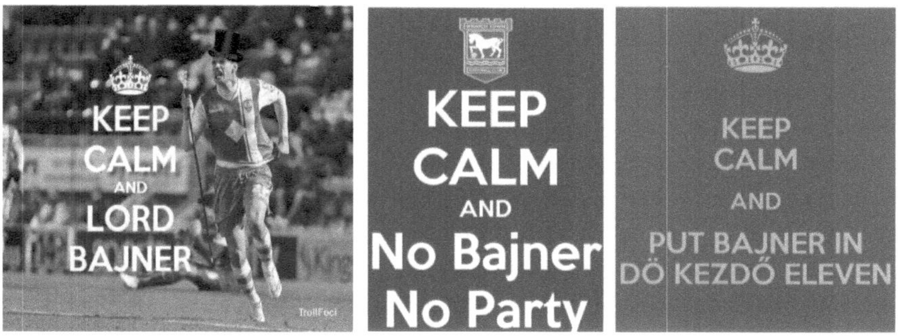

(source: Trollfoci, W5)

The third example of the connection between trolling and visuality is the so-called Trollface image (cf. Veszelszki 2013; *Figure 8*). According to knowyourmeme.com, a website identifying and categorising memes, Trollface is a "comic character wearing a mischievous smile that is meant to represent the facial expression of an internet troll. The image is most commonly used to portray a character as a troll in rage comics, or alternatively, to identify oneself or another participant as such in online discussions" (W6). "Posting a Trollface image into a forum thread is often used to claim that someone was being fooled or intentionally angered" (W3). Thus, the image can be used by trolls for self-identification and by users to reveal a troll.

7 The original poster was made in 1939 in Great Britain to encourage participation in WW2. However, it was only its rediscovery in 2000 when the poster gained international popularity (Lewis 2012). Since then the slogan has become a meme which can be found in the internet in many forms, with and without changes, with and without photo.

Figure 8: Trollface

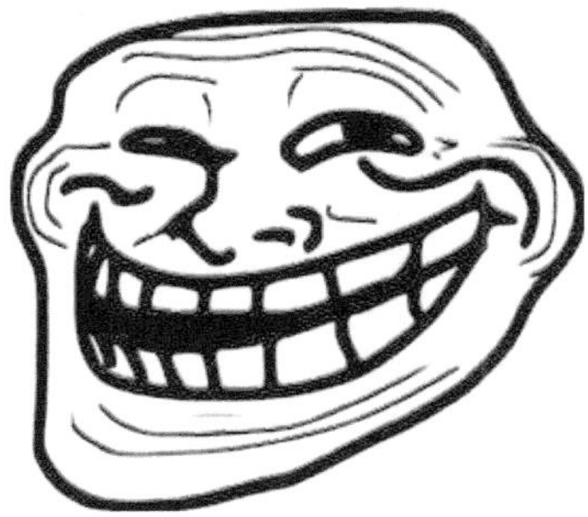

(source: internet meme)

5. Summary

In this paper I outlined the main characteristics of trolling as a behaviour and gave examples to argue that visuality is an integral part of trolling and should be considered when examining this phenomenon.

In conclusion, I would like to suggest a few ways to handle trolls. A number of internet articles are about forms of protection against trolling. Probably the most useful suggestion is that users should stay alert and have a critical view of online information (more generally: media awareness). In relation to trolls, most users recommend the following: „Don't react to deliberately provocative statements. Trolls gonna troll. Don't let yourself rise to obviously inflammatory comments that are only designed to provoke others. If you do, you're giving the trolls what they wanted. Pick your battles—if you suspect someone is just trying to get a rise out of you, don't give him or her the satisfaction" (Elliott 2015). In short: "don't feed the troll".

References

Batár, Levente (2007): A beszólás mint beszédaktus [Teasing as a speech act]. *Magyar Nyelvőr* 131/4: 451–464.

Brock, Alexander (2008): Humor, Jokes, and Irony versus Mocking, Gossip and Black Humor. In: Antos, Gerd – Ventola, Eija (eds.): *Handbook of Interpersonal Communication.* Handbooks of Applied Linguistics, Vol. 2. Berlin – New York: Mouton de Gruyter. 541–565.

Brown, Penelope – Levinson, Stephen C. (1978): Universals in Language Usage. Politeness Phenomena. In: Goody, Esther N. (ed.): *Questions and Politeness. Strategies in Social Interaction.* Cambridge Papers in Social Anthropology 8. Cambridge: Cambridge University Press. 56–232.

Buckels, Erin E. – Trapnell, Paul D. – Paulhus, Delroy L. (2014): Trolls just Want to Have Fun. The Dark Triad of Personality. *Personality and Individual Differences* 67: 97–102.

Camber, Rebecca – Neville, Simon (2011): Sick internet 'troll' who posted vile messages and videos taunting the death of teenagers is jailed for 18 WEEKS. *Daily Mail.* Online: http://www.dailymail.co.uk/news/article-2036935/Natasha-MacBryde-death-Facebook-internet-troll-Sean-Duffy-jailed.html

Danka, István (2016): Mit tanulhatunk a trolltól? Adalékok a trollkodás retorikájához [What can we learn from the troll? On rhetoric of trolling]. In: Horváth, Gizella – Bakó, Rozália Klára (eds.): *Közbeszédaktusok. Argumentor Műhely.* Nagyvárad – Debrecen: Partium Kiadó – Debreceni Egyetemi Kiadó. 57–70.

Domonkosi, Ágnes (2008): A nyelvi agresszió szerepe a személyközi viszonylatokban [The role of verbal aggression in interpersonal communication]. In: Zimányi, Árpád (ed.): *Az agressziókutatásról interdiszciplináris keretben.* Eger: EKF Líceum Kiadó. 53–59.

Donath, Judith (1999): Identity and Deception in the Virtual Community. In: Kollock, Peter – Smith, Marc A. (eds.): *Communities in Cyberspace.* London: Routledge. 29–59.

Doyle, Jennifer (1989): <hick!> Google Groups. 14. 12. 1989. https://groups.google.com/forum/#!msg/alt.callahans/SphfCkUsdtY/FggkP4rvoQEJ.

Elliott, Amy-Mae (2015): How to debate the big issues on social media. *Mashable.* http://mashable.com/2015/03/16/social-media-etiquette-debates/ [15. 09. 2016].

Freud, Sigmund (1905/1985): *Der Witz und seine Beziehung zum Unbewussten.* Leipzig: Gustav Kiepenheuer.

Günthner, Susanne (2008): Interactional Sociolinguistics. In: Antos, Gerd – Ventola, Eija – Weber, Tilo (eds): *Handbook of Interpersonal Communication.* Berlin – New York: Mouton de Gruyter. 53–76.

Hardaker, Claire (2010): Trolling in Asynchronous Computer-Mediated Communication: From User Discussions to Academic Definitions. *Journal of Politeness Research* 6: 215–242.

Hardaker, Claire (2013): Uh....not_to_be_nitpicky_but...the_past. *Journal of Language Aggression and Conflict* 1/1: 58–86.

Heltai, Pál (2016): A sértés beszédaktusának sajátságosságai [Characteristics of insult as a speech act]. In: *Nyelv – nyelvtechnológia – nyelvpedagógia: 21. századi távlatok. XXV. Magyar Alkalmazott Nyelvészeti Kongresszus előadásai.* Budapest: PPKE.

Hughlings-Jackson, J. (1879/1958): On Affections of Speech from Disease of the Brain. In: Taylor, J. (ed.): *Selected Writings of John Hughlings Jackson.* Volume 2. New York: Basic Books. 184–204.

Jeong, Sarah 2015: *The Internet of Garbage*. Forbes Media.

Kegyesné Szekeres, Erika (2008): Verbális agresszió és nemi sztereotípiák [Verbal aggression and gender stereotypes]. In: Zimányi, Árpád (ed.): *Az agressziókutatásról interdiszciplináris keretben*. Eger: EKF Líceum Kiadó. 61–90.

Lewis, Bex (2012): The Renaissance of 'Keep Calm and Carry On'. *The Poster* 2: 7–23.

Maddox, Thomas (1989): Re: CyberSpacee Conference. 22. 10. 1989. Google Groups. https://groups.google.com/forum/#!msg/alt.cyberpunk/976Vj979FPX973Q/973Ytxg-JeCdMJ.

Norrick, Neal R. (2001): Jokes and Joking in Conversation. In: Brinker, Klaus – Antos, Gerd – Heinemann, Wolfgang – Svager, Sven F. (eds.): *Text- und Gesprächslinguistik. Linguistics of Text and Conversation. Ein internationales Handbuch zeitgenössischer Forschung. An International Handbook of Contemporary Research 2*. Berlin – New York: Walter de Gruyter. 1438–1449.

Petykó, Márton (2013): Az internetes troll mint identitás kialakítása politikai blogok diskurzusaiban [Internet troll as an identity assumed in the discourse of political blogs]. *Magyar Nyelvőr* 137/3: 274–313.

Rampton, John (2016): 5 powerful ways social media has forever altered the way we do business. *Mashable*. http://mashable.com/2016/09/14/5-ways-social-media-changed-business/ [06. 10. 2016].

Rudas, Judit (2016): *A trollok nyelvi viselkedésének pragmatikai elemzése* [A pragmatic analysis of the linguistic behaviour of trolls]. BA thesis, manuscript. Consultant: Ágnes Veszelszki. Budapest: ELTE BTK.

Shin, Jiwon (2008): Morality and Internet Behavior: A Study of the Internet Troll and its Relation with Morality on the Internet. *Technology and Teacher Education Annual Review* 5: 28–34.

Szili Katalin (2007): Az udvariasság pragmatikája [The pragmatics of politeness]. *Magyar Nyelvőr* 131/1: 1–17.

Tracy, Karen – Mirivel, Julien C. (2009): Discourse Analysis: The Practice and Practical Value of Taping, Transcribing, and Analyzing Talk. In: Frey, Lawrence R. – Cissna, Kenneth N. (eds.): *Routledge Handbook of Applied Communication Research*. New York: Routledge. 153–178.

Van Dijk, Teun A. (2006): Discourse and Manipulation. *Discourse and Society* 17/2: 359–386.

Veszelszki, Ágnes – Falyuna, Nóra – Fodorné Tóth, Krisztina – Tóth, Aliz (2017, forthcoming): Az internetbiztonság kommunikáció- és nyelvtudományi aspektusból [Internet security from a communication and linguistic perspective]. In: Ollé, János (ed.).

Veszelszki, Ágnes (ed.) (2012): *Netszótár. @-tól a Zukbergnetig* [Net dictionary. From @ to Zukbergnet]. Budapest: ELTE Eötvös Kiadó.

Veszelszki, Ágnes (2013): Promiscuity of Images. Memes from an English-Hungarian contrastive perspective. In: Benedek, András – Nyíri, Kristóf (eds.): *How To Do Things With Pictures: Skill, Practice, Performance.* Frankfurt: Peter Lang.

Veszelszki, Ágnes (2015a): Megfontolások a digitális kommunikáció pragmatikai leírásához [Considerations for the pragmatic description of digital communication]. In: Bárdosi, Vilmos (ed.): *A nyelvi pragmatika kérdései szinkrón és diakrón megközelítésben.* Budapest: Tinta Könyvkiadó. 239–250.

Veszelszki, Ágnes (2015b): Konfliktuskezelés a közösségi médiában. Esettanulmány a Trollfoci vs. Notts County példáján [Conflict resolution in social media. The Trollfoci vs. Notts County case]. *Médiakutató* 2015/2: 39–51.

Veszelszki, Ágnes (2015c): Hogyan kezelhetők a trollok a PR eszközeivel? Online konfliktuskezelés egy futballklub Facebook-oldalán [Handling trolls with PR tools]. In: Sós, Péter János – Szécsi, Gábor (eds.): *Jövőkép és konfliktusok: A Public Relations elmélete és gyakorlata.* Budapest: Alapítvány a Public Relations Fejlesztéséért. 132–147.

Veszelszki, Ágnes – Parapatics, Andrea (2016): From Cooperation to Compassion: Death and Bereavement on Social Networking Websites. In: Knautz, Kathrin – Baran, Katsiaryna S. (eds.): *Facets of Facebook: Use and Users.* Series Knowledge & Information. Berlin – Boston: De Gruyter Mouton. 172–209.

Veszelszki, Ágnes (2017): *Digilect. The Impact of Infocommunication Technology on Language.* Series Knowledge & Information. Berlin – Boston: De Gruyter Mouton.

Wallace, Patricia 1999: *The Psychology of the Internet.* Cambridge: Cambridge University Press.

W1 = Troll. Online Etymology Dictionary. http://www.etymonline.com/index.php?term=troll [26. 10. 2016].

W2 = Troll. Merriam-Webster. http://www.merriam-webster.com/dictionary/troll [26. 10. 2016].

W3 = Trolling. Know your Meme. http://knowyourmeme.com/memes/subcul tures/trolling [26. 10. 2016].

W4 = KFC confirm: Deep Fried Rat is Actually Chicken. *Telegraph.* http://www.telegraph.co.uk/foodanddrink/foodanddrinknews/11695506/KFC-confirm-deep-fried-rat-is-actually-just-chicken.html [06. 10. 2016].

W5 = Trollfoci. https://www.facebook.com/troll0foci/ [26. 10. 2016].

W6 = Trollface. Know your Meme. http://knowyourmeme.com/memes/trollface-coolface-problem [26. 10. 2016].

Apocalyptic, Real, Medial

László Attila Hubbes

Revolution of the Eye. The Spectacular Rhetoric of the Apocalyptic

1. Introduction

The apocalyptic in itself represents a pictorial turn, a "revolution of the eye", already in its ancient anti-iconic context. Relying on projections of the imagination, the apocalyptic produces and reproduces spectacular representations which gain their strong expressiveness from combining images of the real and the uncanny, the monstrous and the desirable. Jewish, Christian or Muslim traditional apocalypses use symbolic and allegoric iconography for an encrypted narrative representation of worldly or transcendental realities, but also project concrete and vivid descriptions of world-ending disasters and reborn new worlds. The allusive, obscure and highly symbolic prophetic-visionary language of apocalyptic texts has always been doubled by the pictographic representations of visual arts. This essay focuses on the question of how the apocalyptic uses the pictorial heritage of various apocalyptic traditions, ancient and contemporary fantastic imagery, recombining them through visual means. The novelty of the essay, however, is the assertion that the essential, indeed revolutionary, strength of the apocalyptic spectacular lies in the masterful rhetorical use of apocalyptic verbal imagery.

For more than a quarter of a century, I have been fascinated with the spell of the apocalyptic mind, especially with the literary and art historical aspects of end-oriented spirituality, striving to bring arguments in favour of a well-defined apocalyptic category in aesthetics. All along my primary research concerning apocalyptic aesthetics, I have been puzzled by the fact that the lush imagery of Western apocalyptic art was essentially rooted in the anti-iconic, if not iconophobic, culture of ancient Judaism (Bychkov 1984). Earlier I reached the conclusion that already Judaic apocalypses (and later Christian ones) were built on a visionary language strange to their own oral-scriptural culture (Hubbes 2008), forming a special genre characterised as 'visionary poetry' (Székely 1923). Still, it seems that images alone cannot explain the success of the strange revelatory visions, and it is necessary to complete our understanding with another aspect: these images are special devices for a highly effective persuasive rhetoric. In this theoretical essay, building on several considerations formulated in earlier studies, I combine the visual and rhetorical aspects of apocalyptic discourse in support of the idea that ancient apocalypses represent a genuine revolution. They are revolutionary just as their contemporary media counterparts, both in the sense of pictorial turn and as subversive discourse. Exactly these two sides of the same expressive paradigm of the imaginary could lead – through their revelatory force – to the visual revolution in religion itself.

2. Apocalyptic, Imagery, Rhetoric – Definitions and Approaches

Before elaborating on my thesis, I want to clarify through brief definitions three basic key notions or ideas supporting this investigation, for a proper understanding of our argumentation: namely *apocalypse* – and even more importantly, the derivative concept of *apocalyptic*; respectively, *imagery* and *rhetoric*, in relation to each other.

2.1 Apocalyptic

Although in colloquial language there is a general tacit agreement on the meaning of *apocalyptic*, the terms *apocalypse*, *apocalyptic* and their derivatives in the academic literature are at least problematic. *Apocalypse* is a Greek word which originally meant 'revealing, lifting of the veil' and it was the introductory word of the *Book of Revelation*[1] left un-translated in the Latin *Vulgata*, thus later perceived as its title. From this initial title-word, *Apokalypsis* came to name a series of religious literary-revelatory writings, denoting the essence of the whole genre, the generic aspects of apocalyptic literature conclusively defined by the workshops of John J. Collins (1979) and David Hellholm (1989). Starting from their definitions I have drawn a general description of apocalyptic as an aesthetic category (Hubbes 2008), which can be applied in arts for iconographic analysis (cf. Hubbes 2011).

Scholarship identified a wider connotation of the term *apocalyptic*, referring to a special worldview and its various representations and expressions not only in religion or arts, but generally in human culture, history and all aspects of social life. This latter, wider meaning forms the apocalyptic paradigm which, as I elaborated elsewhere, is a distinct kind of mentality or structure of the imaginary:

> (t)he apocalyptic paradigm denotes (…) a common religious world view that acts as a reciprocally influencing model of and model for reality, built upon a basic set of beliefs, like the linear development of human history, which is to be disrupted by an imminent

1 '*Apokalypsis Iesou Khristou 'en edoken auto 'o theos*' (The Revelation of Jesus Christ, which God gave unto him) (Rev. 1,1).

> divine intervention; a theodicy-oriented rejection of the world; inseparable from certain fears of destruction and hopes for salvation and regeneration for the elect; being expressed in and manifested through apocalyptic works and movements, messianic, millenarian and utopian ideas; and often (but not necessarily) going hand-in-hand with phenomena of subversiveness, fanatic exaltation, fundamentalism, dualistic exclusivism, paranoia and scapegoating, or demonizing. It is a conglomerate leading to events that provoke massive, radical, long term changes in a given society or culture (Hubbes 2016: 148–149).

2.2. Apocalyptic Imagery

While mythical, and implicitly biblical, images are generally representations or rather expressions of deeply rooted archetypical structures, ordered according to a universal Chaos–Cosmos dichotomy, *apocalyptic images* represent a strikingly different scheme of the imaginary. Apocalyptic images mirror a unique world-view with a strange axiology, where the iconography of the divine forces shows up almost as terrifying as the grim grotesquery of evil. The apocalyptic world-view reverses the original Chaos–Cosmos imagery into a paradoxical inverted dichotomy: "here not the Creation stands as cosmos against a primordial chaos, on the contrary, the corrupt creation (corrupted by the original sin) stands as threatening chaos against a lost, but hoped and promised cosmos! This idea is actually quite the opposite of the general Chaos–Cosmos mythical dualism, and the apocalyptic spirit may be understood only through the prism of this inverted, Manichean-like dualism" (Hubbes 2011).

In such perspective, where apocalypse reveals through vivid images the prospect of an ideal new world to come, as opposed to the frustrating, sometimes even frightening, alienating present world, apocalyptic imagery is the reflection of a transcendent reality. It is in this sense that Northrop Frye (1972: 175–182) argues that apocalyptic imagery expresses or rather reveals the ultimate desires of man – an ordered, paradise-like utopian world in its mineral, vegetal, animal, human and divine aspects – stating that the *Book of Revelation* provides the basic grammar for this biblical archetypal imagery.

This approach, however, poses the same problem as many traditional interpretations of the apocalyptic character: it is unilateral, if from the opposite side. In the same manner, but stressing the darker aspect of apocalyptic imagery, modern Greek philosopher Evanghelos Moutsopoulos brings an argument of aesthetic dimensions, reasoning, "on the contrary, in spite of the obvious prophetic structure of the 'Revelation', we may say that the artworks inspired by it are not to be described as 'biblical' so much the more as the special aesthetic category: the 'apocalyptic' offers itself for characterizing them as anything but attractive and soothing order" (Moutsopoulos 1976: 76). Similar interpretations regarding the fearsome and dark aspect of 'apocalyptic' are found in the works of several scholars, and in everyday language, *apocalyptic* does not refer to paradisiacal images either (cf. Clifford 1997; Wojcik 1997: 11–12).

It is reasonable to approach apocalyptic imagery in a more comprehensive way. Accepting that biblical imagery, and especially the imagery of the apocalypse(s), is a product of visual thinking built upon cognitive metaphors (Lakoff–Johnson 1980; Kövecses 2010; also cf. Szilágyi N. 2010–2012) of analogical logic (Hamvas 1994), then we get closer to the original sense of apocalypse which is no less than showing or rather projecting of the invisible, of what is hidden. Thus, relying heavily on projections of the imagination, the apocalyptic produces and reproduces fantastic representations by analogical images which gain their strong expressiveness from combining visions of the real and the uncanny, the monstrous and the desirable. The strange complexity makes apocalyptic imagery extremely spectacular with grandiose scenery and hosts of sometimes unrecognizably collaged bricolage-beings that might well be most eye-catching, but at the same time mind-bogglingly difficult to interpret due to the abstract symbolism of any elementary detail.

2.3 Apocalyptic Rhetoric

With regards to the visionary apocalyptic language, we have to define the special discursive mode that characterizes it. According to Barry Brummett, apocalyptic rhetoric refers "to the ways in which speakers and writers use apocalyptic themes, forms, arguments, and style to address and to persuade real people in their actual, lived situations" (1991: 10). Frank Borchardt introduces his *Rhetoric of Doomsday* with the following definition of end-time discourses: "(s)peculation about the end of things has a purpose, a goal. Chiefly it is to deal with crisis either by moving an audience to undertake some action to resolve the crisis in its favor or to persuade an audience of the insignificance of the crisis in the grand scheme of things, especially in view of what is yet to come. Speculation about the end of things is therefore a discourse of persuasion and, like all such forms of discourse, it employs a strategy of persuasion — 'a rhetoric'" (1990: 2). Some pages below, he adds that the apocalyptic rhetoric endows the moment of deep crisis with meaning, "first by locating it in a grand scheme, and then by promising imminent surcease with stupendous rewards for endurance [...]" (Borchardt 1990: 20).

While building on the long acknowledged premise that apocalyptic is a mythic narrative model concerned with the issues of time and evil, Stephen O'Leary criticizes both theological exegetic traditions and modern social sciences' interpretations for their failure to understand it as a consistent and dramatic persuasive logical discourse. In such regard, he states that "critics should view apocalyptic discourse as argument that is intended to persuade, focusing attention on specific interpretive practices. This emphasis on logic and rationality might seem misplaced to those disposed to view apocalypticism as an outbreak of irrationality or mass hysteria. However", he concludes, "(a)rgumentative analysis by itself is insufficient [...] for this discourse is produced by human beings who view themselves not only as rational creatures, but as actors in a cosmic drama. The 'logical' form of the discourse thus takes shape within the structure of the participants' dramatic world view. Insofar as rhetors and audiences perceive history and human action in terms of the dramatic narrative of myth, their discourse will exhibit dramatic, as well as argumentative, form" (O'Leary 1998: 15–16). Nevertheless, O'Leary goes beyond merely the logical argumentation as a decisive constituent in the persuasive efficiency of apocalyptic rhetors, and stresses the central importance of authority as a topos of apocalyptic argument, pointing that it is essential to "to examine the eschatological narratives of Christianity for their characteristic modes of symbolizing power and authority, and to discover how institutional structures of religious and political power have shaped and been shaped by these authoritative symbols."

Greg Carey repeatedly pointed out (1999; 2007) that, while earlier scholarship concentrated on issues of form and content, starting from John J. Collins (1976) the problem of function has gained more prominent importance in apocalyptic studies. Thus, Carey claims that rhetoric can offer valuable insights into the roles and functionality of apocalyptic:

> Particular combinations of form and content are more than mere accidents of tradition history; rather, they are configured to serve rhetorical ends. Indeed, the resources of apocalyptic discourse function as what the ancient rhetoricians called topoi, or flexible resources for persuasion. [...] Apocalyptic topoi, such as heavenly and hellish visions, revelations concerning final things, dialogues with angels, cosmic portents, ex eventu prophecy, judgment scenes, and the like, are all possible fuel for apocalyptic argumentation (Carey 1999: 11).

It seems reasonable to conclude that apocalyptic rhetoric is a distinct form of pervasive discourse that uses metaphoric language and mythical narratives, built upon specific eschatological *topoi*, not only to explain the present state of affairs and answer the ultimate question of evil, but also to convince its audience to revert their perspective through a *cathartic metanoia* (cf. Hubbes 2008, 2011) and to recognize that the era of their sufferings will end; and to persuade them by the unquestionable authority of divine revelation to firmly hold their stance or to take some decisive action.

3. Revelatory Revolution – Spectacular Images, Rhetorical Constructions

3.1 Spectacular Images

If we close our eyes and try to internally visualize the scene described below in the fragment taken from the *Book of Ezekiel*, we would certainly meet some difficulties, and not only because of our unfamiliarity with imagination in the ancient Middle East, since such projections had been provoking confusion[2] even for the Judaic scribes interpreting them.

> And I looked, and, behold, a whirlwind came out of the north, a great cloud, and a fire infolding itself, and a brightness was about it, and out of the midst thereof as the colour of amber, out of the midst of the fire. Also out of the midst thereof came the likeness of four living creatures. And this was their appearance; they had the likeness of a man. And every one had four faces, and every one had four wings. And their feet were straight feet; and the sole of their feet was like the sole of a calf's foot: and they sparkled like the colour of burnished brass. And they had the hands of a man under their wings on their four sides; and they four had their faces and their wings. Their wings were joined one to another; they turned not when they went; they went every one straight forward. As for the likeness of their faces, they four had the face of a man, and the face of a lion, on the right side: and they four had the face of an ox on the left side; they four also had the face of an eagle. Thus were their faces: and their wings were stretched upward; two wings of every one were joined one to another, and two covered their bodies (Ezek. 1:4-11) (KJV).

These images stand out even today not only by their strangeness, but also by their visual grandeur – they are truly spectacular. The soothing heavenly images with their blinding angelic apparitions and the horrific cataclysm landscapes together with the nightmarish demons sprang up from an oral and aural textual tradition in which religious rigor banished every figurative visual expression. In spite of the traditional interpretation of ancient Judaism as an anti-iconic culture, utterly hostile to images (cf. Bychkov 1984), already Judaic apocalypses (and later Christian ones) were built on a visionary language. Archaeologist-iconographers like Othmar Keel and Christoph Uehlinger (1998) or Izaak Josias de Hulster (2008) have clearly shown the rich figurative imagery of Middle Eastern mythical representations in arts and artefacts from "behind the scenes" that organically constitute

2 As Cristian Bădiliță notes, even later, the rabbinic tradition approached with wary suspicion all apocalyptic writings and felt confused even when explaining the dreams in the canonized *Book of Daniel*, not to speak about the un-interpreted visions, which they deemed as dangerous for the uninitiated (Bădiliță 1998: 73).

the material forms of biblical images. On the other hand, contrary to the rigorous iconoclastic provisions concerning figurative representations, biblical scriptures abound in visual metaphors. As David Gelernter explains, Judaism actually has got a passionate affection towards images (Gelernter 2009, cited by Nyíri 2011: 89).

In his *Open Heaven*, Christopher Rowland describes in detail how visual as well as oral traditions have contributed to the formation of apocalyptic imagery, pointing out that beyond the direct naturalism and fantastic of the revelatory images, symbolism is essential. As he exposes:

> (C)ertain visions in the apocalypses contain imagery which is used by the apocalypticist as a means of presenting a particular truth about existence. In visions of this type there is usually no doubt as to what the seer thinks his imagery meant, as an angelic interpretation of the dream or vision is included as well to explain the contents of the vision. It becomes more difficult when we have a vision which does not purport to communicate the truth about earthly realities in symbolic form but the actual contents of the heavenly world (Rowland 1982: 58).

I still think that the conclusions I have reached in my earlier work (Hubbes 2008) namely that, paradoxically, apocalyptic imagination was the catalyst of the visual turn in late Biblical times, still apply. In the third chapter of my thesis, where I followed the way from the prohibition of images to the reign of images I argued: "through apocalypse, visions not only gained legitimacy but they acquired a particular force in the Jewish mentality repugnant of any (even if 'only' literary) imagery" (Hubbes 2008: 84–85). There I developed the idea of the penetration of images into the predominantly anti-iconic Middle Eastern religious culture from the surrounding environments through various channels, but also from its own extant ancient iconographic traditions. The train of thought included arguments that showed the existence of figurative depictions from early Biblical periods to Roman times – a wide repertory of iconographical exegesis (Keel – Uehlinger 1998; de Hulster 2008) – ranging from animal figures up to the zodiacs and narrative bible story illustrations of the late Hellenistic Jewish mosaics and frescoes in synagogues in Dura Europos, Beth-Shearim and other places. In the development of the visual language, an important role was played by fantastic mystical creatures like the cherubim, seraphim and other guardian beings, otherworldly beasts, central to the merkabah–throne visions (cf. Orlov 2007; Rowland 1982) of Isaiah, Ezekiel and the Enochian metatron-tradition (continued in Christianity through the tetramorph-visions of the *Book of Revelation* and the great Last Judgment compositions). On the other hand, strong visual impulses reached the Judaic theology from the Persian/Zoroastrian dualist eschatology, demonology and heavenly visions, as well as the other Middle Eastern (Assyrian – Babylonian) prophetic traditions acting in the direction of the formation of a new apocalyptic fervor and rhetoric. It would be wrong to underestimate the significance of this turn by arguing that these apocalyptic images, visions lived only in the letters of the Scriptures, and thus they do not really relate to the veneration or rejection of figurative images – the least so as these images got projected into ink and parchment from the real visions of the seer prophets, or from the imagination of apocalyptic writers (which presupposes some inner vision anyway). These visions grossly contributed to the opening of the strictly anti-iconic religiosity of ancient Judaism towards the world of vision, towards the sensibility of the eye to images – since, the apocalyptic, the apocalypse (as the very name shows) means revelation: the showing, revealing of invisible things and hidden mysteries by lifting the veil, and thus the opening of the eye for seeing. Although this argumentation may seem too farfetched, mystifying, and interpretable in a figurative sense, we should not forget that this semiotic process brought also practical, or even physiological, consequences. On the other hand, we know from Paul that "Jews demand signs" (1 Cor 1.22) and these (miracle) signs are actually visible, or rather, spectacular things, which could persuade the unbelieving. It is exactly this miracle-seeing, this spectacle of signs what the apocalypses offered in virtual form for the initiated religious communities: and these signs also reinforced the believers in their faith. Thus, these processes contributed both to the softening of ancient Judaic culture in its stance towards images, and in consequence, a bizarre yet strongly impressive imagery woke alive and started its own way not only in the Biblical Jewry but in Gnosticism, and even more characteristically in Christianity – up to our contemporary secular culture. Apocalyptic visionary in itself, by its very concrete revelatory nature of showing the unseen, the unimaginable, represents a pictorial turn: *Revelation* being a "revolution of the eye" by which the spectacular gradually invaded the ancient anti-iconic Middle East and later Christianity.

3.2 Spectacular Constructions

Images, however, do not suffice by themselves to explain the efficiency and success of the apocalyptic. As stated above already, apocalyptic imagery – being whatever strange and special within the biblical visions – is a product of the metaphorical language of analogical logic, and along my earlier studies I was firmly convinced that the direct impact of its weird and terrifying nature could account for the revolutionary force of apocalyptic discourses. Still, no visual revelation alone might be mighty enough to bring ultimate catharsis and persuade to change attitude or take up even extreme action.[3]

In order to be effective, images need to be part of a complex, coherent system, to form a characteristic apocalyptic language, as explained by Austin Farrer:

> An image thrown in isolation on the screen means nothing, because it may mean anything: and everyone who has touched the interpretation of images has experienced this bewilderment. In a long concatenation of images, each fixes the sense of the others, and is itself determined by them. If we appreciate the connexion rightly, we feel the new image emerging out of the hidden mind under the evocation of the images already in place, as St. John saw the figure of the Beast come up out of the deep when the Dragon's feet touched the sand of the sea. At a first reading the complexity of images in the Apocalypse may baffle and confuse us, but if we persevere we shall become thankful of it. It means that no image stands alone, but has its place and sense determined by a whole surrounding world of images. In the Apocalypse every image is bound to all the others by a delicate web of interrelated significance, almost as every point in physical nature is bound to the rest by lines of causal force (Farrer 2007: 18).

Going further on this idea, not even the coherence of the system, the power of this great visual language can account for the success of the apocalyptic. Kristóf Nyíri (2011) reminds us that Herder interprets the Bible as being written in the language of images, saying that the angel of the Apocalypse "neither speaks nor conceals, but merely points in images (semanei). The images must, therefore, have had a meaning, and been intelligible in themselves" (as cited by von Balthasar 1982: 85). Well, the Angel may point to images, but the apocalyptic prophet must interpret and, as Rowland (1982: 58) points out, in the very diverse Judaic and Christian apocalyptic literature, with the exception of John's *Revelation*, there is only one example where the symbolic images are left unexplained: the so-called animal-apocalypse in *1 Enoch* 85ff. It seems, then, that apocalyptic images, however grandiose, symbolic, intelligible, or revelatory, need to be organized, disposed, elaborated, just as they need interpretation, explanation. They need rhetorical formulation.

It is exactly this need that resulted in the spectacular compositions that characterize apocalyptic works like 1 Enoch and especially the *Book of Revelation*. If we look at the familiar throne-tetramorph vision of *Revelation* known from of Ezekiel 1 (quoted above) we can see how St. John re-invokes the prophet's vision:

---

3 By no means does this statement suggest, however, that I regard the language of prophetic and apocalyptic images as inferior (cf. Luther 1530 as referred by Belting 1994: 549). On the contrary, it is exactly their visionary nature that confers their penetrating pervasive force.

> And before the throne there was a sea of glass like unto crystal: and in the midst of the throne, and round about the throne, were four beasts full of eyes before and behind. And the first beast was like a lion, and the second beast like a calf, and the third beast had a face as a man, and the fourth beast was like a flying eagle. And the four beasts had each of them six wings about him; and they were full of eyes within: and they rest not day and night, saying, Holy, holy, holy, Lord God Almighty, which was, and is, and is to come. (Rev 4.6-8) (KJV)

However, we can also see that St. John not only uses (and simplifies) Ezekiel's fearful vision of the four fantastic creatures but he also goes beyond using them as only a powerful introductory, descriptive image of God's glory, as his predecessor did, and adapts the tetramorph beings as a stylistic, rhetorical device throughout his work. He uses the four creatures with multiple functions: as visual tropes – like cosmic symbols or heavenly allegories, as a repeating leitmotiv, as a dramatic chorus emphasizing given actions or enunciations, or even dramatis personae (Rev. 4–9, 11, 14–16, 19–21). Moreover, one can observe a deliberate paralleling use of the number four in the topoi of the four horsemen, the four winds, the four horns, the four angels of the Euphrates, four corners and four walls[4] – and above all, a four-fold structure of the text itself. In a similar way, other images are constructed into consequent numerical series and patterns of threes and sevens and dozens. We have good reason to believe that beyond aesthetical playfulness, these devices are used for a clear argumentative purpose: repeating and intensifying the messages, ordering them into logical coherence, and investing them with sacred authority.[5]

Given its outstanding importance in Christianity as the only canonized apocalypse in the *New Testament*, and also as a name-giver prototype for the genre, *Revelation* has been analysed and interpreted from countless aspects during church history. In the twentieth century an increased interest stepped beyond the actualizing inquiry of its content and symbols and messages; and subjected it to a meticulous structural investigation, thus theological exegesis, philosophical criticism and scholarly interpretation has repeatedly shown that the *Apocalypsis* has got a conscious and very rigorous composition. For example, Austin Farrer (2007 [1949]) sees in it a series of genially applied numerical patterns building on Old Testament prefigurements and traditions, while D. H. Lawrence subjectively (1932) criticizes it (amongst other faults) for its incoherent structure and clumsy adaptations of Hellenic pagan imagery. Whatever their attitude, they both

4 Exact references: Rev. 4.6–9; 5.6, 8, 14; 6.1, 6, 7; 7.1–3, 11; 8.12; 9.13–15; 11.16; 14.3; 15.7; 16.8; 19.4; 20.8; 21.16–19.

5 Fulfilling thus the three Aristotelian criteria of rhetorical art: pathos, logos, and ethos.

emphasize the conscious use and intentional composition for giving meaningful reason to the spectacular images in the *Book of Revelation* – and Christopher Rowland (1982) extends this compositional idea to the entire apocalyptic genre.

We can agree with both Austin Farrer (2007 [1949]) and D. H. Lawrence (1932) that John's *Revelation* and, in general, the entire apocalypse genre is literature, or visionary poetry as defined by István Székely (1923). I would, however, go one step further: we face here not only an elaborate textual composition, but also a genuine visual rhetoric, that is the conscious, deliberate construction of the images, and their rhetorical elocution into a persuasive narrative of spectacular projections.

3.3 Rhetorical Modes

On the other hand, Stephen O'Leary takes the perspective of a rhetorician and identifies a distinct logic in the complex compositional use of apocalyptic images: "While the potent metaphoric images generated by apocalypse over the centuries are indeed a significant resource for religious and public argument [...], apocalyptic metaphor cannot be understood apart from apocalyptic logic. [...] while mythic imagery forms our original stock for metaphoric invention, such imagery can itself be viewed not only as a predecessor to logical thought, but also as a product of a certain kind of logic" (1998: 21). It is exactly this distinct logic that constructs the meaning of apocalyptic metaphors; that uses them rhetorically to elaborate not only emotionally moving but rationally plausible, pervasive messages.

Apocalyptic discourse in itself represents a special way of argumentation, and there are several authors who, either explicitly or implicitly, approach or interpret apocalyptic texts and traditions from a rhetorical-discursive perspective, as I have shown earlier: "Several authors concentrate on the narrative or rhetoric aspect of apocalypticism and it is true that this apocalyptic web is best understandable through the surviving texts and images it produced, since those reflect most directly and authentically the nature of the apocalyptic mind [...] they all start from the implicit presumption that apocalypticism (whatever term they use for its denotation) is a predictive narrative or a persuasive discourse" (Hubbes 2016: 166). Discussing artistic representations of apocalyptic imagery István Székely opposed soothing, consoling compositions of early Christianity at the end of antiquity, with the threatening messages of medieval Last Judgments (Székely 1923). Delimiting Tyconius' and Augustine's explanations from millenarian interpretations of late antiquity, Paula Fredriksen (1992) opposes allegorizing and actualizing the apocalyptic, while for the Middle Ages, Bernard McGinn differentiates between *a priori* and *a posteriori* uses of apocalyptic discourse, to validate imperial or clerical politics, or to mobilize revolutionary audiences (1974; 1979). In distinguishing medieval apocalyptic rhetorical modes concerning the first turn of millennia, Richard Landes speaks metaphorically of roosters and owls, the former preaching while the latter denying the imminent end (Landes 1996). Stephen O'Leary interprets contemporary millennial rhetoric in Burke's dramatic terms of tragic or comic frames (O'Leary 1998). Frank L. Borchardt analyses Doomsday speculation as a strategy of persuasion and predictive narrative (Borchardt 1990). In terms of modern discursive approaches, we may consider to differentiate preterist versus dispensationalist rhetoric (Naugle, sa), and from another aspect, avertive versus catastrophic discourses (Wojcik 2016).

As we can see from this short and incomplete overview, modern scholarship approaches the apocalyptic inherently as a narrative or rhetoric way of discourse. It is the more curious that in this regard one can scarcely find approaches – excepting maybe iconographic analyses in art history – that would treat apocalypses as a specific, highly spectacular rhetoric of images. I have attempted such an approach, without an explicit rhetoric terminology, on two occasions (Hubbes 2011, 2015), where my main aim was to demonstrate the parallel existence of two reciprocally influencing modes: a dramatic and a narrative tradition of representation in pre-modern art inspired by the *Book of Revelation* and other apocalyptic texts, characterized by specific symbols and purposes of persuasion. We can distinguish between a plastic figurative line of depictions materialized in Last Judgments, illuminations, in *Dies Irae* movements in music, Day of Wrath poems in literature; while, on the other hand, a dramatic-narrative line, overwhelmingly present in literature, medieval drama, manuscript illuminations, in music by the Oratories built on the *Revelation*, and, in recent times, movies: Antichrist-stories or Armageddon wars, Rapture scenarios, and many popular culture or video games built on them (Hubbes 2015). While it seems that such a distinction between the two traditions is based on considerations of form and content, they primarily serve different pervasive purposes and apply correspondingly different rhetorical devices and imagistic constructions.

4. Conclusion

Images have a direct strong appeal on the irrational. In dreams, fantasies, visions, the images appear in a continuous flow, seemingly unorganized, segmented only by the inherent rhythm of the imagination – and comprehensible only for the intuitive mind (Szilágyi 2012). Apocalyptic imagination, rising from atavistic archetypes of fear, wish, and hope, creates powerful images of destruction and renewal, of demonic, monstrous foes and salvation, of horrific desolation and sublime, blinding theophanies. Laden with symbolic meaning, these same images, if ordered according to some external, arbitrary but rational structure, may become intelligible for the abstract logic – somewhat to the detriment of their transparency. Organizing the apocalyptic images by analogical, metaphorical correspondences, according to some culturally inherited relevant patterns, confers them coherence and highlights their interrelations as well as points to their liaisons with scriptural traditions and contemporary contexts of their surrounding reality. In such compositions, heavenly secrets of the divine world are revealed and the true nature of earthly powers is exposed in a universal, panoptic spectacle. Still, no visual revelation alone, however well constructed, might be mighty enough to bring ultimate catharsis and persuade people to persevere, change their attitudes or to even take extreme action. Whether painted, projected or written, the mythic images of the apocalyptic spectacle must be made to speak. Not by sophisticated exegetical interpretation (which often spoils their effect as explication does to a punch line) but by careful elaboration and composition of the images, the use of rhetorical techniques by adapting the logical and stylistic devices from *ars oratoria* to *ars monstraria*.

References

Bădiliță, Cristian (1998): *Apocalipsa lui Ioan în tradiția iudeo-creștină*. București: Humanitas.

Balthasar, Hans Urs von (1982): *Glory of the Lord. Vol. I: Seeing The Form*. Edinburgh: T&T Clark.

Belting, Hans (1994): *Likeness and Presence: A History of the Image Before the Era of Art*. Chicago: University of Chicago Press.

Borchardt, Frank L. (1990): *The Rhetoric of Doomsday. Doomsday Speculation as a Strategy of Persuasion: A Study of Apocalypticism as Rhetoric*. New York: Lewiston.

Brummett, Barry (1991): *Contemporary Apocalyptic Rhetoric*. New York et al.: Praeger.

Bychkov, Viktor (1984): *Estetica antichitatii tirzii. Secolele II–III* (*Aesthetics of Late Antiquity, II–III centuries*). Bucuresti: Editura Meridiane. (Original: Бычков, В. В. 1981: *Эстетика поздней античности. II—III века*. Москва: Наука.)

Carey, Gregory (1999): Introduction. Apocalyptic Discourse, Apocalyptic Rhetoric. In: Carey, Gregory – Bloomquist, L. Gregory (eds.): *Vision and Persuasion: Rhetorical Dimensions of Apocalyptic Discourse*. St. Louis, MO: Chalice Press. 1–15.

Carey, Gregory (2014): Early Christian Apocalyptic Rhetoric. In: Collins, John J. (ed.): *The Oxford Handbook of Apocalyptic Literature*. Oxford: Oxford University Press. 218–234.

Clifford, Paula (1997): *A Brief History of End-Time*. Oxford: Lion Books.

Collins, John J. (ed.) (1979): Apocalypse: The Morphology of a Genre. The Jewish Apocalypses. *Semeia 14*. Missoula, MT: Scholars Press.

de Hulster, Izaak Josias (2007): *Illuminating Images: an Iconographic Method of Old Testament Exegesis with Three Case Studies from Third Isaiah*. Utrecht: Utrecht University.

Farrer, Austin (2007): *A Rebirth of Images: The Making of St. John's Apocalypse*. 3rd reprint edition. Eugene, OR: Wipf & Stock.

Fredriksen, Paula (1992): Tyconius and Augustine on the Apocalypse. In: Emmerson, Richard K. – McGinn, Bernard (eds.): *The Apocalypse in the Middle Ages*. Ithaca, NY: Cornell University Press.

Frye, Northrop (1972): *Anatomia criticii*. Bucuresti: Univers. (Original: *The Anatomy of Criticism: Four Essays*. New Jersey: Princeton University Press, 1957. Consulted online version: http://northropfrye-theanatomyofcriticism.blogspot.ro/ [25. 07. 2013]).

Hellholm, David (ed.) (1989): *Apocalypticism in the Mediterranean World and the Near East. Proceedings of the International Colloquium on Apocalypticism, Uppsala, August 12–17, 1979*. 2nd edition, Tübingen: Mohr Verlag.

Hubbes, László Attila (2008): *Látomások a vég bűvöletében. Az apokalipszis a vallásirodalmi műfajtól a művészet egy kifejezésmódjáig*. Marosvásárhely: Mentor Kiadó.

Hubbes, László Attila (2011): Apocalyptic Motifs in the Early Christian Literature and Art. In: Labahn, Michael – Lehtipuu, Outi (eds.): *Imagery in the Book of Revelation*. Contributions to Biblical Exegesis and Theology 60. Leuven: Peeters. 55–78.

Hubbes, László Attila (2015): A harag Napja és a Fenevad Haragja / The Day of Wrath and the Wrath of the Beast. In: Pápai, Lívia (ed.): *Kárpit3. Apokalipszis vagy globális fenntarthatóság / Apocalypse or Global Sustainability*. Budapest: Magyar Kárpitművészek Egyesülete. 24–46.

Hubbes, László Attila (2016): Apocalyptic as a New Mental Paradigm of the Middle Ages. In: Ryan, Michael A. (ed.): *A Companion to Premodern Apocalypse*. Leiden: Brill. 144–176.

Keel, Othmar – Uehlinger, Christoph (1998): *Gods, Goddesses and Images of God in Ancient Israel*. Translated by Thomas H. Trapp. Philadelphia: Fortress.

Lakoff, George – Johnson, Mark (1980): *Metaphors We Live By*. Chicago: University of Chicago Press.

Lawrence, David Herbert (1932): *Apocalypse*. Hamburg: The Albatross Modern Continental Library.

Moutsopoulos, Evanghelos (1976): *Categoriile estetice*. Bucuresti: Univers. (Original: Αί αισθητικαι κατηγορίαι. Είσαγωγή είς μίαν άξιολογίαν τού αισθητικού άντικειμένου; Αθινα, 1970.)

Naugle, David (s.a.): *The Apocalyptic Rhetoric of Dispensational Premillennialism*. Paper, Dallas Baptist University. Online: http://www3.dbu.edu/naugle/pdf/apocalyptic_rhetoric.pdf [20. 03. 2017].

Nyíri, Kristóf (2011): *Kép és idő* [Image and time]. Budapest: Magyar Mercurius.

O'Leary, Stephen D. (1998): *Arguing the Apocalypse: A Theory of Millennial Rhetoric*. New York: Oxford University Press.

Orlov, Andrei A. (2007): *From Apocalypticism to Merkabah Mysticism. Studies in the Slavonic Pseudepigrapha*. Leiden – Boston: Brill.

Rowland, Christopher (1982): *The Open Heaven. A Study of Apocalyptic in Judaism and Early Christianity*. London: SPCK.

Székely, István (1923): *Az apokalyptika a világirodalomban*. Értekezések a filozófiai és társadalmi tudományok köréből, II/5. Budapest: Magyar Tudományos Akadémia.

Wojcik, Daniel (1997): *The End of the World as We Know It. Faith, Fatalism, and Apocalypse in America*. New York – London: New York University Press.

Wojcik, Daniel (2016): Avertive Apocalypticism. In: Wessinger, Catherine (ed.): *The Oxford Handbook on Millennialism*. New York – Oxford: Oxford University Press. 66–88.

Philipp Stoellger

"In Images We Trust". On Belief in Images as the Real Reality[1]

1. Trust

We usually trust in people. Trust is normally an interpersonal relation: we trust our parents not to seduce us, but to wish our best. We trust whom we love—no love without trust. But there is also trust without love. We trust—hopefully—our colleagues not to deceive us but to be honest. This means trust can be total, as in love, and it can be partial or perspectival, when we trust someone with regard to something in particular.

Whatever trust may be, it is difficult to say 'how to make it'. Trust-making is a mystery of social coherence. Without trust, no living together, no cohabitation or communication is possible. Trust may be a gift that we get (like recognition) and give back. Thus, it is a kind of 'gift-exchange' that entails a mysterious obligation: If you trust me, I have no choice but to trust you. Trust is a response to the trust of the other. The 'origin' of trust is earlier than we are. In a way, it is 'prevenient'.

This means that trust is not simply made but rather given or inherited. If there are cultural heritages, trust should be on the list. And if there is no more trust given, social life becomes quite difficult. Then we need contracts and lawyers for everything: for marriage and for friendships. The pervasive 'legalization', the law penetrating our life may be the symptom of a problem: lack of trust.

However, I don't want to complain about the lack of trust or moral sense but simply hint to a social paradox: trust is necessary but impossible to make. It is given, inherited and responsive. But if it is gone, the way to 'recall' it is a mystery. In the sphere of mistrust, trust becomes impossible but it remains a necessary impossibility, because only by this strange gift becomes social life possible. Otherwise, life would be merely 'natural', not a social 'being together' (in German, Mitsein).

2. Trust in God and Myself?

How trust works is a field of research of its own, quite a wide and open one. However, the basic idea of interpersonal trust and trust as a basic factor of social

---

1 See also Stoellger 2010.

life entails some problems. If trust is given and not made, it becomes unavailable or unaffordable. So, one may search for the real root of trust and may start 'in the beginning', with God and may end up with 'oneself'. 'In God we trust' and 'I trust only and exclusively in myself' are the two dominant options.

Remember Descartes' marvellous invention, the 'sum cogitans': the one and only foundation of secure knowledge is the certainty of myself, while I am thinking. This certainty did not last very long. In Romanticism (Schlegel) or at last in Nietzsche and Freud, this basic trust in the foundational character of the 'I' was already disseminated. What the 'I' may ever have been is either too dark or too much, either too lonely or too fragile to be the basic foundation of everything. It failed in the functioning of essentialist foundationalism.

This is a kind of repetition of an older story. Once ago, we believed in God. This belief was named faith, just to mark its extraordinary character. Faith was thought to sustain the cultural world: justice and institutions, morality and mercy, society and community. It was a quite fruitful period in art, culture, economy, and society as well as in colonialism and warfare. Basic beliefs seem to *enable* us to achieve what otherwise would remain impossible. Some beliefs make the impossible possible, whether Heaven or Hell.

However, this unquestionable belief *was* questioned nevertheless and became doubtful or even suspicious. And the same story happened with the belief in 'myself', in the ominous 'I'. Suspicion against deep beliefs and any trust leads to suspicion against suspicion against suspicion... There seems to be no more ground, foundation or basic belief left.

Is there anyone nowadays who really and still believes in 'oneself'? For sure, this is a prominent thesis out of the Jurassic Park of philosophy's history. And it is today a topic of 'self-promotion': of the economies of trust in yourself, either in management or in new religions. But can you ever have read Freud and Nietzsche and still really believe in yourself?

3. Trust in Immediacy and Media-trust

What now, what after such foundationalisms? What remained after God and 'I' as 'self-evident' beliefs? There are beliefs nevertheless but in such a plurality, fragility and transiency that no one can give or get any guarantees. The old model of basic belief and guaranteed certainty is a lovely idea, but it is gone. And even where it is still present, it is a quite postmodern revival of pre-modern options. Essentialism in times of late modernity *is* a postmodern position, like the so-called 'radical orthodoxy'.

Essentialism and foundationalism have failed, but does that lead necessarily to pluralism and relativism? I doubt it does and I would prefer not to follow this pattern, not to revitalise this metaphysical and anti-metaphysical discourse: either essentialism or relativism. Not least because it bewitches our intelligence and belief as well. The necessary 'brainwork' is beyond this 'old' and 'postmodern' alternative: it is the quest for figures of the third, neither foundationalist nor essentialist.

The pragmatist traditions (like Putnam) and interpretationism (Goodman, Abel, Lenk) offered a mediation: All reality is mediated, but media are not all of reality. In our context, we might slightly transform this insight: The real is an image and the image is real, but it is not *the* real, the only reality. The reality of the image and the image of reality are two aspects of the basic *mediality* of reality. This means to proceed from symbolic realism to image-realism.

In politics as well as in economy, law, our daily life, in science and religion, we trust in images as basic media of 'the real' (whatever that may be). This basic trust can be understood as 'belief in images' or 'image-belief'. This means we live in belief systems which are created and formed by images.

The images we live by (as explicated in my 2014 Budapest talk) are images we trust and believe in. Along the lines of Wittgenstein's *On Certainty*, we cannot escape the basic certainties as the likewise labile and stable ground of our forms of life (Wittgenstein 1969). However, this 'ground' is not a hard and physical 'real' but rather a dynamic of mediation, as in visual communication. So, Wittgenstein should be pushed a little bit further: the ground we live on is quite more labile than stable, more image than 'physics and mathematics' or more mediality than immediate certainty.

One decisive failure of the 'old' patterns of belief is the quest for *immediacy*: The belief in God looked for an immediate vision or contact or for rational self-evidence (natural theology). Similarly to modern subjectivity, it was claimed to be infallible and really certain because of its so-called immediacy (unmittelbares Selbstbewusstsein, in German). Both quests looked for something impossible: immediacy as last grounding of all belief, certainty, and trust. In the name of a 'real immediacy', all mediality may be under suspicion and at last claimed to be fallible, just an artefact, not 'nature' or real reason. But the claimed immediacy remains an empty and broken promise.

Both options failed in the 'condition of all possibility': in their lack of sense for mediality, or even more, their contempt for mediality. Since the desire for and believe in immediacy was quite firm: we trust and believe in God, not in an image, not even in an image of him. Or we believe in the self-certainty of the 'I', not in any images or media. And so on, the story remains structurally the same. In the name of a great immediacy, all mediality comes under suspicion—and this is as promising as deceptive.

The condition of all possibility and hence reality is mediality. The 'Kittsteiner' thesis of 'media a priori' claims that whatever and whenever we think and act, we do so under the conditions of the contemporary media. This may be plausible but one should go a little further: not the an-iconic immediacy is the basic foundation, but iconic mediality is the basic relation of all possibilities and realities. One may say where there is difference, there is mediality. But the opposite is also true: Where there is mediality, there is a difference before (whether in death or life).

4. Veridiction as Appearance and Monstration

This becomes relevant regarding 'veridiction': the veridical is *not* an immediate authenticity but a media formation. Veridiction *appears* only in and by media, whether verbal or visual (or any other form). What is believed to be veridical is a verbal-visual appearance. On the one hand, this makes it fallible. Think of the political strategies to *show* veridiction: It becomes a political show. Or with Daniel Dayan: The appearance of veridiction becomes a monstration if it is shown in a show (Dayan 2009). The will to show, i.e. to monstration may produce monsters, either bright stars and leaders, or dark enemies. On the other hand, the mediality of veridiction makes it possible—no view from outside. The 'view', the appearance of veridiction is given by the media, which makes it at the same time fallible. Thus, visuality (and verbality) are the conditions of veridiction. They make it both possible and fallible.

This is embodied in the figure of the 'witness': a visual and verbal figure who embodies a piece of evidence, not in authentic immediacy but in all fallibility of mediality. The witness appears and shows what he has seen, but if the witness is shown and demonstrated, it becomes suspicious. Heroes or saints, for example, may embody what they witness, but shown and demonstrated, they become little monsters.

We believe in the witness, when he (or she) *appears* to be veridical. In other words, the appearance is decisive (and manipulable, as US judicial processes show). We trust in his experience and his embodiment of an event. But we never trust blindly in this visual appearance. We have to look precisely for what is shown. As a visual figure the witness becomes an image of himself and his experience, a bodily trace of an event or story. But the connection to the event is as fallible as are images and embodiments.

The witness is a figure of the third: not God or the 'I' myself, but an Other who claims our trust and belief. But this figure of the witness becomes part of an institutional process. In court he or she is part of an institutional strategy of veridiction.

Thereby the witness is an example of a 'trust-shift': from personal interaction to institutional procedures. And this is a problem: When the witness becomes an image of himself, when this image is part of an institutional setting like a law court, what is going on there?

Beyond the interpersonal relation of trust, one may ask for institutional substitutes, and ends up in a 'second order trust' in institutions and structures (cf. Luhmann). In complex societies and communications, interpersonality or bodily presence do not work. But are media like institutions satisfactory substitutes? Can trust in a present witness be supplemented by papers and images, like 'media-trust' or can it be institutionalized? After reading Kafka's *The Castle* or after some years at the university, almost nobody can honestly trust institutions (exceptions confirm the rule). Trust is gone and lost in this shift: the substitute is not trustworthy because institutions are not 'trustworthy' but at best perhaps reliable. The shift from trust to reliance is at stake. This also holds for images.

When in late modernity trust in institutions becomes more and more questionable, various supplements of interpersonal trust appear: things, machines and techniques, like my Mac or my cell-phone, my bike or my smart home. All these little fetishes we like and love, so much that we cannot imagine life without them. We get things we never needed before and they become necessary for our life.

However, there is an obvious need for the critique of trust. We do not trust institutions as substitutes; we *rely on* them at best. It's the same with the supplements: we rely on our phone and Mac, but we do not *trust* them, especially in times of the NSA. Shall one go further and claim that there is not even reliability left but only usability or usefulness? The user doesn't trust or rely on the media, only uses them. Thus, mere usefulness would be the pragmatistic 'rest'. What is left?

5. Trust in Images as Image-belief

The difference between trust and reliance becomes relevant regarding images. In many cases, we just rely on images: that they depict what they ought to, as in the case of the ID card, even if we don't recognize ourselves anymore after some decades. But what about news and their images on TV or on the web? Do we just rely on them or do we trust their truth? Do we believe them? I guess, we do, if not without reservations, nevertheless we trust and believe them. That means 'news images' are quite usual and secular media of image-belief. What about medical images, like X-ray, MRT and PET? Do we only rely on them, or is there more at stake? We trust their depictive truth, and based on this trust the surgeon relies on them.

On the ground of pragmatistic reliance, there is a trust or belief: in the technique, in the image itself and in the whole structure of visual communication. And the patient? An image of one's own cancer is shocking and changes your life. So it's fair to say, it is ground-breaking and it leads to conversion. It is not only indexical and depictive (that is its referential truth), but it is also moving and monstrative. It has not only an epistemic but also an ethical and emotional impact of deepest relevance. May one call such images trust-maker? Trust in images is trust in the times of visual communication.

The main thesis is that to trust images ('image-belief') is present and vivid. It's the modality of trust in times of visual communication. We cannot help trusting images, even if we primarily trust present persons. However, such presence and presumed immediacy and authenticity are always mediated, and thereby as fallible as possible.

The decisive task, then, is the quest for the validity of such image-belief and its risks and limits. But images? Do we *believe* in images? To trust images is a form of image-belief simply because trust is a form of belief. If we trust someone, we can believe that they will not harm us. Because trust is a form of belief, trust has become a basic metaphor for religious belief, named faith. To trust in God means to believe in God (both *fides quae* and *fides qua*). Trust *is* belief because belief is trust. Whatever we may do, when we trust we believe, in a way, what we trust (at least, we believe that it is 'trustworthy').

'Image-belief' is not new: remember Egypt, the pharaoh as a visual presence of God; or remember the golden calf as the presumed presence of Yahweh; remember Rome and the image policy of Augustus and his followers: the image of Caesar *is* Caesar, as Louis Marin explicated in the *Portrait of the King* via the Logique de Port Royal (Marin 1988). Remember also Christ as the image of God and all the images of Christ and all the Saints. And so on: iconic presence is the conductive medium where visual communication is present. This is currently relevant in the 'new media' but not new.

Therefore, the problems with iconic presence (or omnipresence) are not new either. The struggles and conflicts around the image have their histories, between Rome and Byzantium, between Wittenberg and Rome, between the Reformations (Calvin, Zwingli, Luther), and reinforced during the Enlightenment and the Baroque period. As the Western tradition of Rome claimed, the image *is* a medium of presence (of God, Saints), therefore it deserves veneration but no adoration. We adore only God, but the veneration of an image leads veneration to the depicted (Christ, Mary or the saints). The image functions as an instrumental medium of presence and like a channel, conducting the presence to the venerated. This is probably useful but quite too simple because the image as a medium of presence is not nothing, not a lifeless instrument but a living image. The distinction between the veneration and adoration of an image can be reframed: there is no *faith* in images but *belief* is allowed. This distinction is normative, not descriptive: there shall be no faith in images. But the distinction is also 'soporific': it calms down what can be hot and exciting, hot because faith in God and his Saints may be gone, but the belief in image is still vivid, perhaps as vivid as rarely before in history. Belief in images is belief in the realm of visual communication.

6. Versions of Image-belief

For the sake of orientation, I suggest distinguishing some forms of image-belief:

1. There is a general image-belief already among animals that extends not only to the *animal rationale*. A dog recognizes a dog in the mirror and barks. It effectively believes in seeing a dog barking. This is like our belief in depictions: We have the feeling to be seen when the image looks at us. What we see looks back at us (but doesn't see us).
2. There is an anthropological image-belief, perhaps coming from the dominance of visual perception. The sensual certainty is present when we believe what we see. The natural phenomenon is that we cannot help believing 'our eyes' even if we criticise it afterwards. A consequence of this natural belief in what we see is the 'witness' in court or in religion. We believe the witness, at least when there is more than one.
3. There is a methodical image-belief addressed, for example, whenever something is shown with and by images. In teaching, for example, sometimes we try to show by images what we say. Saying and showing shall come together and the image is shown to make the students believe in what they have been told. A consequence of this method is that 'to show' can also mean 'to prove', to give evidence: in mathematics or medicine with its imaging procedures.
4. There is also a popular and media use of image-belief: for example, when brain scans are used to make us believe that someone is a criminal because they lack mirror neurons; or that God is naturally present in the brain (like in the so-called neuro-theology). One use, of course, is also advertising or strategies of 'event-shopping'.
5. There is a political image-belief, as discussed by Marin: the image of the King. The old idea that the image of Caesar *is* Caesar. Then the image becomes a presence-maker or even more: a king-maker. Note that the second body of the king *is* an image, the effigy.

6. The political interacts with the religious image belief: that God is present in visual media, in the Torah or in Christ, in the Temple or in the cult, in (orthodox) icons or in the sacred host. Christ as an image of God is repeated and repeated in supplementary images as the embodiments of Christ.
7. Not to forget: 'dark' image-belief. I don't think here of Satanists or the like but of iconoclasts. The deep mistrust in images or even the phobia and destruction of images shows a deep belief in images, just reversed in its destructive veneration. The image-critique in enlightenment-traditions is also a consequence of this phobia. The epistemology and ontology since Kant tends to a deep scepticism about images. They are not what they show, at least, they are mere 'seeming', 'mere' appearance. The denial of the image is a subtle and gentle form of mistrust in images. And every form of mistrust is a distorted trust.

A strange thing about image-belief is that it works, even if we don't believe in the image. We believe in images, because we cannot help believing in them. Even in the times of critique and mistrust, the image works as a trust-maker. We believe even when we believe not to believe. One may call it image-magic or simply 'imagic'.

What does it mean to believe in an image? Generally speaking, it means to follow the image: to buy (in economy), to elect (in politics), to venerate it (in aesthetics) or to live in the shown way (in religion). Wittgenstein's idea of 'following a rule' is a pragmatist concept of image-belief. To follow an image shows one's belief.

Image-belief is *not* the naïve idea to believe that the image *is* what it shows. Instead, it is the not-so-naïve idea that the image is *a bit* what it shows. It is not what it shows, not a mere and empty representation but rather a presence: whether the aesthetic presence of an artefact, political presence (of power or 'the king'), or the religious presence of God. However, *not* naïve is such a belief only when the presence is different. It is not a real presence but a presence in withdrawal.

The promise of advertising that the promised is really present through the label and image is never kept. It would be naïve to believe that you get the final iPhone by buying the newest one. Even economically, presence is driven by withdrawal. This also holds for politics. What you see is never what you get. Withdrawal is the motion in the political sphere.

It is similar, albeit slightly different, in the religious sphere. Presence is not the final presence but its anticipation: the beginning of the new world. This anticipative presence also has its withdrawal: no foul and definitive presence but just the beginning. This model has been taken over by economy and politics. But who keeps the promise? Who keeps the truth-promise?

7. The Ambivalence of Image-belief: Some Examples

What images do we trust today? The most widely spread and everyday image of the world is as well the most desired: 'the dollar'. Even if the dollar note confesses 'In God we trust', it embodies another trust and belief: trust in the little green images of value. Its image-belief is the belief in the globally shared desire and acceptance of this value. Generally speaking, money is a belief system, dependent on trust in the little images called 'notes' and 'coins'.

It is similar with labels like Apple, Prada, and others. Labels are markers for images of trust (and of trusts). We trust images of value: the labels function as globally shared attention markers and codes of visual communication.

And this is not totally different from the so-called 'high' art and strong images. They are distributed and shared *like* labels: Gerhard Richter, Polke, and others. The recognition may be grounded in a belief in their aesthetic value. However, the 'aura' and veneration (or even adoration) of these images is like that of a saint's relic: an image of real presence, of value, not in the least of economic value.

Less about economy but rather about power is the belief in public figures, politicians, stars, heroes, and new saints, who function like labels and images. The 'leaders of the free world' are images of themselves or of ideas and ideals, traditions and nations.

The code of visual communication in economy and politics is, of course, not about 'veridiction' but about power (political and economic power). So veridiction is just a side-effect or a secondary gesture and habit for the sake of power. This means do not trust the gestures of a public figure as in personal interaction. The whole system of communication is about something else. But it seems to be successful to design politics as if it cared about veridiction. The visual design of politicians and public performances makes an intense use of trust-markers and even religious gestures or rhetoric, but this is part of another game. The rhetoric of 'pure and impure', 'God's own nation' and about sin, guilt and forgiveness are useful because they evoke interpersonal belief; however, the system-shift uses these cultural patterns for power-questions. Veridiction then becomes a fake, even if it seems honest.

However, what about visual communication in religion? Take, for example, the present Pope: Is he not an icon of veridiction? He *as pope* embodies the veridical, a true image of truth and trustfulness. He *is* a public image and *has* a public image of honesty and truthfulness like just few others. It may seem that he is the candidate to become a saint already in his lifetime. This is not mockery: the Pope really appears honest and truthful, but the problem is a basic ambivalence of being an image: He as a person may be so but as an office bearer, as a church official (with Agamben: in and ex officio), he is not only a personal appearance but also an institutional monstration. The veridical of his person becomes part of institutional image-politics. His little home, his modest car, his use of public transportation, his authenticity and so on: All these markers of visual veridiction become *at the same time* political and (unintentionally?) a means to an end: for the Church's sake.

This ambivalence of the Pope also pertains to Christ himself, regrettably. Christ as *the* visual image of God, as an embodiment of God's essence which means simply the embodiment of radical love: Christ himself became a public figure and an image of religious communication. This may be quite a veridical image-use, like in church service, communion and diakonia, but the personal appearance of the veridical becomes political monstration in competition with other religions and politics.

8. Three Differences: Aesthetic, Political and Religious Difference

What can we learn from this dilemma, from this reduplication of personal and institutional images? An image is never just an image. It is an appearance, like in a personal interaction. But an appearance never remains just an appearance. Embedded in different spheres or systems of communication, it shifts and becomes 'itself as another': it is altered and othered. In image-theory we are used to 'aesthetic difference': Magritte's pipe is not a pipe but an aesthetic intervention. By the way, I don't think that the pipe *is just not* a pipe. The aesthetic image is not what it shows. In image-theory we also use a 'political difference': the image is not just an image, but a political intervention, too. The personal gestures of veridiction become public *images* of veridiction in the political sphere. The appearance becomes monstration, and sometimes monstrous if trustfulness is used for personal power interests. This means to believe in such images of veridiction can be an easy deception, if and immediately if the political difference is forgotten.

And what about religion? Shouldn't we expect that the veridical is really present in religious communication? In analogy to the aesthetic and political difference, I suggest a religious difference in image theory. The religious image is also affected by the aesthetic and political difference. Of course, Gerhard Richter's window in the Dome in Cologne is an aesthetic appearance (and it is venerated because of that). It is also a political intervention (because it challenges the symbolic order of the Church and the Bishop by introducing contingency in the order of necessities). However, the religious difference is something different: in the religious sphere the image pretends to be(come) a trace of God or, generally speaking, an immanence of transcendence. This means it pretends to be access to God or, vice versa, God's access to us. The image as a religious medium pretends to become a medium of transcendence by transcendence of the medium. This means to transcend the image in becoming an image of transcendence.

9. The Truth-claim of Images

This is not an aesthetic claim or a political power claim but a special kind of truth-claim: to become a metaphor from world to God and vice versa, to become a little incarnation of transcendence. More specifically, in the Christian sphere, to become a marked space of a special veridical of grace and mercy, even more specifically, to embody Christ's spirit. This is *not* a mere proposition, as if the image claims a propositional truth. It is not a truth that is said or shown (not a vérité à dire) but it is a truth that is done, a practical truth, one may say with Merleau-Ponty a 'vérité à faire', or even better: a truth to live by, like the 'Christian freedom'.

Nevertheless, this *salvific* truth-claim is open for ratification or for critique. Such a special truth-claim is not self-evident but rather embedded in religious practice with all the ambivalences mentioned above. The power-claim may become dominant, or as well the aesthetic reception by the tourist; venerating religious art may become dominant as well. At last, every religious image (image in the religious sphere) is affected by the ambivalence of monstration. The image 'wants' to be a 'passive medium' of Christ's 'self-presentation', but it has to show itself in order to hint to Christ. This is a dilemma represented by John the Baptist: to show and to point at Christ is only possible by showing himself, by becoming present as an image.

In order to open up a 'marked space' for transcendence, the image has to show itself, and even more: it has to be shown and presented in public space. The religious truth-claim of an image becomes demonstrative or 'monstrative'. This means, it is shown and is in danger to become a show. One may think of some kinds of charismatic shows, or of official celebrations in Rome, or as well of the celebration of the Reformation these days in Europe.

This dilemma of showing oneself even by pointing away to Christ is a reason for the intrinsic iconoclasm in Christian image-practice (especially, of the Lutheran kind): To avoid or at least to limit the self-presentation of the image as an image, the medium has to become invisible in order to open up the marked space of transcendence. The example is the host of the Eucharist: it has to disappear to be eaten up. Accordingly, 'art' in the religious sphere is at last for consumption, not for eternal conservation.

Regarding verbal and visual media, one may argue for a specific 'relativism', or rather a specific pragmatism. There is no intrinsic truth (either in words or in images) but the truth is 'external'. I would prefer to call it religious pragmatism: the image is whatever it may be only and exclusively in its use and consumption.

But then again, the use makes the difference: A mere aesthetic use is undercutting its truth-claim, a mere political or institutional use as well; also a mere pedagogic use. One may object that images, even in the religious sphere, are open for many uses, and that's true. But to become aware of their specific truth-claim, a special use is the decisive access. To give a simple example, art history will never access the truth-claim of a religious image.

PS: Images as truth-makers or as sense-makers and trust-makers? If we believe in images, since we cannot help believing in them, every mistrust and critique comes belatedly or with a delay, images are belief-makers: They make us believe, for example, 'what happened' or 'who the enemy is' or 'who is right'. As belief-makers images seem also to be trust-makers, in economy and politics as well as in the religious context.

However, may they be also 'truth-makers'? Is truth not an iconoclastic concept: referring to what is 'really' true? Perhaps the perspectivity of truth might help here: truth is only given in and through perspectives. This also means that truth is given in and through images (remember Plato's myths). To believe in a truth beyond all words and images leads to metaphysics. To identify a perspective or an image with the full truth, however, leads to a totalitarian claim.

What then about *the* central image in Christianity: Christ as *the* image of God? As one full of truth and grace? One can easily make an absolute claim of truth out of it: that 'the Church' possesses the full truth… But the better use seems to be a critical, a self-critical one: No one, apart from Christ himself, is the truth. The consequence is critique: of all identification, like the identification of truth and institution, of truth and image or of truth and one's own confession. This use may be called antiabsolutism (or a specific relativism: relativizing absolute positions). There is a qualified negativism in this antiabsolutism: no concept (of the absolute) is capable of this truth, either.

Does a critical belief in images mean to believe in a truth beyond all images as well? Yes, but only if this external truth is accessible in and by verbal and visual communication.

References

Dayan, Daniel (2009): Sharing and Showing. Television as Monstration. *The Annals of the American Academy of Political and Social Science* 625: 19–31.

Marin, Louis (1988): *Portrait of the King.* Language, Discourse, Society. Trans. Martha M. Houle. Basingstoke: Palgrave.

Stoellger, Philipp (2010): 'In God we trust'. Trust in the Making—and in Becoming. In: Grøn, Arne – Welz, Claudia (eds.): *Trust, Sociality, Selfhood*. Religion in Philosophy and Theology 52. Tübingen: Mohr Siebeck. 153–169.

Wittgenstein, Ludwig (1969): *On Certainty*. Translated by Denis Paul and G.E.M. Anscombe. Oxford: Blackwell.

Notes on Contributors

ACZÉL, PETRA is a Professor at Corvinus University of Budapest and Head of the Institute of Behavioral Science and Communication Theory, as well as a member of the Social Communication Doctoral School. She studied at Eötvös Loránd University, Budapest, earned her PhD degree in Linguistics with the thesis *Winning with Word: Classical and Modern Argumentation Theory* in 2003, and gave her habilitation lecture in 2011. Her research interests focus on the theory and practice of rhetoric. She is author and co-author of four books and numerous essays on verbal and visual argumentation, persuasive communication and (new) media communication. Her recent publications include contributions to the debate on "new rhetoric" and new media rhetoric, such as *Enchanting Bewilderment: Concerns for Visual Rhetoric* (in series VISUAL LEARNING, vol. 1, 2011), *Mediarhetoric: Complex Visual Literacy* (in series VISUAL LEARNING, vol. 2, 2012); *Visionary Rhetoric: Teaching Imagistic Communication* (in series VISUAL LEARNING, vol. 3, 2013); *Expressivity and Emotion in Visionary Rhetoric* (in series VISUAL LEARNING, vol. 4, 2014), and *Ingenious Rhetoric: The Visual Secret of Rhetoricality* (in series VISUAL LEARNING, vol. 5, 2015). She is the chair and member of various Hungarian and international communication associations and boards. Email: petra.aczel@uni-corvinus.hu.

BENEDEK, ANDRÁS, born 1950, is Professor of Education of the Department of Technical Education, Budapest University of Technology and Economics, and DSc of the Hungarian Academy of Sciences. From 1976 to 1979 he studied systems analysis on a scholarship and acquired a PhD at the Academy of Sciences in Moscow. During the 1980s he was a scientific advisor for the Hungarian Academy of Sciences. He was the Director of Vocational Training (from 1984 to 1989), then Director General (from 1989 to 1990) at the National Pedagogical Institute. As its first Director General in 1990, he established the National Institute for Vocational Education. He was involved in numerous UNESCO and ILO projects and continues to participate in the preparation of various World Bank and Phare projects in the area of human resource development. His main fields of research are the theory of learning, the history and development of vocational qualifications, the impact of new technologies on visual and mobile learning and teaching. To date he has published approximately 150 papers on human resource development, including the essays *New Vistas of Learning in the Mobile Age* (in Kristóf Nyíri ed. 2006: Mobile Understanding: The Epistemology of Ubiquitous Communication. Vienna: Passagen Verlag), *Mobile Learning: New Horizons and Unstable Summits* (in Kristóf Nyíri ed. 2009: Engagement and Exposure: Mobile Communication and the Ethics of Social Networking. Vienna: Passagen Verlag), and *Visual Education: Old and New Dilemmas* (in series VISUAL LEARNING, vol. 4, 2014). Further information: www.benedekandras.hu. Email: benedek.a@eik.bme.hu

DANKA, ISTVÁN, born 1978, is an Assistant Professor at the Department of Philosophy and History of Science, Budapest University of Technology. He earned his MA in Philosophy at the University of Pécs, Hungary, and his PhD at the University of Leeds, UK. A former junior researcher at the Research Institute for Philosophy, Hungarian Academy of Sciences, he held various research positions at the LMU Munich; Wittgenstein Archives, Bergen; and the University of Vienna. His current research interests include the relation between realism, constructivism and relativism; visual argumentation and rhetoric; and the philosophy of online education. Email: danka.istvan@gmail.hu.

DELI, ESZTER, born 1989, is an Assistant Lecturer at the Institute of Behavioral Sciences and Communication Theory at Corvinus University of Budapest. At the same time, she is a part-time lecturer at Pázmány Péter Catholic University, Saint Ignatius Jesuit College, and Mathias Corvinus College. Her teaching career at these institutions has given her a chance of continuous development and gaining new experiences as a researcher. She obtained her Master's degree at Budapest University of Technology and Economics, and was a member of the Social Communication Doctoral School of Corvinus University. She has a lifelong passion for rhetoric, which inspired her PhD research, and her participation at the Debate Club of Cambridge University in 2014 just made her commitment even stronger. Her main fields of research are visual rhetoric and the philosophy of images in disaster news. Email: eszter.deli@uni-corvinus.hu.

ENDRŐDY-NAGY, ORSOLYA, born 1977, is an Associate Professor at the Department of Education of the Faculty of Primary and Preschool Education of Eötvös Loránd University of Budapest. She obtained her PhD in Education, her MA in Education, her BA in Hungarian and Cultural Management at ELTE. As a student she won the Hungarian State Scholarship, Hungarian Initiatives Fund, Washington DC and Doctoral Scholarships of ELTE, doing research at INRP, Lyon, and Archiginnasio, Bologna. In 2016 she became Associate Editor of Volume 7 of the *International Journal of Image* and Volume 10 of *The International Journal of Visual Design*. Her main research fields are history of childhood, iconography and multiculturalism. Her first monograph was published in 2015, on *Conceptions of Childhood in the Renaissance. An Iconographic analysis* (Budapest: Eötvös Press). Her research areas include iconography, childhood studies, and cross-cultural comparative analysis. Email: endrodyorsolya@gmail.com.

HALPERN, DANIEL is a professor at the Catholic University of Santiago, Chile. He completed his doctoral studies at Rutgers University in the field of communication. He has been actively involved in exploring the effects of online activity on social relationships, among many other topics such as visual aspects of museum attendance and viewing. E-mail: halperndaniel@gmail.com.

HUBBES, LÁSZLÓ ATTILA is a lecturer of Religious Studies, Semiotics, Rhetoric and other communication disciplines at the Faculty of Economic, Socio-Human Sciences and Engineering of the Sapientia Hungarian University of Transylvania, Miercurea Ciuc, Romania. In 2006 he defended his PhD thesis in Philology (apocalyptic studies) at Babeş-Bolyai University of Cluj-Napoca, which was later published as a monographic volume (in Hungarian): *Látomások a végső dolgok bűvöletében. Az apokalipszis a vallásos irodalmi műfajtól a művészeti kifejezésmódig (Visions under the Spell of the End. Apocalypse from a Genre of the Religious Literature to a Way of Artistic Expression.* Marosvásárhely, 2008). Since then he has maintained his research interest in apocalypticism. Other publications in the field include *Apocalyptic Motifs in the Early Christian Literature and Art* (2011); *'Signs of Times' – A Semiotic Content-Analysis of Visual Apocalyptic Rhetoric on Hungarian Conspiracist Websites* (2010); *Debating Contemporary Internet-based Apocalyptic Discourse in Class* (2010); *Apocalyptic as a New Mental Paradigm of the Middle Ages* (2016). He maintains a Hungarian and English bilingual online resource collection on apocalyptic at: www.apokaliptikum.lap.hu. In recent years he has also been involved in the research of contemporary myths, online rituals and discourses of various religious or nationalistic networks, communities, particularly ethno-paganism. Email: hubbeslaszlo@gmail.com.

KATZ, JAMES E., PhD, is the Feld Family Professor of Emerging Media at Boston University's College of Communication, where he is Director of the Center for Mobile Communication Studies and Division of Emerging Media. His research on the internet, social media and mobile communication has been internationally recognized, and he is frequently invited to address high-level industry, governmental and academic groups on his findings. His latest book is *Philosophy of Emerging Media: Understanding, Appreciation, Application*, edited with Juliet Floyd (Oxford University Press), which includes contributions from Kristóf Nyíri and Zsuzsanna Kondor. He is also the co-author of *The Social Media President: Barack Obama and the Politics of Citizen Engagement,* published in 2013 by Palgrave Macmillan. Prior to his Boston University appointment, he was the Governors Distinguished Professor of Communication at Rutgers University (the title being the highest honor that Rutgers can bestow on one of its faculty) and served two terms as chair of its Department of Communication. Preceding his tenure at Rutgers, Katz was a Distinguished Member of Staff and Director of the Social Science Research Unit at Bell Communications Research (Bellcore). Earlier, Katz taught at other universities, including the University of Texas, Austin, where he was elected Chair of the Austin World Affairs Council. His many other books include *Magic in the Air: Mobile Communication and the Transformation of Social Life, Social Consequences of Internet Use: Access, Involvement, Expression* (with Ronald E. Rice), and *Handbook of Mobile Communication Studies*. Author of more than 100 scientific articles and papers, his publications have been translated into seven languages.

KATZ, RACHEL A. is a doctoral researcher in the Sociology Department at the University of Manchester, UK. She completed her master's degree in Gender Studies at the University of Cambridge and received her bachelor's degree from Columbia University/Barnard College. Her research addresses dating app technologies' consequences for communication, identity, and everyday social interaction. Email: rachel.katz@postgrad.manchester.ac.uk; website: http://www.socialsciences.manchester.ac.uk/sociology/research/postgraduate-research/current-phd-students/rachel-katz/.

KÖVECSES, ZOLTÁN is Professor Emeritus in the School of English and American Studies, Eötvös Loránd University. His research interests include metaphor, metonymy, emotion language, American English and culture, and the relationship between metaphoric conceptualization and context. His major publications include *Metaphor and Emotion* (2000, Cambridge UP), *American English. An Introduction* (2000, Broadview Press), *Metaphor. A Practical Introduction* (2002/2010, Oxford UP), *Metaphor in Culture* (2005, Cambridge UP), *Language, Mind, and Culture* (2006, Oxford UP), and *Where Metaphors Come From* (2015, Oxford UP). Email: kovecses.zoltan@btk.elte.hu.

MOKTEFI, AMIROUCHE is Lecturer of Philosophy at Tallinn University of Technology, Estonia. He is a member of the Ragnar Nurkse Department of Innovation and Governance. He holds a PhD in the History and Philosophy of Science from the University of Strasbourg (2007). His research interests include science communication, the history of logic, visual reasoning, and the philosophy of mathematical practice. Main publications include '*What the Tortoise Said to Achilles*'*: Lewis Carroll's Paradox of Inference* (with Francine F. Abeles eds., London: The Lewis Carroll Society, 2016); *Visual Reasoning with Diagrams* (with Sun-Joo Shin eds., Basel: Birkhäuser, 2013); *Définir l'Image Scientifique* (with Catherine Allamel-Raffin eds., Limoges: Presses Universitaires de Limoges, 2011).

MOLNÁR, GYÖRGY, PhD, is an associate professor, head of department, vice dean, director general, electrical engineer, teacher of engineering, medical biologist engineer, qualified public education manager, who works at the Department of Technical Education of the Faculty of Economic and Social Sciences of Budapest University of Technology and Economics (BME), and at the Teacher Training Centre of Budapest University of Technology. After graduation from BME as an electrical engineer in 2000, he gained a multidisciplinary university medical biologist engineer degree at BME. Subsequently, he started work as an engineer and, in parallel, another training program in pedagogy as a teacher of engineering from 2001. Since then, he has carried out his academic studies and teaching activities at the Department of Technical Education, successor of the ever-prestigious Institute of Pedagogy. He also applied for admission to the PhD program of the same department and completed it at the Doctoral School of Education of Eötvös Loránd University. He has been teaching at the Department of Technical Education since 2001. His fields of research include the basic aspects of ICT, the methodological and innovative issues of vocational teaching, which have enabled him to research new, atypical and electronic teaching-learning paths. Email: molnar.gy@eik.bme.hu.

NYÍRI, KRISTÓF, born 1944, is Member of the Hungarian Academy of Sciences. He was Leibniz Professor of the University of Leipzig for the winter term 2006/07. His main fields of research are the history of philosophy in the 19th and 20th centuries, the impact of communication technologies on the organization of ideas and on society, the philosophy of images, and the philosophy of time. Some main publications: *Tradition and Individuality* (Dordrecht: Kluwer, 1992); *Electronic Networking and the Unity of Knowledge* (in Stephanie Kenna and Seamus Ross eds.: Networking in the Humanities. London: Bowker-Saur; 1995); *The Picture Theory of Reason* (in Berit Brogaard and Barry Smith eds.: Rationality and Irrationality. Wien: öbv-hpt, 2001); *Vernetztes Wissen: Philosophie im Zeitalter des Internets* (Vienna: Passagen Verlag, 2004); *Zeit und Bild: Philosophische Studien zur Wirklichkeit des Werdens* (Bielefeld: transcript, 2012); *Meaning and Motoricity: Essays on Image and Time* (Frankfurt/M.: Peter Lang, 2014). Further information: www.hunfi.hu/nyiri. Email: knyiri@t-email.hu.

STOELLGER, PHILIPP, born 1967, is Professor of Systematic Theology: Dogmatics and Philosophy of Religion at Heidelberg University and Fellow at the Marsilius Kolleg in Heidelberg. He was speaker of the graduate college "Deutungsmacht" at the University of Rostock in 2014 and he founded the Institute for Iconicity (Institut für Bildtheorie, ifi) in 2007. His main fields of research are Christology and anthropology, hermeneutics, phenomenology and philosophy of religion, and image and media theory. Some main publications: *Metapher und Lebenswelt. Hans Blumenbergs Metaphorologie als Lebenswelthermeneutik und ihr religionsphänomenologischer Horizont* (Tübingen: Mohr Siebeck, 2000); *Passivität aus Passion. Zur Problemgeschichte einer categoria non grata* (Tübingen: Mohr Siebeck, 2010); *Deutungsmacht. Religion und belief systems in Deutungsmachtkonflikten* (ed., Tübingen: Mohr Siebeck, 2014); *Bild und Tod. Grundfragen der Bildanthropologie* (ed., 2 vol., Tübingen: Mohr Siebeck, 2016). Further information: www.uni-heidelberg.de/fakultaeten/theologie/einrichtungen/ts/faecher/st/dogmatik.html. Email: ps@wts.uni-heidelberg.de.

VESZELSZKI, ÁGNES, PhD, is an Associate Professor in Hungarian Linguistics and Communication at Corvinus University of Budapest and editor of the online periodical *Filológia.hu* (Hungarian Academy of Sciences). Research fields: the impacts of infocommunication technology on the Hungarian language (digilect), modern philology, grammar of spoken language, interdisciplinary connections between marketing and linguistics. Her publications include *Image and Self-representation* (in series Visual Learning, vol. 1, 2011); *Connection of Image and Text in Digital and Handwritten Documents* (in series Visual Learning, vol. 2, 2012); *Promiscuity of Images: Memes from an English-Hungarian Contrastive Perspective* (in series Visual Learning, vol. 3, 2013); *Information Visualization: Infographics from a Linguistic Point of View* (in series Visual Learning, vol. 4, 2014); *Emoticons vs. Reaction-Gifs. Non-Verbal Communication on the Internet from the Aspects of Visuality, Verbality and Time* (in series Visual Learning, vol. 5, 2015); most recently: *#time, #truth, #tradition. An Image-text Relationship on Instagram: photo and hashtag* (in series Visual Learning, vol. 6, 2016); *Digilect: The Impact of Infocommunication Technology on Language* (De Gruyter Saur, 2017). Website: www.veszelszki.hu. Email: agnes.veszelszki@uni-corvinus.hu.

Index

A
Aczél, Petra 8, 9, 29, 30, 32, 36, 37, 38, 47, 56, 189
apocalyptic 13, 157, 159, 160, 161, 162, 163, 164, 165, 166, 167, 168, 169, 170, 171, 172, 173, 191
argumentation 9, 36, 40, 41, 42, 43, 44, 45, 46, 47, 160, 163, 166, 169, 189, 190
Arnheim, Rudolf 9, 47, 51, 52, 53, 54, 56, 91, 99
augmented reality 11, 31, 114, 115

B
Benedek, András 7, 11, 38, 39, 47, 48, 57, 77, 91, 92, 99, 115, 116, 155, 189

C
childhood 10, 71, 72, 76, 77, 78, 190
CMT. *see* conceptual metaphor theory
common-sense realism 9, 10, 51, 57, 59, 60, 61
Compatibility Criterion 61, 62
computer-mediated communication 30, 141, 143, 153
concept of smell 23, 24, 25, 26, 27, 28
conceptual metaphor theory 8, 17, 18, 21, 22, 23, 27
Connectivity Criterion 62
CSR. *see* common-sense realism
cyberspace 11, 33, 39, 101

D
Danka, István 9, 59, 190
dating app 131, 132, 133, 134, 135, 136, 137, 138, 192
Deli, Eszter 9, 41, 56, 57, 190
diagram 10, 81, 82, 83, 84, 85, 86, 87, 88, 89, 94, 114, 192
digital dating 12, 131

E
Elkins, James 7
Endrődy-Nagy, Orsolya 10, 71, 72, 77, 190
essentialism 176, 177

F
Facebook 12, 92, 100, 101, 122, 123, 124, 128, 129, 130, 135, 138, 141, 143, 146, 148, 149, 151, 153, 155
figurative conceptualization 17, 23
figurative meaning 17, 27
film 54, 145

G
Gombrich, Ernst H. 9, 42, 47, 48, 51, 52, 53, 56, 77

H
Halpern, Daniel 11, 121, 123, 125, 126, 129, 130, 191
Hubbes, László Attila 13, 159, 160, 161, 163, 165, 169, 170, 172, 191
Hug, Theo 7
humour 144, 145

I
IBDA. *see* image-based dating apps
iconography 10, 71, 77
ICT. *see* info-communication technology

image 42, 44, 45, 46, 52, 53, 54, 55, 56, 72, 87, 91, 92, 96, 123, 125, 128, 131, 132, 134, 135, 136, 137, 138, 144, 145, 147, 149, 151, 167, 168, 177, 178, 179, 180, 181, 182, 183, 184, 185, 186, 194
image-based dating apps 131, 132, 138
image-belief 177, 179, 180, 181, 182, 183
immersion 29, 30, 31, 32, 33, 34, 35, 36, 37, 38, 39
info-communication technology 91, 92, 93, 99, 101, 116, 193

J
Japan 10, 71, 72, 73, 74, 75, 76

K
Katz, James E. 11, 121, 129, 130, 191
Katz, Rachel A. 12, 131, 192
Kövecses, Zoltán 8, 17, 23, 28, 162, 192

L
Lakoff, George 18, 19, 22, 28, 162, 172
Langacker, Ronald 24, 27, 28
learning environment 93, 116
learning management system 91
literal meaning 17, 18, 20, 22, 27
LMS. *see* learning management system

M
mathematics 81, 82, 83, 84, 85, 86, 87, 88, 89, 95, 97, 98, 177, 181, 192
mediality 177, 178
mental image 51
metaphor 14, 17, 18, 19, 20, 21, 22, 23, 24, 25, 26, 27, 28, 37, 38, 51, 54, 55, 59, 74, 91, 162, 165, 169, 180, 185, 192
metonymy 17, 20, 27, 192
Moktefi, Amirouche 10, 81, 83, 84, 87, 88, 89, 192
Molnár, György 11, 92, 93, 99, 101, 116, 193

N
Nyíri, Kristóf 7, 9, 14, 29, 38, 39, 47, 48, 51, 52, 57, 59, 60, 77, 91, 99, 116, 155, 165, 167, 173, 189, 190, 191, 193

O
OCD. *see* Open Content Development
OER. *see* Open Educational Resources
OLR. *see* Open Learning Resources
online aggression 141
Open Content Development 11, 91, 93, 94, 95, 96, 99
Open Educational Resources 93, 95
Open Learning Resources 91

P
painting 51, 53, 55
perspectivism 60, 61
persuasion 8, 9, 29, 30, 31, 32, 33, 35, 38, 39, 41, 162, 163, 170, 171
pictorial truth 51, 54, 56
pictorial turn 41, 159, 160, 166
pictoriality 9, 10, 59
profile picture 131, 132, 136

R
realism 9, 10, 52, 53, 57, 59, 60, 61, 62, 77, 177, 190
relativism 9, 51, 52, 59, 60, 61, 62, 177, 185, 186, 190
rhetoric 8, 9, 13, 29, 30, 32, 35, 36, 37, 38, 39, 40, 41, 43, 47, 48, 56, 144, 153, 159, 160, 162, 163, 166, 169, 170, 171, 172, 173, 183, 189, 190, 191
Röttgers, Kurt 7

S
selfie 12, 121, 122, 123, 124, 125, 126, 128, 129, 130, 131
self-presentation 123, 125, 128, 130, 185
Sipos, Júlia 56, 57
social media 12, 122, 123, 124, 125, 126, 128, 135, 137, 141, 146, 150, 153, 154, 155, 191
Stoellger, Philipp 13, 175, 187, 193
SysBook 95, 96, 97, 98, 100

T
time 11, 18, 19, 28, 33, 62, 71, 86, 93, 101, 115, 128, 143, 162, 178, 184, 190, 193, 194
Tinder 131, 132, 134, 135, 136, 138, 139
Triviality Thesis 60
trolling 141, 143, 144, 145, 146, 147, 148, 149, 151, 152, 153, 154, 155
trust 135, 175, 176, 177, 178, 179, 180, 182, 183, 186, 187

V
verbal aggression 13, 142, 143, 153
veridiction 178, 179, 183, 184
Veszelszki, Ágnes 8, 12, 14, 57, 77, 116, 117, 141, 143, 144, 146, 149, 151, 154, 155, 194
VET. *see* vocational education and training
virtual reality 11, 29, 31, 32, 40, 101, 115
virtual rhetoric 9, 30
virtuality 8, 9, 14, 29, 30, 31, 32, 34, 38, 39, 40, 59, 114, 115, 116, 122, 153
visual aggression 12
Visual Learning Lab 7, 11, 56, 57, 91
visual literacy 131, 137, 138
visual trolling 141, 149
visuality 7, 8, 10, 11, 12, 14, 29, 30, 41, 46, 101, 115, 148, 151, 152, 178
VLL. *see* Visual Learning Lab
vocational education and training 92, 93, 96

W
Wittgenstein, Ludwig 9, 52, 53, 57, 177, 182, 187, 190
WWF (World Wildlife Fund) 9, 41, 43, 44, 45, 46

Visual Learning

Edited by András Benedek and Ágnes Veszelszki

Vol. 1 András Benedek / Kristóf Nyíri (eds.): Images in Language. Metaphors and Metamorphoses. 2011.

Vol. 2 András Benedek / Kristóf Nyíri (eds.): The Iconic Turn in Education. 2012.

Vol. 3 András Benedek / Kristóf Nyíri (eds.): How to Do Things with Pictures. Skill, Practice, Performance. 2013.

Vol. 4 András Benedek / Kristóf Nyíri (eds.): The Power of the Image. Emotion, Expression, Explanation. 2014.

Vol. 5 András Benedek / Kristóf Nyíri (eds.): Beyond Words. Pictures, Parables, Paradoxes. 2015.

Vol. 6 András Benedek / Ágnes Veszelszki (eds.): In the Beginning was the Image: The Omnipresence of Pictures. Time, Truth, Tradition. 2016.

Vol. 7 András Benedek / Ágnes Veszelszki (eds.): Virtual Reality – Real Visuality. Virtual, Visual, Veridical. 2017.

www.peterlang.com

www.ingramcontent.com/pod-product-compliance
Ingram Content Group UK Ltd.
Pitfield, Milton Keynes, MK11 3LW, UK
UKHW041826031026
15587UKWH00002B/593

9 783631 731048